# SOCIAL JUSTICE ISSUES AND RACISM IN THE COLLEGE CLASSROOM: PERSPECTIVES FROM DIFFERENT VOICES

# INTERNATIONAL PERSPECTIVES ON HIGHER EDUCATION RESEARCH

Series Editor: Malcolm Tight

Recent Volumes:

INTERNATIONAL PERSPECTIVES ON HIGHER
EDUCATION RESEARCH   VOLUME 8

# SOCIAL JUSTICE ISSUES AND RACISM IN THE COLLEGE CLASSROOM: PERSPECTIVES FROM DIFFERENT VOICES

EDITED BY

## PATRICIA G. BOYER

*University of Missouri – St. Louis,
St. Louis, MO, USA*

## DANNIELLE JOY DAVIS

*Middle Tennessee State University,
Murfreesboro, TN, USA*

United Kingdom – North America – Japan
India – Malaysia – China

Emerald Group Publishing Limited
Howard House, Wagon Lane, Bingley BD16 1WA, UK

First edition 2013



**British Library Cataloguing in Publication Data**
A catalogue record for this book is available from the British Library

ISBN: 978-1-78190-499-2
ISSN: 1479-3628 (Series)

# CONTENTS

**SECTION III: VOICES FROM FACULTY AND STUDENTS:
FOCUS UPON STUDENTS**

# LIST OF CONTRIBUTORS


| | |
|---|---|
| *Patricia G. Boyer* | University of Missouri – St. Louis, St. Louis, MO, USA |
| *Annette M. Burris* | University of Missouri – St. Louis, St. Louis, MO, USA |
| *Bonita K. Butner* | University of Missouri – Kansas City, Kansas City, MO, USA |
| *Dannielle Joy Davis* | Middle Tennessee State University, Murfreesboro, TN, USA |
| *Matthew D. Davis* | University of Missouri – St. Louis, St. Louis, MO, USA |
| *Ty-Ron M. O. Douglas* | University of Missouri – Columbia, Columbia, MO, USA |
| *Marybeth Gasman* | University of Pennsylvania, Philadelphia, PA, USA |
| *Juan Carlos González* | California State University – Fresno, Fresno, CA, USA |
| *Ashley L. Gray* | University of Missouri – St. Louis, St. Louis, MO, USA |
| *Aimee Howley* | Ohio University, Athens, OH, USA |
| *Marged Howley* | Pulaski County Special School District, Little Rock, AR, USA |
| *Katrina M. Hubbard* | University of Missouri – St. Louis, St. Louis, MO, USA |
| *Amy A. Hunter* | University of Missouri – St. Louis, St. Louis, MO, USA |

| | |
|---|---|
| *Kathleen M. Kanz-White* | University of Missouri – St. Louis, St. Louis, MO, USA |
| *Eunyoung Kim* | Seton Hall University, South Orange, NJ, USA |
| *Renée A. Middleton* | Ohio University, Athens, OH, USA |
| *Christine W. Nganga* | South Dakota State University, Brookings, SD, USA |
| *Abul Pitre* | North Carolina A&T State University, Greensboro, NC, USA |
| *Edwardo L. Portillos* | University of Colorado, Colorado Springs, CO, USA |
| *Laura Jeanette Pressley* | Ohio University, Athens, OH, USA |
| *Linda Sue Warner* | Northeastern Oklahoma A&M Jr College, Miami, OK, USA |
| *Natalie F. Williams* | Ohio University, Athens, OH, USA |

# SECTION I
# INTRODUCTION

# CHAPTER 1

# INTRODUCTION

Patricia G. Boyer

> *Just agreeing that social justice is important is not enough. Educators must practice social justice or else the concept is meaningless*
>
> — (Sensoy & DiAngelo, 2009, p. 345)

Historically, women and people of color in the United States were not given access to education. It is sometimes taboo to discuss race in our society because of our history. Since the United States has elected an African American president, many believe that racism is eradicated and it is no longer necessary to continue conversations about race. In 1994, Cornel West told us that race matters. Race still matters in every facet of our lives including the college campus, but some academicians avoid dialogue about this issue in the classroom.

Today we live in a diverse society and therefore, our colleges and universities are becoming more racially and ethnically diverse than ever before. Due to this diverse population, various difficulties evolve regarding the campus climate. Yes, in this day and time, institutional racism is alive and well on our campuses. Many faculty and students of color assert that some campus environments are unwelcoming and intolerant and they feel a sense of not belonging. Recently, I was privy to data that revealed some people of color personally experienced offensive, hostile, and intimidating conduct on a college campus. Unfortunately, these behaviors are not an anomaly; but they are consistent with behaviors found in many institutions of higher learning. Our institutions are supposed to be a safe and civil

**Social Justice Issues and Racism in the College Classroom: Perspectives from Different Voices**
**International Perspectives on Higher Education Research, Volume 8, 3–10**
Copyright © 2013 by Emerald Group Publishing Limited
All rights of reproduction in any form reserved
ISSN: 1479-3628/doi:10.1108/S1479-3628(2013)0000008003

environment to express beliefs, opinions, and feelings. Additionally, our campuses are safe and civil environments for students, faculty, and staff to express their personal beliefs, educating students about race and racism. Regrettably, this experience is not necessarily true for faculty and students of color. Anecdotal accounts of overt and covert acts of racism against people of color such as discrimination, disparity, hostility, and other such problems reported on our college and university campuses. Specifically, isolated incidents have occurred on various campuses such as noose hangings, "Blackface" on Halloween, and other insensitive depictions. Nevertheless, for faculty of color, the more frequent and disparaging issues include but are not limited to salary disparities, workplace discrimination in hiring, and denial of tenure and promotion. Institutions usually handle isolated incidents but tend not to address overarching discrimination experienced by their faculty of color.

Although institutional missions tend to include a diversity statement, classroom discussions of race relations and racism are often an overlooked part of our educational process. One way to address issues of race and racism is to have open discussions in the classroom. When faculty present the topic of race and racism in the classroom they often encounter resistance from students and are challenged. In some instances student' resistance is related to their lack of experience with the topic; they often question the relevance of race and racism to their given fields, and yet others openly state, "I am tired of talking about race." Some students of color have expressed discontent with the expectation of that they should be "the" authority on matters related to their particular race or ethnicity. Some students of color have expressed discontent with the expectation that they should be the "authority" on matters related to their particular race or ethnicity.

In some cases, faculty may avoid the topic of race and racism or search for reasons not to have the "race talk" because *they* are uncomfortable with discussing this topic. They also steer clear of including topics of race and racism in their courses. Despite the fears, avoidances, and discomfort, it is imperative to engage in conversations in the classrooms and integrate race and racism into the curriculum. The benefits of being proactive and forward thinking about such topics may lead to open and honest communication among students and promote a greater acceptance of diversity. Additionally, the classroom offers a safe environment for this type of dialogue.

Research reveals that by engaging in difficult dialogues such as race and racism in the classroom enhances student development. For example, chang as cited by Pascarella and Terenzini (2005) revealed "The extent to which faculty emphasize diversity in their teaching and research and the overall institutional orientation to diversity also positively influence student persistence" (p. 419). Researchers also claimed, "evidence that perceptions of racial discrimination and prejudice in the classroom and on campus were negatively related to continued enrollment" (Cabera et al., as cited by Pascarella & Terenzini, p. 419).

Some researchers have explored campus racial climate, yet social justice issues and racism in the college classroom have not been investigated simultaneously to the same extent. Neither faculty nor students are always willing, able, or comfortable to adequately communicate on issues related to race. Typically, in classroom settings when discussing social justice topics related to gender or age, discussions tend to flow freely. In contrast, if the topic changes to social justice and racism, the classroom is silent, everyone holds their breath, and one can sense the tension. Why in 2012 are we still struggling with comfort in discussing race? It has been years since authors like Tim Wise or Beverly Tatum described how to manage discomfort in discussing race and moving to an action plan, but yet not much has changed.

This edited book include faculty and students of various racial and ethnic backgrounds from postsecondary institutions who provide personal testimonies about racial challenges they encounter in college classrooms. There are several distinctive features of this work. Other social justice books have focused on K-12 issues related to one race/ethnicity, postsecondary institutions' climates, and/or culture. Other social justice books tend to focus on "isms" such as sexism, classism, and ableism or even biomedical ethics or religion as they relate to race and social justice. This book will include on the voices of various racial/ethnic groups of faculty and students, including international scholars. In light of the shortcomings of many postsecondary institutions, this book focuses on providing information to assist students and faculty of color with survival skills in complex environments. Additionally, the book will inform and bring attention to nonminority faculty and students of social justice issues related to race in the classroom and offer suggestions on how to be supportive of people of color.

Questions posed for this edited book are as follows: (1) How do faculty members include social justice issues related to race/ethnicity in their curricula? (2) How are issues associated with race or ethnicity discussed in the classroom by students, as well as minority and nonminority faculty? (3) What are the experiences of students of color in the classroom working with faculty of different races and ethnicities?

Several frameworks will be utilized throughout this book to assist readers in better understanding ideas, concepts, and practices (see Cross, 1971;

Helms, 1995; Sensoy & DiAngelo, 2009; St. John, 2009). Specifically, the framework adapted for this book is from Cochran-Smith, who presents a framework to assist with multicultural teacher education. Additionally, critical race theory, and White privilege are used to better explore the featured topics. Both quantitative and qualitative (e.g., auto-ethnographic, interviews, etc.) data will be utilized in the book to give voice to the authors.

As previously stated, the framework for this book is based on the work of Cochran-Smith (2003). Her conceptual framework can be used to examine and sort out existing or envisioned teaching approaches by investigating the stance taken on the key issues and the way these are influenced by external forces. The framework can also be used as a tool for colleges and universities for analyzing the theoretical and/or empirical research related to multi-cultural teaching. This social justice framework can provide a structure for analyzing teaching for culturally and linguistically diverse populations. A significant contribution of the framework allows the reader to observe the deep complexities and multiple meanings involved in understanding multicultural teaching and at what critical junctures the major differences and similarities exist as well as which aspects are emphasized and ignored (p. 20). Our focus upon higher education and the use of a social justice framework in understating outcomes of teaching race renders this work unique and appealing to administrators, scholars, and students of post-secondary institutions. The material in this book will prove to be useful in terms of both theory and practice.

## OVERVIEW

The contributors for this book consist of different voices from students and faculty, by different race/ethnicity, even nationality, as well as feelings and instructions on various perspective on discussing race in classroom. It is important to have a conversation about race in a "safe setting" to prepare our students for a diverse society and workforce.

Chapter 2 "Teaching for Social Justice through Embracing Identity Tensions" by Christine W. Nganga uses the interrelated knowledge base of multicultural education and critical pedagogy to offer possibilities for identity negotiations among students and educators. As an international scholar of color, the author also interweaves how her own identity is negotiated by comparing and contrasting her teaching experiences in her home country and in the United States. The author argues that it is important for educators to interrogate their identity and embrace the tensions that arise in the process, in order to enact a critically engaged dialogue in their classrooms.

Chapter 3 "Teaching Race, Pushing Back, and Making Meaningful Change" by Marybeth Gasman discusses the role of the author as a White woman who studies race in the academy. She examines her ability to use her status, including her tenured status, to make change that can have a positive impact on faculty and students of color, especially African Americans. Moreover, she discusses her approach to teaching about race in the classroom. She also explores the limitations of her role and the reactions to her role by both Whites and people of color.

Chapter 4 "Advocating for Change: A Reflection on My Journey to Social Justice Education" is by Bonita K. Butner

*It takes a deep commitment to change and an even deeper commitment to grow.*
— Ralph Ellison

This quote from Ralph Ellison highlights the complexity of the concepts of change and growth. As faculty, we are constantly called on to facilitate the growth and change of our students through their academic work. This article provides a narrative of one faculty member's growth toward understanding and the incorporation of social justice concepts and structures into her classroom.

Chapter 5 "Confessions of a Border-Crossing Brotha-scholar: Teaching Race With All of Me" is by Ty-Ron M. O. Douglas. Drawing on the author's experiences in various educative spaces, the purpose of this chapter is to share how the author utilizes his positionality as a border crossing brotha-scholar to teach about social justice and racism in university classrooms. In sharing how he employs his identity to help students negotiate various ideological borders in his courses, he also models how socially just pedagogical practices can emerge out of who we are.

Chapter 6 "The Experiences of Marginalized Academics and Understanding the Majority: Implications for Institutional Policy and Practice" by Dannielle Joy Davis features a minority faculty member's interactions with White students and female colleagues from two regions in the United States. Helm's Racial Identity Model for Whites offers a conceptual lens to understand classroom and workplace dynamics between Blacks and Whites in predominantly White postsecondary settings, regardless of national context. Findings suggest that the quality of the featured academic's experiences with White colleagues and students often reflected the status the individuals held in terms of their own racial identity development. These findings promise to inform institutional policy and faculty evaluation practices.

Chapter 7 "Chicanos Teaching Social Justice in Higher Education/ Chicanos Enseñando Justicia Social en la Universidad: Experiences at Predominately White and Hispanic Serving Institutions" by Juan Carlos González and Edwardo L. Portillos provides examples of how Chicano faculty teach and practice social justice in the U.S. college classroom, where subtle forms of racism operate through White privilege, and influence faculty credibility and authority. From a Latino Critical Theory (LatCrit) perspective, the authors address the question, "What are the similarities and differences in classroom experiences of Chicano faculty in Predominately White Institutions (PWI) and Hispanic Serving Institutions (HSI)?" In addressing this question, the authors provide examples from their teaching experiences at both PWIs and HSIs, and how a Chicana/o-centered social justice perspective can help to mediate and overcome classroom challenges. The chapter ends with a discussion of how a social justice framework is necessary in college classrooms that are becoming increasingly diverse; and recommendations for how PWIs and HSIs can support Chicana/o faculty in endeavors to institutionalize a social justice framework in the college curriculum.

Chapter 8 "Revolutionary Reforestation and White Privilege in a 'Critical Race' Doctoral Program" by Amy A. Hunter and Matthew D. Davis examines and analyzes several key race related moments during a doctoral program's existence. The chapter's second author (a White male) leads the program in which the first author (an African American female) has been a student. They utilize the overarching umbrella theory of Cochran-Smith's social justice in education framework, as well as a Critical Race Theory grounding in sharing their experiences.

Chapter 9 "Research As Activism" by Linda Sue Warner discusses the similarities and differences between native research methods and western social science research as it impacts American Indians in the academy. The chapter reflects on the requirements needed by young practitioners and their responsibilities to their tribal communities to produce research that is both informative and available. The chapter contextualizes the discussion in examples of indigenous activism.

Chapter 10 "Reflective Journaling in a College Multicultural Education Classroom: Looking Past, Present, and Future" by Eunyoung Kim seeks to understand how a group of graduate students from diverse backgrounds in terms of race, ethnicity, class, gender, and culture locate and negotiate their identities within the context of a multicultural education course. Through reflective journaling, students engaged in reflection on their practice (classroom dynamics and interactions) by examining their own values, listening to others, challenging others, and being challenged in regard to issues related to diversity, oppression, White privilege, and racism. Reflective journaling is a powerful tool for promoting students' voices, developing their understanding, as well as a way for students to construct meanings and knowledge that guide their actions in the classroom.

Chapter 11 "Classroom Experiences Through the Lens of Social Justice: The Post-secondary Experiences of Three Black Female Students" is by Katrina M. Hubbard, Annette M. Burris, and Ashley L. Gray. The U.S. educational system has a long history of racial discrimination, creating an environment that is in many ways hostile to those who are different. For some students of color, negotiating this culturally hostile environment can lead to feelings of invisibility and isolation. This chapter examines the educational perspective of three Black, female graduate students within the context of a social justice framework. We will explore these dynamics and their influences upon individual educational, social, and personal development from the perspective of nondominants in a dominant culture.

Chapter 12 "The Experience of Conducting a Study of Racial or Ethnic Dynamics: Voices of Doctoral Students in Colleges of Education" by Renée Middleton reports the findings of a qualitative study featuring doctoral students in a College of Education and Human Services completing or who were close to completing dissertations in which racial and ethnic dynamics were major foci. For some of the doctoral students, critical race theory formed an organizing set of concepts guiding the development of research questions. For others, inductive methods surfaced particular racial or ethnic dynamics that either fit with or differed from well-accepted theories. In both cases, the doctoral students experienced the challenge, as well as the exhilaration of using systematic inquiry in order to navigate the intellectual territory circumscribed by their own racial and/or ethnic identities, as well as those of their informants.

Chapter 13 "Perspective of a Majority Student" by Kathleen M. Kanz-White examines the importance of social justice courses from a majority student's perspective and outlines some of the difficulties in offering these courses. It discusses the benefits of social justice courses for both minority and majority students and focuses on the challenges of understanding and acknowledging the impact of the types of privilege and power that majority individuals experience. The concept of intersectionality, the compounding of injustice for individuals who have multiple minority identities, is explored. Finally, a four phase model is proposed which can be used to describe the journey that majority students experience as they begin to understand the impact of privilege both on a personal and societal level.

Chapter 14 "Reflections on a Critical Race Theory Project with Educational Leaders" by Abul Pitre reflects on the author's experiences with doctoral students in a cultural diversity and ethical and legal issues course. As a major part of the course, students were required to write a paper that would later be used as a contribution for a book addressing multicultural education for educational leaders. During the course, several of the conversations presented a type of shock and awe for these educational leaders. In part, much of the dilemma lies in the fact that professors in educational leadership programs may have limited knowledge in multi-cultural education and critical theory.

The primary audience for this work includes postsecondary educators, faculty development specialists, administrators interested in diversity within the campus curricula, and students within the social sciences. Faculty development librarians comprise a key secondary audience. Courses in which this book is likely to be adopted include higher education curricula, social justice, race, diversity, and other social science classes. This book informs both policy and practice by highlighting the triumphs and challenges of teaching about social justice and race. Understanding the complexities involved in teaching these subjects may influence policies related to tenure and promotion of faculty and offer insight for best practices. The book promises to hold utility across disciplines given the diverse fields of the authors.

# REFERENCES


Cochran-Smith, M. (2003). The multiple meanings of multicultural teacher education: A conceptual framework. *Teacher Education Quarterly, 30*(2), 7. Retrieved from http://eric.ed.gov/PDFS/EJ852354.pdf

Cross, W. (1971). *Black racial identity development model.* Retrieved from http://www.tilford.ksu.edu/cultural_self/AfricanAmerican.pdf

Helms, J. (1995). *Helm's White racial identity development model.* Retrieved from http://edweb.csus.edu/edc/class-downloads/senna/edc171_white_id.pdf

Pascarella, E. T., & Terenzini, P. T. (2005). *How college affects students. A third decade of research* (Vol. 2). San Francisco, CA: Jossey-Bass.

St. John, E. P. (2009). *Action, reflection, and social justice: Integrating moral reasoning into professional development.* Cresskill, NJ: Hampton Press.

Sensoy, Ö, & DiAngelo, R. (2009, January). Developing social justice literacy: An open letter to our faculty colleagues. *Phi Delta Kappan, 90*(5), 345–352.

# SECTION II
# VOICES OF FACULTY IN THE CLASSROOM

# CHAPTER 2

# TEACHING FOR SOCIAL JUSTICE THROUGH EMBRACING IDENTITY TENSIONS

Christine W. Nganga

## ABSTRACT

*In this chapter, the author uses the interrelated knowledge base of multicultural education and critical pedagogy to offer possibilities for identity negotiations among students and educators. As an international scholar of color, she also interweaves how her own identity is negotiated by comparing and contrasting her teaching experiences in her home country and in the United States. The author argues that it is important for educators to interrogate their identity and embrace the tensions that arise in the process, in order to enact a critically engaged dialogue in their classrooms.*

Notions of social justice have gained prominence in educational research, teacher preparation, and educational leadership programs. The literature on leadership for social justice has focused on themes such as school leaders who demonstrate social justice leadership with notable academic success for all students, including those from racially, culturally, and linguistically diverse populations (e.g., Maynes & Sarbit, 2000; Riester, Pursch, & Skrla,

Social Justice Issues and Racism in the College Classroom: Perspectives from Different Voices
International Perspectives on Higher Education Research, Volume 8, 13–32
Copyright © 2013 by Emerald Group Publishing Limited

ISSN: 1479-3628/doi:10.1108/S1479-3628(2013)0000008004

2002; Scheurich, 1998). Another body of literature has given attention to theoretical frameworks for social justice leadership (e.g., Brown, 2004, 2006; Theoharis, 2007) while an additional line of research includes educational leadership program endeavors that focus on preparing school leaders who enact social justice principles in their practice (e.g., Bogotch, 2002; Theoharis & Caston-Theoharis, 2008). In the recent past, research on teaching and leadership for social justice in international contexts has emerged to include African nations (Bosu, Dare, Dachi, & Fertig, 2011).

The teacher education literature on social justice had also focused on various themes ranging from documenting experiences of teachers learning to teach for social justice (Darling-Hammond, French, Garcia-Lopez, 2002) application to specific content areas (Gutstein, 2003), and an analysis of school wide social justice models (Kraft, 2007). Some scholars have given attention to teacher educators' professional commitment to social justice (Cochran-Smith et al., 1999) and teacher preparation program conceptions of social justice (Cochran-Smith, Shakman, Jong, Terrell, Barnatt, & McQuillan, 2009; Enterline, Cochran-Smith, Ludlow, & Mitescu, 2008; McDonald, 2005, 2007).

Various traditions such as Black/ethnic studies, critical pedagogy, critical race theory, feminist theories, international education, multicultural education, postcolonial theory, and teacher education among others also extend the conceptual and pedagogical frameworks of social justice (Adams, Bell, & Griffin, 2007). Although scholars and researchers on social justice in education may lean on different theoretical traditions in their conceptualization and practice, many would generally agree that,

> Social justice education does not merely examine difference or diversity but pays careful attention to the systems of power and privilege that give rise to social inequality, and encourages students to critically examine oppression on institutional, cultural, and individual levels in search of opportunities for social action in the service of social change. (Hackman, 2005, p. 104)

Therefore although social justice education includes respecting and valuing cultural pluralism, an analysis of systemic inequities in order to advocate and take action for social change is crucial. With that in mind, teachers and leaders who perceive themselves to be agents of social change create learning communities whereby their daily practice is connected to promoting equitable participation, access to learning resources, and uplift for all students.

Bell (2007) views social justice as "a vision of society in which the distribution of resources is equitable and all members feel physically safe and secure" (p. 1). At the center of their vision and practice, teachers and leaders of social justice keep issues of race, class, gender, disability, sexual orientation, linguistic diversity, and other historically marginalizing conditions at the forefront of their work (Theoharis, 2004). Such educators work toward democratic, participatory, and inclusive schooling practices. Hackman (2005) argues that a social justice educational approach can be characterized by five essential characteristics – content mastery, tools for critical analysis, tools for social change, tools for personal reflection, and an awareness of multicultural group dynamics. Educators in schools of education can reflect on how their individual courses utilize either one or multiple components of these characteristics.

This chapter extends the literature on teaching and learning for social justice while paying particular attention to how the positionality of the students and the instructor in teacher preparation programs impact the classroom experience both for the instructor and the student.

In this chapter I utilize concepts from multicultural education literature and critical pedagogy to illuminate how though beneficial, such pedagogies need to incorporate the positionality of the teacher/instructor in the college classroom because the classroom is not necessarily a neutral space. I suggest that perspectives from these two bodies of literature coupled with addressing issues of positionality and identity of faculty and students can further inform the practice of teaching for social justice. Additionally, I posit that teaching and learning is also context dependent and encompasses identity tensions that cannot be ignored. As an international female faculty of color, I also narrate how my own identity negotiation process of growth as an educator who teaches through a social justice lens has evolved. I begin with showcasing a demographic imperative that highlights the call for K-12 educators to teach with a focus on social justice. I highlight the impact of the positionality of the instructor and the students in the teaching and learning classroom environment.

## DEMOGRAPHIC CHANGES

Educators in the 21st century are facing a demographic imperative. According to the National Center for Educational Statistics (2011), between 1989 and 2009, the percentage of public school students who were White decreased from 68 to 55 percent, and the percentage of those who were Hispanic doubled from 11 to 22 percent. By 2009, Hispanic enrollment had exceeded 11 million students. Additionally, the total number of Black students increased from 7.1 to 7.8 million, their share of enrollment decreased slightly during this time. Hispanic enrollment surpassed Black enrollment for the first time between 2001 and 2003 and has remained higher than Black enrollment in each year through 2009. Although the racial/ethnic distribution of public school enrollment differs from region to region, the statistics point toward the imperative for educators to prepare students from diverse populations in a changing society. In 2009, 12 states and the District of Columbia had an enrollment of less than 50 percent White students. Black students had the largest share of enrollment in Mississippi and the District of Columbia. Hispanic students had the largest share of public school enrollment in Arizona, California, New Mexico, and Texas. While the demographics of the students continues to shift, the racial/ethnic and gender make-up of the teaching work force, though changing, has only had slight shifts. For instance, the percentage of teachers who were Hispanic rose from 6 to 8 percent for elementary and 5 to 7 percent for secondary, from 1999–2000 to 2007–2008. At the elementary level, there was no notable change to the percentage of teachers who were White and those who were Black during this time period. However at the secondary level, the percentage of teachers who were White was lower in 2007–2008 (83 percent) than in 1999–2000 (86 percent). These demographics indicate that as the student population becomes more diverse, the teaching workforce has largely remained White and female. Pedagogical practices that ensure the academic success of all students, including those who are ethnically, culturally, and linguistically diverse remain a central component of teacher preparation and leadership programs.

In addition to the racial, ethnic, and linguistic diversity that the U.S. public schools continue to experience, the number of school age children who are living in poverty has been on the rise. The National Center for Education Statistics (2011) indicated that in 2009, 19 percent of 5- to 17-year-olds were in families living in poverty, compared with 15 percent in 2000 and 17 percent in 1990. The statistics also revealed that the child poverty rate was higher in 2009 than in 2000 in 36 states, although the percentages differ depending on the regions. These indicators again call for a continued conversation about how public school can meet its democratic aims of educating all students. Although the demographic imperative is not a new phenomenon to educators, faculty who prepare teachers to work in such culturally diverse schools as Zeichner (2003) suggests, often lack the experience in teaching such schools. Additionally there is a lack of diversity among students, faculty, and staff in teacher education programs majority of them being White, monolingual, and English speaking. While responses to the demographic imperative have included programmatic changes such as those in Boston College (Cochran-Smith et al., 2009) among others, the typical response has been to add a course or two in the teacher education program that focuses on multicultural education, cultural diversity, and teaching English Language Learners (Ladson-Billings, 1999; Villegas & Lucas, 2001; Zeichner & Hoeft, 1996). Hence multicultural education courses and courses on cultural, racial, ethnic, and linguistic diversity still play a major role in equipping teachers to teach in diverse schools.

It has been documented that nationally, there is a disproportionate number of instructors of color (faculty members or graduate student instructors) who are engaged in teaching diversity courses in the academe (Mckinley & Brayboy, 2003; Perry, Moore, Acosta, Edwards, & Frey, 2009). Although all instructors can face resistance in the classroom, especially while teaching diversity courses, research has shown that experiences of instructors of color are closely and negatively linked to their outsider status in predominantly White institutions (Butler, 2000; Vargas, 1999). The positionality of faculty of color in the academe is closely connected with how they experience the classroom as a space for developing critical consciousness especially when teaching courses that call for students to question the normative patterns of privilege, power, and oppression in schools and society.

On the other hand White scholars have also engaged in research on how racial power is reified in education classrooms (Hytten & Warren, 2003) including how discourses in teacher education that address issues of race can inadvertently propagate color blindness when White faculty do not acknowledge their own racial identity (Gordon, 2005). White faculty and teachers also need to do identity work as Lawrence and Tatum (1997) assert that "when White teachers fail to acknowledge their own racial identity, this lack of acknowledgement becomes a barrier for understanding and connecting with the developmental needs of children of color" (p. 163). Therefore interrogating our identities and positionalities is crucial for both faculty from the dominant culture and faculty of color.

Teacher education programs have a broad range of courses that focus on social justice, racial, ethnic, cultural, and linguistic diversity. Some schools of education specifically offer multicultural teacher education courses as the required course that equips preservice and inservice teachers to teach students from diverse populations. I now turn to how multicultural education is conceptualized in teacher education programs.

# MULTICULTURAL EDUCATION

Although there are many different approaches, statements, and aims and definitions of multicultural education, there is a high consensus that the goal of multicultural education is to reform the school and other educational institutions so that students from diverse racial, ethnic, and social class groups including gender diversity, will experience educational equity (Banks, 1993, 2010). Additionally multicultural theorists are also interested in how the intersections of race, class, and gender influence educational practices and outcomes (Grant & Sleeter, 2006).

Banks and Banks (2010) discuss five dimensions of multicultural education – content integration, prejudice reduction, knowledge construction process, an equity pedagogy, an empowering school structure, and culture. Content integration looks at the extent to which teachers use examples and information from other cultures and groups to illustrate key concepts in their subject content. However, time and resources are impediments to teaching for social justice because teaching materials that integrate information and examples from other cultures are not always readily available and take time to access (Gaudelli, 2001; Moller, 2002). Due to these constraints fewer teachers infuse social justice in their curriculum. The knowledge construction process helps students understand that knowledge is value laden, how some forms of knowledge are valued while others are rendered invisible. Knowledge is also impacted by ethnic, racial, gender, and social class positions (Banks, 1993). The prejudice reduction dimension helps students understand the values, dispositions, and attitudes they attach to different racial groups and work toward more positive racial attitudes that are democratic and inclusive. Equity pedagogy involves teachers using techniques and methods that aid the academic achievement of all students including those who are from diverse populations. Teachers cannot work through these dimensions of multicultural education without the support of an empowering school culture and structure. Institutional factors need to be reformed in order for students from diverse communities to excel and for teachers to feel supported in meeting their needs.

Gollnick and Chinn (2009) define multicultural education as "an educational strategy in which students' cultures are used to develop effective classroom instruction and school environments. It supports and extends the concepts of culture, diversity, equality, social justice, and democracy into the school setting" (p. 4). In this regard, culturally relevant teaching (Gay, 2010; Villegas & Lucas, 2002) and culturally relevant pedagogy

(Ladson-Billings, 1995) have been used as hallmarks for pedagogical frameworks to prepare preservice teachers to teach a diverse population.

In his review of the different conceptualizations of multicultural education from leading pioneers that included Nieto (2004), Sleeter (1996), Grant and Sleeter (2006), and Banks (2004), Gorski (2006) found that while each had their own unique conceptualization of multicultural education, they all agreed on the following key principles:

(1) Multicultural education is a political movement and process that attempts to secure social justice for historically and presently under-served students.
(2) Multicultural education recognizes that, while some individual classroom practices are consistent with multicultural education philosophies, social justice is an institutional matter and as such, can be secured only through comprehensive school reform.
(3) Multicultural education insists that comprehensive school reform can be achieved only through a critical analysis of systems of power and privilege.
(4) The underlying goal of multicultural education – the purpose of this critical analysis – is the elimination of educational inequities.
(5) Multicultural education is good education for all students. (pp. 164–165)

However Gorski concluded that many multicultural education professionals, though with good intentions, "conservatize multicultural education" to simply learning about other cultures and celebrate diversity but hardly explicitly teach about eradicating sexism, classism, racism, and other forms of oppression.

In his analysis of 45 course work syllabi, for multicultural teacher education, Gorski (2009) investigated the theories and philosophies underlying multicultural education course designs. His analysis revealed that most of the courses were designed to prepare teachers with pragmatic skills and personal awareness, but not to prepare them in accordance with the key principles of multicultural education, such as critical consciousness and a commitment to educational equity. Sixteen percent of the syllabi were consistent with Jenks, Lee, and Kanpol (2001), conservative multiculturalism, of assimilationist notions of the Other, but there was no explicit attention to the systemic inequities and how these informed classroom practice. Fifty-eight percent of the syllabi were largely dominated by elements of liberal multiculturalism whereby "difference and self-awareness were celebrated" (Gorki, 2009, p. 313). Approximately 29 percent of the syllabi fell under Jenks et al.'s critical multiculturalism in which education was discussed within a sociopolitical context. These syllabi indicated that the teacher education students explored power relationships, oppression in society and schools, and the ways in which educators could act as agents of social change by challenging inequities. It was disturbing that though what Gorksi analyzed in his syllabi indicated that they were teaching a multi-cultural education course, 71 percent of the syllabi were inconsistent with the basic aims of multicultural education.

Multicultural teacher educators need to reflect on their practice in order to understand the gaps between their teaching and the ideals of multicultural education. However, as earlier stated, if teacher education programs incorporate one or two multicultural education courses in their curriculum, it is difficult for one course to be sufficient in covering all dimensions of multicultural education and cultural pluralism. Some scholars have suggested to the infusion of multicultural concepts throughout teacher education curricula (Talbert-Johnson & Tillman, 1999). Additionally, considering the emotional toll that teaching such courses may take on the part of the instructor, faculty who teach such courses need to find an avenue of personal and professional renewal.

In addition to teaching multicultural education courses as a way to equip teachers to teach for social justice, teacher educators also incorporate critical pedagogy as a lens through which students can understand the larger systemic inequities. Such educators incorporate in their syllabus the work of critical theorists such as Paul Freire, Henry Giroux, and bell hooks among others.


## CRITICAL PEDAGOGY


Geneva Gay (1995) has noted that there are "ideological, conceptual, and operational parallels between multicultural education and critical peda-gogy" (p. 155). She asserts that "while these two movements are not identical, many of the concerns, perspectives, and proposals are analogous with respect to issues of educational access, equity, and excellence in a culturally pluralistic society and world" (p. 155). Further, she points out that the distinction may largely be about the scale and specificity rather than ideological distinctions and intentions. To this end, critical pedagogues tend to be generalists in their proposals for action applying these to the U.S. education as a whole. On the other hand, multiculturalists are more particularistic in their intentions and goals such as curriculum change and classroom instruction that is equitable for all students including those who are racially, ethnically, and linguistically diverse, those with disability and effective for both sexes.

> Villaverde (2008) describes the aims of critical pedagogy in the following statement: Critical pedagogy aims to develop and nurture critical consciousness to address larger political struggles and transformations in dealing with rampant oppressive social conditions. It works from Paulo Freire's critique on the banking concept of education to chart new pedagogical experiences, carefully mining popular culture for a wide range of learning possibilities. (p. 129)

Several scholars in teacher education have cited the importance of infusing critical pedagogical principles into teacher education. Bartolomé (2004) refers to the process of developing critical consciousness as acquiring ideological and political clarity. Political clarity "is the ongoing process by which individuals achieve ever-deepening consciousness of the sociopolitical and economic realities that shape their lives and their capacity to transform such material and symbolic conditions," while ideological clarity refers to "the process by which individuals struggle to identify and compare their own explanations for the existing socioeconomic and political hierarchy with the dominant society's" conceptions (Bartolomé, 2004, p. 98).

Developing a critical consciousness about racial, ethnic, and cultural diversity should be a major component of preservice teacher education (Gay & Kirkland, 2003; Howard, 2003; McDonough, 2009; Milner, 2003). Self-reflection and critical consciousness are keys to understanding the gap between one's practice and beliefs about improving educational opportunities for diverse populations. Critical reflection "requires one to seek deeper levels of self-knowledge and to acknowledge how one's own worldview can shape students' conceptions of self" (Howard, 2003, p. 198). Toward this goal, Milner (2003) points out that reflection on race and diversity among preservice teachers should be practiced and proposes a *critically engaged dialogue* and *race reflective journaling* as an instructional process. Freire (1998) encourages simultaneous reflection on self and the world and emphasizes that "authentic reflection considers neither abstract man nor the world without people, but people in their relations with the world. In these relations, consciousness and world are simultaneous: consciousness neither precedes the world nor follows it" (p. 62). Therefore preservice teachers need to reflect on who they are in relation to their students. Race reflections, then becomes "a process to understand hidden values, biases, and beliefs about race that were not to the fore in a teacher's thinking prior to conscious attempts to think about race" (Milner, 2003, p. 196).

Critically engaged dialogue in a college classroom and specifically with preservice teachers, can serve as a transformative process whereby students debate on their different positions on issues of equity, justice, and oppression, allowing them to connect with each other and the classroom lesson. hooks (1994) on engaged pedagogy which bears similarities to critically engaged dialogue, recognizes the importance of acknowledging the experience that students bring to the college classroom and the value of allowing their voices to be heard including those from minority populations:

> As a teacher, I recognize that students…enter classrooms within institutions where their voices have been neither heard nor welcomed, whether these students discuss facts – those that any of us might know – or personal experience. My pedagogy has been shaped to respond to this reality. If I do not wish to see these students use the "authority of experience" as a means of asserting voice, I can circumvent this possible misuse of power by bringing to the classroom pedagogical strategies that affirm their presence, their right to speak, in multiple ways on diverse topics. (p. 84)

In the next section, I address the impact of the identities represented in the classroom that can have on practice of critical engaged dialogue. As Rodriguez (2009) suggests, though there have been major contributions to critical theories and multicultural education by scholars in the field, most studies have failed to address the racialized and gendered identity of the instructor. I posit that the positionality of the instructor and that of her/his students can complicate the practice of critically engaged dialogue, teaching and learning for social justice.

## POSITIONALITY AND IDENTITY TENSIONS

Villaverde (2008) describes *positionality* as "how one is situated through the intersection of power and the politics of gender, race, class, sexuality, ethnicity, culture, language, and other social factors" (p. 10). The positionality of teachers and instructors is implicated in their practice, implicitly or explicitly (Martin & Guten, 2002). As Parker Palmer (1998) affirms, teachers teach who they are. Maher and Tetreault (1995) noted that "the concept of positionality points to the contextual and relational factors as crucial for defining not only our identities but also our knowledge as teachers and teacher educators and students in any given situation" (p. 165). Similarly, Britzman (1991) reminds us:

> We are all situated by race, class, and gender, and without an understanding of the social meaning that over determines how we invite and suppress the differences, the complexity

of biography is reduced to the dreary essentialism that beneath the skin we are all the same, or to the insistence that difference can be overcome through sheer individual effort. (p. 223)

One cannot teach classes that focus on social justice, multicultural education, critical pedagogy, or any other approaches that advocate for equitable distribution of resources, paying attention to privilege and oppression in schools without dealing with the power relationships that are already represented in the college classroom. Tisdell (2001) points out that how college instructors navigate power relationships with students, often privilege constructions of knowledge based on rationality and ways of interrelating more typical and comfortable for members of the White dominant culture. Additionally race is a critical positionality in a classroom context where the dynamics are contested (hooks, 1994).

In a qualitative study, Vargas (1999) interviewed 15 women teachers of color, 19 professors of color, and included 567 student evaluations in which 267 had narrative commentary. The participants in her study taught in predominantly White institutions. Her study revealed that being seen as the "Other" teacher in the classroom could lead to complex classroom dynamics as the "Other" teacher's values and beliefs are likely to differ from those of White middle class students and "may interpret such differences as a lack of objectivity on the part of the Other Teacher" (p. 365). Vargas also pointed out how students in their evaluations indicated that they saw her critique of aspects of the American society as constantly bashing American culture and how she should acknowledge how fortunate she was to live in the United States. Students saw her as having a strong sense of bias because of her background. In their interviews, some professors reflected on how students assigned less expertise to them as compared to their colleagues. Additionally, challenging racist behavior resulted in less positive evaluations.

Although most participants in Vargas' (1999) study felt that ethnic/racial identity did not influence their professional role, they believed that their race and ethnic identity impacted their everyday interactions with students. While each woman of color experiences academe differently, the prevailing conclusion emerging from the data was that the intersections of gender, race, ethnicity, class, and other social distinctions matter and not in positive ways in reference to women of color. Johnson-Bailey and Lee (2005) discussed some similar struggles and narrated an incidence when their authority was undermined as they were asked to show their vita to a White male student before he could accept to sign up for a class they were co-teaching.

Similarly, in her reflective essay on teaching diversity courses, Shrake (2006) narrated on how she learned to maintain a "mask" as an act of defense against the racism and sexism she encountered in the college classroom. As a form of identity negotiation, she tried to put on a face that she thought would be "acceptable" to the dominant society. However, the act of masking who she really was created a cognitive dissonance which resulted to her experiencing inner conflict as she felt limited in exercising her freedom as an educator. She wrote about her journey to "unmasking" herself:

> My journey toward reclaiming myself as strong not weak, proactive not passive, expressive not reticent and self-aware not self-conscious is far from over. However, what I have learned is that to be myself is the key. Now I believe that all female faculty should understand that self-confidence and a strong sense of ourselves are needed to sustain is in the field. (p. 192)

Female faculty of color who share power by inviting students into a dialogue may seem as though they are not the authority and lack the intellectual expertise, as opposed to a White male professor relinquishing his status in the classroom and inviting students to become authorities in the subject. Indeed, "for those Other Teachers who strive to be transformative intellectuals, who engage themselves in social criticism, and who practice critical pedagogy, the classroom performance represents a true pedagogical dilemma" (Vargas, 1999, p. 376). For professors of color, their presence disrupts the normative social order in the academy. Nevertheless minority faculty need to engage with difference rather than resist the differences they face in terms of race, class, gender, and other markers of identity and go beyond the binary of "self" and "other" (Asher, 2003). Then they will in turn be able to model for their students a more humanizing way of being in relation with each other.

## TEACHING FOR SOCIAL JUSTICE: MY JOURNEY

Darling-Hammond et al. (2002) frames learning to teach for social justice as a lifelong undertaking:

> It involves coming to understand oneself in relation to others; examining how society constructs privilege and inequality and examining how this affects one's own opportunities as well as those of different people; exploring the experiences of others and appreciating how those inform their world views, perspectives and opportunities and examining how schools and classrooms operate and can be structured to value diverse human experiences and to enable learning for all students. (p. 201)

My inclination toward teaching was inspired by the love of language and literature. As a young voracious reader, I wanted to become a teacher in order to have the opportunity to access different social spaces through literature from different parts of the world. Becoming a teacher then served as an avenue for me to share with students the capacity to see the world through the lens of different authors of literary works. This gave them the opportunity to understand the experiences of others by analyzing poetry, drama, and novel. I believed that, from their textual analysis and infusing their own perspectives, while drawing from different authors, students would gain knowledge of other cultures and the way of life of different people. Thus, as a high school and middle school teacher, I taught because I wanted to help students understand the world they live in and the realities of others.

Looking back, I realize how naïve I was in my ambitions. I had inadvertently fallen into the trap that Britzman (2003) refers to as the three cultural myths – everything depends on the teacher, the teacher is always a subject matter expert, and that teachers are self-made. When a beginning teacher buys into the myth that everything that happens in the classroom depends on him/her, even with good intentions of embracing a nonauthoritarian teaching style a teacher often reverts to teacher-centered pedagogical styles. This myth situates uncertainty in classroom encounters as a flaw. Teachers, who position themselves as subject matter experts, face the constant fear of not "knowing how to teach" and not "knowing everything there is about the material" (Britzman, 2003, p. 227). The myth that teachers are self-made constructs the "natural teacher" as one who somehow processes "talent, intuition, and common sense" while the historical and institutional structures that normalize this subjectivity are not taken into consideration (Briztman, 2003, p. 230). In my quest to be a "good" English and Literature teacher, I fell into the trap of embracing all these three myths. Hence, I failed to view the socioeconomic struggles of my students and the surrounding community within the larger political structures of the country. Though I realized that there was a socioeconomic gap between my students and myself, I had little knowledge of their lived experiences and the sociopolitical structures that created the inequities I saw in the school and my country. Upon joining graduate school and becoming curious about systemic inequities in my country and in the United States, I later learned that providing education was not a guarantee to creating equitable outcomes for all children (Wane & Gathenya, 2003). Additionally, ethnic frameworks were and still are an important determinant in tracking development patterns in Africa, including in my home country Kenya

(Alwy & Schech, 2004). During colonization, the British divided the country into eight provinces along ethnic lines. Further, the postcolonial government aligned parliamentary constituencies along ethnic boundaries which remain part of the political system today and consequently continues to determine how resources are allocated. Hence ethnicity and allocation of educational resources have been intertwined since colonization. As a young teacher I did not ponder on such issues. While teaching in a low socioeconomic school, I did not equate the lack of resources to the larger political structures in my country. My training in teacher education accorded me the privilege to hide in the word and not really look at the world through critical eyes. Poetry, literature, and the novel were stories and themes that had a historical context but I failed to link these to the current issues such as the impact of neocolonialism and globalization on developing countries.

Upon joining graduate school in the United States my teaching philosophy of "understanding the one's world and the world of others through literature and poetry" with little contextual application began to crumble. My first awakening to issues of social injustice in the United States was when Katrina occurred in 2005. On the surface Katrina seemed like a "natural catastrophe" however I slowly began to unlearn the difference between natural catastrophes and social injustices within the U.S. context. As Giroux (2006) eloquently pointed out, "In the aftermath of Hurricane Katrina, the biopolitical calculus of massive power differentials and iniquitous market relations put the scourge of poverty and racism on full display" (p.192). It was during my second year as a master student after being introduced to the works of Paulo Freire, Henry Giroux, and Cornell West that I began to realize that although America was a free and democratic society, it was a country where social injustices still occurred. While living in Africa, we rarely heard of the injustices and inequitable distribution of resources in the American society. The media portrayed the United States as a nation that fought for inequalities whereby everyone could make it if they worked hard – meritocracy was the ideal and practice of many. After this awakening, and the subsequent discussions that ensued in my graduate classes, I began to inform myself of the inequities that exist in U.S. public schools. Although public education was free, the intersections of race, class, and linguistic diversity was a site for struggle in educating *all* children.

As a doctoral student in an Educational Leadership program that was explicit about its social justice goals, my practice as an educator began to shift. I wanted to embrace the struggle and become a part of the solution.

One senior professor from the teacher education department, who saw my inner drive began to groom me to teach a course *Diverse Learners*, which is offered to preservice, alternative licensure, and graduate students. This course is designed to provide students with a broad base of knowledge and skills that will facilitate their effectiveness in meeting the needs of diverse student populations through appropriate instructional, curricular, and behavioral strategies. Students also explore diversity with respect to race, ethnicity, socioeconomic class, language, gender, and exceptionalities. In her intentionality to mentor me, she invited me to shadow her classroom for a semester before she recommended that I teach the same course. I subsequently began to teach this course as a first year doctoral student.

Students come to the university classroom with varying personal and professional experiences. The students consist of different age groups ranging from 22 to over 50. Discussing issues of race, class, and gender and the intersections among these in such a diverse age group can be a complex endeavor. Additionally, I am cognizant of the one or two minorities in the classroom. While I do not want them to feel silenced, neither do I want them to take the position of a native informant and speak as a representative of their people and in so doing essentialize their identities. Hence, I have to be cognizant of how to handle identity tensions in the classroom and keep in mind that though the classroom has limitations it is also a site for possibilities of growth.

Although I would consider my teaching to be fairly successful (with evaluations averaging 4.6/5) over the five years, I was a doctoral student and later an instructor in the same university. I have faced some of the tensions and oppositions that other female faculty of color have discussed in the literature. I have had to constantly evaluate my authority as a teacher and question my sharing of that authority. I have dealt with the fear of not being seen as the expert in the field just as I did as a beginning teacher, even as I embrace Paulo Freire's liberatory and dialogic pedagogy whereby teachers and students share power and authority in the classroom.

However, I have come to learn to ground my confidence not in how much I "know" about social justice work or multicultural education, but in embodying a true passion for social change. With this in mind, I no longer try to impress my students with my knowledge expertise about teaching for social justice but offer students the opportunity to critic the roots of their knowledge base about diverse learners. Initially many students are resistant about being self-reflective and would rather have the course only focus on equipping them with strategies for teaching diverse learners. I point out to them at the beginning of class that strategies are great about are not context free and the teacher of diverse learners also shares certain beliefs, about the students they teach.

## CONCLUDING REMARKS

When teacher educators and scholars commit themselves to teaching for and about social justice in order to prepare teachers who can serve in diverse school communities, encountering identity tensions is almost inevitable. They then need to continuously be self-reflective of who they are and their pedagogical practices so that they can embrace their own multifaceted identities and the identities that students bring to their classroom.

Evidently teaching that disrupts the social order and addresses issues about systemic inequities makes the classroom sometimes feel "unsafe" and contradicts the ethos of a safe teaching and learning environment. However, in embracing a critically engaged dialogue with students one must have a "deeply reflective interpretation of the dialectical relationship between our cultural existence as individuals and our political and economic existence as social beings" (Darder, 2009, p. 568). Hence understanding our positionalities and speaking of the marginalized when we sometimes feel marginalized is a negotiation of our identities and the tensions that arise. Although identity tensions cannot be fully eradicated, teaching for social justice is a call to embrace the risks that go along with the practice:

> If as the teacher of multiculturalism, [or social justice] I am to awaken in my students the teacher of multiculturalism within them, I know that I cannot do so without my own self-awareness. After all, if I am not aware of how various forces of oppression affect me and how I respond to them, how would I be able to get my students to think about the same? (Asher, 2003, pp. 245–256)

## REFERENCES


Adams, M., Bell, L. A., & Griffin, P. (Eds.). (2007). *Teaching for diversity and social justice*. New York, NY: Routledge.

Alwy, A., & Schech, S. (2004). Ethnic inequalities in education in Kenya. *International Educational Journal, 2*(5), 266–274.

Asher, N. (2003). Engaging difference: Towards a pedagogy of interbeing. *Teaching Education, 14*(3), 235–247.

Banks, J. (2004). Approaches to multicultural curriculum reform. In J. Banks & C. Banks (Eds.), *Multicultural education: Issues and perspectives* (pp. 242–264). San Francisco, CA: Jossey-Bass.

Banks, J. M. (1993). Multicultural education: Historical development dimensions and practice. *Review of Research in Education, 9*, 3–49.

Banks, J. M., & Banks, C. M. (Eds.). (2010). *Multicultural education: Issues and perspectives* (7th ed.). Hoboken, NJ: Wiley.

Bartolomé, L. (2004). Critical pedagogy and teacher education: Radicalizing prospective teachers. *Teacher Education Quarterly, 31*(1), 97–122.

Bogotch, I. E. (2002). Educational leadership and social justice: Practice into theory. *Journal of School Leadership, 12*(2), 138–156.

Bosu, R., Dare, A., Dachi, H., & Fertig, M. (2011). School leadership and social justice: Evidence from Ghana and Tanzania. *International Journal of Educational Development, 31*(1), 67–77.

Britzman, D. (1991). *Practice makes practice.* Albany, NY: State University of New York Press.

Britzman, D. (2003). *Practice makes practice* (2nd ed.). Albany, NY: State University of New York Press.

Brown, K. M. (2004). Leadership for social justice and equity: Weaving a transformative framework and pedagogy. *Educational Administrative Quarterly, 40*(1), 79–110.

Brown, K. M. (2006). Leadership for social justice and equity: Evaluating a transformative framework and andragogy. *Education Administration Quarterly, 42*(5), 700–745.

Butler, J. (2000). Reflections on borderlands and the color line. In S. Lim & M. Herrera-Sobek (Eds.), *Power, race, and gender in academe: Strangers in the tower?* (pp. 8–31). New York, NY: Modern Language Association.

Cochran-Smith, M., Albert, L., Dimattia, P., Freedman, S., Jackson, R., Mooney, J., … Zollers, N. (1999). Seeking social justice: A teacher education faculty's self-study. *International Journal of Leadership in Education, 2*(3), 229–253.

Cochran-Smith, M., Shakman, K., Jong, C., Terrell, D. G., Barnat, J., & McQuillan, P. (2009). Good and just teaching: The case for social justice in teacher education. *American Journal of Education, 115*(3), 347–377.

Darder, A. (2009). Teaching as an act of love: Reflections on Paulo Freire and his contribution to our lives and our work. In A. Darder, M. P. Barltodano & R. D. Torres (Eds.), *The critical pedagogy reader* (pp. 567–578). New York, NY: Routledge.

Darling-Hammond, L., French, J., & Garcia-Lopez, S. P. (Eds.). (2002). *Learning to teach for social justice.* New York, NY: Teachers College Press.

Enterline, S., Cochran-Smith, M., Ludlow, L., & Mitescu, E. (2008). Learning to teach for social justice: Measuring change in the beliefs of teacher candidates. *The New Educator, 4*(4), 267–290.

Freire, P. (1998). *Pedagogy of the oppressed.* New York, NY: Continuum.

Gaudelli, W. (2001). Reflection on multicultural education: A teacher's experience. *Multicultural Education, 8*(4), 35–37.

Gay, G. (1995). Mirror images on common issues: Parallels between multicultural education and critical pedagogy. In C. E. Sleeter & P. McLaren (Eds.), *Multicultural education: Critical pedagogy and the politics of difference.* Albany, NY: State University of New York Press.

Gay, G. (2010). *Culturally responsive teaching: Theory and practice* (2nd ed.). New York, NY: Teachers College Press.

Gay, G., & Kirkland, K. (2003). Developing cultural critical consciousness and self-reflection in preservice teacher education. *Theory into Practice, 42*(3), 181–187.

                                                    

Giroux, H. A. (2006, Summer). Reading hurricane katrina: Race, class, and the biopolitics of disposability. *College Literature, 33*(3), 171–196.

Gollnick, D. M., & Chinn, P. C. (2009). *Multicultural education in a pluralistic society* (8th ed.). Upper Saddle River, NJ: Pearson Education Inc.

Gordon, J. (2005). Inadvertent complicity: Colorblindness in teacher education. *Educational Studies, 38*(2), 135–153.

Gorski, P. C. (2006). Complicity with conservatism: The de politicizing of multicultural and intercultural education. *Intercultural Education, 17*(2), 163–177.

Gorski, P. C. (2009). What we are teaching teachers: An analysis of multicultural teacher education coursework syllabi. *Teaching and Teacher Education, 25*, 309–318.

Grant, C., & Sleeter, C. (2006). *Turning on learning: Five approaches to multicultural teaching plans for race, class, gender, and disability.* Upper Saddle River, NJ: Prentice-Hall.

Gustein, E. (2003). Teaching and learning mathematics for social justice in an urban, Latino school. *Journal for Research in Mathematics Education, 34*(1), 37–73.

Hackman, H. W. (2005). Five essential components for social justice education. *Equity & Excellence in Education, 38*(2), 103–109.

hooks, b. (1994). *Teaching to transgress: Education as the practice of freedom.* New York, NY: Routledge.

Howard, T. C. (2003). Culturally relevant pedagogy: Ingredients for critical teacher reflection. *Theory into Practice, 3*(42), 195–202.

Hytten, K., & Warren, J. (2003). Engaging whiteness: How racial power gets reified in education. *International Journal of Qualitative Studies in Education, 16*(1), 65–89.

Jenks, C., Lee, J. O., & Kanpol, B. (2001). Approaches to multicultural education in preservice teacher education: Philosophical frameworks and models for teaching. *Urban Review, 33*(2), 87–105.

Johnson-Bailey, J., & Lee, M. (2005). Women of color in the academy: Where's our authority in the classroom? *Feminist Teacher, 15*(2), 111–122.

Kraft, M. (2007). Toward a school-wide model of teaching for social justice: An examination of the best practices of two small public schools. *Equity & Excellence in Education, 40*(1), 77–86.

Ladson-Billings, G. (1995). Toward a theory of culturally relevant pedagogy. *American Educational Research Journal, 32*(3), 465–491.

Ladson-Billings, G. (1999). Preparing teachers for diversity: Historical perspectives, current trends, and future directions. In L. Darling-Hammond & G. Sykes (Eds.), *Teaching as the learning profession: Handbook of policy and practice* (pp. 86–124). San Francisco, CA: Jossey Bass.

Lawrence, S. M., & Tatum, D. M. (1997). Teachers in transition: The impact of antiracist professional development on classroom practice. *Teachers College Record, 99*, 162–178.

Maher, F. A., & Tetreault, M. K. (1995). *The feminist classroom.* New York, NY: Basic Books.

Martin, R. J., & Van Gunten, D. M. (2002). Reflected identities: Applying positionality and multicultural social reconstructionism in teacher education. *Journal of Teacher Education, 53*(1), 44–54.

Maynes, B., & Sarbit, B. (2000). Schooling children living in poverty: Perspectives on social justice. *Exceptionality Education Canada, 10*(1–2), 37–61.

McDonald, M. A. (2005). Integration of social justice in dimensions of prospective teachers' opportunities to learn. *Journal of Teacher Education, 56*(5), 418–435.

McDonald, M. A. (2007). The joint enterprise of social justice education. *Teachers College Record, 109*(8), 2047–2081.

Mcdonough, K. (2009). Pathways to critical consciousness: A first year teacher's engagement with issues of race and equity. *Journal of Teacher Education, 60*(5), 528–537.

McKinley, B., & Brayboy, J. (2003). The implementation of diversity in predominantly white colleges and universities. *Journal of Black Studies, 34*(1), 72–86.

Milner, R. H. (2003). Reflection, racial competence, and critical pedagogy: How do we prepare pre-service teachers to pose tough questions? *Race Ethnicity and Education, 2*(6), 193–208.

Moller, K. J. (2002). Providing support for dialogue in literature discussions about social justice. *Language Arts, 79*(6), 467–477.

National Center for Educational Statistics. (2011, May). *The condition of education 2011.* Retrieved from http://nces.ed.gov/pubs2011/2011033.pdf. Accessed on April 28.

Nieto, S. (2004). *Affirming diversity: The sociopolitical context of multicultural education.* Boston, MA: Pearson Inc.

Palmer, P. (1998). *The courage to teach: The inner landscape of a teacher's life.* San Francisco, CA: Jossey-Bass.

Perry, G., Moore, H. A., Acosta, K., & Fry, C. (2009). Maintaining credibility and authority as an instructor of color in diversity-education classrooms: A qualitative inquiry. *Journal of Higher Education, 80*(1), 80–105.

Riester, A. F., Pursch, V., & Skrla, L. (2002). Principals for social justice: Leaders of school success for children from low-income homes. *Journal of School Leadership, 12*(3), 281–304.

Rodriguez, D. (2009). The usual suspect: Negotiating white student resistance and teacher authority in a predominantly white classroom. *Critical Methodologies, 9*(4), 483–508.

Scheurich, J. J. (1998). Highly successful and loving, public elementary schools populated mainly by low-ses children of color: Core beliefs and cultural characteristics. *Urban Education, 33*(4), 451–491.

Shrake, E. K. (2006). Unmasking the self: Struggling with the model minority stereotype and the lotus blossom image. In G. Li & G. H. Beckett (Eds.), *"Strangers" in the academy: Asian women scholars in higher education* (pp. 178–194). Sterling, VA: Stylus Publishing.

Sleeter, C. (1996). *Multicultural education as social activism.* Albany, NY: State University of New York Press.

Talbert-Johnson, C., & Tillman, B. (1999). Perspectives on color in teacher education programs: Prominent issues. *Journal of Teacher Education, 50*(3), 200–208.

Theoharis, G. (2007). Social justice educational leaders and resistance: Towards a theory of social justice leadership. *Education Administration Quarterly, 23*(2), 221–238.

Theoharis, T. (2004, November). The rough road to justice: A meta-analysis of the barriers to teaching and leading for social justice. Paper presented at the University Council of Educational Administration, Kansas City, MO.

Theoharis, T., & Causton-Theoharis, J. N. (2008). Oppressors or emancipators: Critical dispositions for preparing inclusive school leaders. *Equity & Excellence in Education, 41*(2), 230–246.

Tisdell, E. (2001). The politics of positionality: Teaching for social change in higher education. In R. M. Cervero (Ed.), *Power in practice: Adult education and the struggle for knowledge and power in society.* San Fransisco, CA: Jossey Bass Publishers Inc.

Vargas, L. (1999). When the "other" is the teacher: Implications of teacher diversity in higher education. *Urban Review, 31*(4), 359–383.

Villaverde, L. (2008). *Feminist primer*. New York, NY: Peter Lang.

Villegas, A. M., & Lucas, T. (2001). Preparing culturally responsive teachers: Rethinking the curriculum. *Journal of Teacher Education, 53*(1), 20–32.

Villegas, A. M., & Lucas, T. (2002). *Educating culturally responsive teachers: A coherent approach*. Albany, NY: State University of New York Press.

Wane, N. N., & Gathenya, W. T. (2003). The yokes of gender and class: The policy reforms and implications for equitable access to education in Kenya. *Managing Global Transitions, 1*(2), 169–194.

Zeichner, K. (2003). The adequacies and inadequacies of three current strategies to recruit, prepare, and retain the best teachers for all students. *Teachers College Record, 105*(3), 490–519.

Zeichner, K., & Hoeft, K. (1996). Teacher socialization for cultural diversity. In J. Sikula (Ed.), *Handbook of research on teacher education* (2nd ed., pp. 176–198). New York, NY: Macmillan.

# CHAPTER 3

# TEACHING RACE, PUSHING BACK, AND MAKING MEANINGFUL CHANGE

Marybeth Gasman

## ABSTRACT

*In this chapter, I discuss my role as a White woman who studies race in the academy. I examine my ability to use my status, including my tenured status, to make change that can have a positive impact on faculty and students of color, especially African Americans. Moreover, I discuss my approach to teaching about race in the classroom. I also explore the limitations of my role and the reactions to my role by both Whites and people of color.*

When most people look at my curriculum vitae they make the assumption that I am an African American woman. Of course my name makes people wonder, but names are not always an accurate signifier for race. Truth is that I am White. However, I've never quite been able to relate to other White women in the ways that society says I am supposed to. I have White female friends but not a lot of them and none of my closest friends are White females with the exception of my daughter and my mom. I used to question

Social Justice Issues and Racism in the College Classroom: Perspectives from Different Voices
International Perspectives on Higher Education Research, Volume 8, 33–44
Copyright © 2013 by Emerald Group Publishing Limited
All rights of reproduction in any form reserved
ISSN: 1479-3628/doi:10.1108/S1479-3628(2013)0000008005

this fact but as I have grown older, I have realized that friends are where you find them – much like love.

In this chapter, I discuss my role as a White woman who studies race in the academy. I examine my ability to use my status, including my tenured status, to make change that can have a positive impact on faculty and students of color, especially African Americans. Moreover, I discuss my approach to teaching about race in the classroom. I also explore the limitations of my role and the reactions to my role by both Whites and people of color.

## GROWING UP RURAL AND WHITE

I grew up in a family of 10 children in a very rural area of the Upper Peninsula of Michigan. We were horribly poor. I often tell people, "We were so poor that when my mom made chipped beef on toast, there wasn't any beef." My mom did the best she could on about $7,000 a year. People often ask how 10 children and their parents could survive on so little money – the answer – we grew and made everything. As a child, I learned how to can fruits, make jams and jellies, wax vegetables for winter, cut sides of meat, gut fish and deer, and bake pies. Ironically, as an adult I do not eat meat and my husband is the cook in the house (enough is enough). As children, we entertained ourselves. We did not have a television or any fancy games; we made up games. We climbed apple trees and shook them for fun, flooded the backyard to make an ice rink during winter, played "kick the can," and rode the tractor for sport. I remember making homes for my blond, bikini-clad Barbies out of old record albums and tape. My little sister and I entertained each other for hours with these make-shift Barbie homes.

We had no idea that we were poor. Of course our parents knew, but we kids thought everyone lived this way. It was not until eighth grade when our house burned to the ground and we had to live in temporary housing in a nearby small city that we realized we were poor. I noticed what others had and the access that money gave people. It was then that I discovered that I was on free lunch and that my school uniforms had been worn by my brothers and sisters before I wore them. I wondered why my blouses were not white and why my tights had holes in the knees. I did not say much about my thoughts and feelings to anyone because I knew it would hurt my mom and dad.

My mom was lovely although she cried a lot. She tried her best to hide her tears but her struggle was hard. My father was an adequate husband. Yet, he was resentful and jealous of the accomplishments of others. He was bitter and this emotion resulted in very little love shown toward my mother. Instead, he verbally abused her, labeling her stupid because of her lack of education. She did what she needed to raise her children and get through the madness that had her trapped in a life she had never envisioned. Perhaps what I admire most about my mom and why I am talking about her in an essay about using one's Whiteness to speak truth to power, is that she spoke up and pushed back. In a provincial town, where most people conformed and took part in hatred and bigotry, my mom did not.

Sadly, my father did. When I wrote that he was bitter earlier, I was referring to his hatred of others, be they Blacks, Latinos, or Asians. Native Americans were spared for some reason (more than likely, my mother says, because my father was actually part American Indian). I grew up hearing my father say nigger, spic, jap, and chink. But, I also grew up with a mother who told me that these words were wrong and hurtful. She washed our mouths out with soap if we ever repeated these words. I saw my older brothers endure the *Zest* or *Dove* bar many times. In my heart I knew those words were wrong and did not say them. My mom told us that hatred of someone based on race, or color, or wealth was wrong. Of note, there were NO African Americans, Latinos, or Asians living in our town or within 150 miles from us at any point during my childhood (and even today – the town has not changed much). But, that didn't stop my father or many of the other residents of our town from hating these racial and ethnic groups. Oh, they were fun to laugh at on *Sanford and Son* and *Chico and the Man,* but you wouldn't want "those people" as friends. Minorities were easy targets.

My father did anything he could to convince us that African Americans were bad and that we should always hold them suspect. "Martin Luther King was a rabble rouser and didn't really believe in peaceful protest." "Malcolm X was anti-American." "Blacks were dirty and lazy; they just wanted a hand out." Ironically, my father was always trying to get government cheese and he stole from his employer time and time again. Many of my school teachers reinforced these stereotypical, racist ideas. I learned nothing about African American history and culture with the exception of slavery (and that was whisked over and romanticized and of course, there was no blame to be had). I heard teachers say derogatory things about Blacks. My Catholic grade school had a slave auction and was not apologetic about it. As a small child, I didn't see a problem with the slave auction. I didn't even know what slavery was let alone the horrors of Jim Crow. Our local coffee shop was called "Little Black Sambos" and had a young African boy being chased by a tiger on the sign and on the menus.

I thought Sambo was cute. The local bakery had big fat cookie jars decorated like a Black woman. I dug my hand in for a cookie never thinking twice about the image on the jar. I went to "Sambos" and the bakery with my father; my mother never took me to these places.

As my mom saw my father's influence on her children, she worked to counter it – ever so patiently. She told us not to listen to him. She confided in us – telling us how my dad blamed minorities for his lack of success, for his problems. She told us that she had grown up in Flint, Michigan, living next door to a Black family and that they were "just like you and me." When she married my father she had no idea that he held such racist views. Many times these views do not surface for years and by that time she had too many kids to make it on her own. She felt trapped. And as a result, she endured his hostile and shameful verbiage. Through our mother, some of us learned that prejudice is wrong and that we should speak up for others and confront injustice. Unfortunately, not all of my siblings learned this lesson – some of them harbor horrible thoughts and school their children in racist ideas. I no longer speak to these siblings – a choice I had to make when I had my own child.

Because of my mother, despite growing up in a racist and exclusionary environment, I chose to pursue a research agenda and scholarly life dedicated to issues of race. It makes sense to my mother. My father couldn't understand until very late in his life why his daughter would care so much about equity. In the spirit of true irony, my father had a stroke and we placed him in a nursing home near my sister in Tennessee. Unlike the Upper Peninsula of Michigan, there are African Americans in Tennessee and my father's roommate in the nursing home (he had a roommate because he could not afford a private room) was an African American man. Although disgusted and belligerent about the idea at first, my father grew to love the man and the man's family. They became close friends and when I would visit him, the two of them would be sitting in rocking chairs laughing and sharing stories. A few months before my father died, he told me that he had been wrong about Blacks. He cried in my arms about the life of anger and hatred he had lived for over 80 years; he was proud of me for standing up against his racist beliefs. Sadly, he never acknowledged the work of my mother – a poor, abused, White woman who could have grown bitter – to push back against his influence over her children; he continued to resent her.

Given the example of my mother (and my father for that matter), my interest in race and equity might make sense. Despite not knowing anyone of another race or ethnicity (outside of Native Americans) until graduate school, I felt compelled to make a difference in the world. I idealistically believed (and still believe) that we should "be the change we want to see." I make no apologies for having this perspective. Yes, it might color my viewpoint – it might make a difference in what I choose to research. But, it does not mean that I will cover up findings to appease my ideology. It does not mean that I'll avoid asking questions that run counter to my hopes. I believe that it is entirely possible to pursue a research agenda steeped in a commitment to justice.

## PUSHING BACK AND MAKING CHANGE

I am a firm believer in doing research about which you are passionate and with which you can make a difference. For me, issues of race, class, and gender have been salient in my life. Growing up in poverty with a trapped mother and a racist father gives me a unique insight into these issues – not the only insight, but an interesting one. For example, I could have become the type of person who carries the "pulled myself up by my bootstraps" narrative, questioning the work ethic of minorities. I know many White women who carry this narrative. I do not hold this perspective because I have come to understand that racial prejudice is much harder to overcome in the United States; whereas Whites can mask class differences.

Although the majority of my research is focused on Historically Black Colleges and Universities (HBCUs) and African American philanthropy, for this chapter I want to focus on the research that I have done related to students of color. This research interest grew out of my experience at the University of Pennsylvania, an elite, Ivy League institution with a less than desirable percentage of African American students (interestingly, Caribbeans and Africans are counted in this group). When I first arrived at Penn, I encountered a barrage of students who sought solace from their past experiences within my department. Faculty members, who have long since retired, drove them crazy. One young woman, who now teaches at another Ivy League institution, was told she was "dead in the water" upon admission – that she would never make it at Penn. Of course, when she graduated with distinction, she was a "phoenix rising from the ashes." Other African American students were discouraged from studying topics related to race. Classes revolved around White, Eurocentric ideas and rarely did anyone notice. Above all of that, admissions decisions were made with no commitment to bringing in a diverse class and as a result, I found myself looking out upon a sea of whiteness in the classroom.

I care deeply about the future make-up of the professoriate because I believe firmly in equity. I also believe that a diverse professoriate is the responsibility of all faculty and not just faculty of color. As such, I have focused much of my scholarly efforts on issues that will help bolster the future professoriate. Interestingly, my actions here are connected to my historical work on Black colleges. My dissertation was on an African American leader of a Black college named Charles Spurgeon Johnson. One of his goals was to change the face of the academy and to prepare future scholars and leaders. I decided to follow his lead. Of course, making a decision to change the status quo is not without its critics. Those who want to protect the status quo guard it with their lives. And taking on these individuals can mean coming to terms with your sense of integrity. Although I am fortunate to have, for the most part, good colleagues at Penn, there have been times during which I had to assert my perspective on equity in order to stop the extreme perpetuation of privilege.

One of my first efforts to make change at Penn relates to admissions decisions. I was uncomfortable teaching an all White class and as such, I banded together with one of my White, male colleagues to make much needed change. I knew that we would have more power working together. We conspired on ways to increase not only diversity in the applicant pool, but how to push back against our senior colleagues who wanted to maintain the status quo. When the time came for the meeting in which admissions decisions were made we pushed back at our colleague who had separated the candidates into acceptable and nonacceptable. Of course, the majority of the nonacceptable students were students of color. Together, we forced our colleagues to review each candidate in a holistic way, emphasizing the need for a diverse class and our commitment to access for more than merely White students from the Northeast. Our efforts started out slowly, with some success, but eventually (today), we have the most diverse programs in our school. Our cohorts are truly representative of the nation as a whole. Moreover, our faculty, which has changed and is much more diverse in terms of race and gender, is now committed to enrolling a diverse class. We no longer have to push with such intensity.

Based on my knowledge of higher education and especially the experiences of African American students both within Black colleges and historically White institutions, I know that learning in an environment that embraces one's ideals and culture is beneficial. In addition, as someone who also wants to be part of an environment that cares about issues of race and tries to move forward in its ability to understand and manage these issues, I wanted to create an open conversation around race. With the help of the

Dean of Students in my school, we started a Race in the Academy series that showcased research on race and also highlighted films and plays pertaining to race. Although the attendance was slow in the beginning, it picked up and students began to look forward to the events. They saw the gatherings as a safe space in which they could share their thoughts and frustrations. Of note, White students participated in these events as often as African Americans and saw them as a supplement to their classroom instruction. When the Race in the Academy series started there was some backlash from a few faculty and staff members who "didn't think race was a problem" or "wanted to see more talks on Whiteness because that is a race as well." We tried our best to embrace these faculty members and offer programs that met their needs too. Unlike some scholars, I believe that people who are resistant to change and the infusion of conversations around race should be included in discussions. The only way for learning to take place is through exposure. That said, with some faculty, we just could not change their minds.

Over time perhaps we have changed minds. Shortly after the launching of the Race in the Academy series, with the support of our dean at the time, we began a series of informal discussions about race among the faculty. We met once a month over breakfast and talked about issues of race in our research, teaching, and interactions with students and each other. Interestingly, different people showed up for the discussion every month. Sometimes those people who we knew were committed attended; we knew they were committed from student comments, from their research, and from their actions in the school. Other times those people who never spoke up in a meeting or never attended any race-related events showed up. They did not talk, but they listened to the conversation. I think that just listening to others talk about the manifestations of race was helpful to those who live in fear of taking a risk. These monthly conversations about race and the Race in the Academy series bring the conversation to the surface and it bubbles up and from time to time there is a breakthrough.

Recently, I feel that we had a breakthrough in terms of an individual's understanding of her own perpetuation of oppression. During a faculty meeting, we had a discussion about issues of race in the classroom and one White, female professor who is notorious for ignoring these issues, silencing others, and making deeply insensitive comments to students, spoke up. She said, in a trembling voice, something so important – "How do I know if I am one of the people making our African American students feel uncomfortable? I think I might be but how will I know unless someone tells me." Interestingly, this professor is one of the most powerful faculty members in our school and commands immense respect externally and within the university – yet, she does not know how to manage her thoughts about race and does not know how to facilitate conversations around this issue in the classroom. She did, however, take the first step and admit her inability. Bringing issues of race (as well as class, gender, and sexuality – which is something we do) out into the open is vital and creates an environment in which people (eventually) feel comfortable asking for help, admitting fault, and expressing a desire to change. For those of us doing research related to race, it is crucial that we create these opportunities in our local environments. It's not JUST enough to do research – the research should engender change.

Perhaps the area in which a professor and researcher can have the most impact is in his or her teaching. Of course, this is a choice. One can merely present information and let students take from it what they want and move forward. Or, one can present information and ask probing questions to make students think – critically think. Or, one can teach with a particular ideological approach and ignore other perspectives. I want to make it clear that although I believe in discussing issues of race in the classroom, I do not believe in jamming an ideology down students' throats. I use the second approach I described above.

For example, in my History of American Higher Education course, I provide students with readings that speak to issues of race, class, gender, sexuality, ethnicity, and religion. Within these readings, I present many sides of each issue and a variety of perspectives. So, if I am teaching about the civil rights and student protests of the 1960s, I present readings from the right, left, and center. I want students to analyze these readings and understand the various perspectives. I want them to study the language – there is a difference between calling students "activists" and "radicals," for instance. Why are the different words used and how does the use of one word rather than the other color the reader's perspective?

In addition to presenting different perspectives, I try to push students to understand their role in the world and more specifically, in American history. So often, students think that they are powerless. Not true! I provide my students with many examples of how students have changed many aspects of academe as well as the larger society. One need look no further than the Black college students who sat at a lunch counters in Greensboro, North Carolina and endured ridicule and abuse in order to desegregate eating facilities (and so much more) (Branch, 1989). Students have had a great impact on the make up of the faculty at many colleges and universities, pushing for greater diversity. They have also shaped the curricula, asking for offerings that represent their perspectives and serve their needs. Sometimes students doubt the ability of one person to make change. In response, I talk about those well-known individuals who have led movements for change – Nelson Mandela, Martin Luther King, Jr., Caesar Chavez, among others. But, I also talk about those leaders, many people of color but also Whites, who have made change on a daily basis within their local communities, schools, and universities. The readings I provide to students focus on these people and their efforts. I also talk about the ways that I have pushed back to make positive change as a White woman. Of course, regardless of one's politics, all of my students now have a contemporary example of how one person can make a difference and make great change – Barack Obama – a person who started out making change in local communities and is now the leader of the United States. And, of note, students at colleges and universities across the country are partially responsible for Obama's success – students who many assumed were passive and lacked any inclination to step up and take responsibility for their country.

Although I only tell the students once that I want them to live their lives for something bigger than themselves, I secretly hope that my message will get through to them. I hope that they will choose to fight for justice in many areas – some do, some don't. I try to role model this behavior.

From time to time, students do not like my approach to teaching history. They are angered that I don't teach the traditional "White men and wars" curriculum. When I was younger, those students who disagreed with my approach got on my nerves – got under my skin. However, now I just let people know on the first day of class that my approach to teaching history is an inclusive approach. I let them know that I want each student to see him or her self-represented in the readings. And, I bluntly let students know that they might want to drop the class if they are not comfortable with this approach. Rarely do people drop. Rumor has it that my class pushes people to think different – that students leave feeling refreshed and energized about making change. They may not agree with everything I say, but they understand that "to be educated is to be conscientiously uncomfortable" (Peterkin, 2008, n.p.).

## THE POWER OF TENURE

Thus far, all of the examples I have given in this essay took place before I had tenure. I have always been a fighter and a feisty one and as such, when I started at Penn, I told the dean at the time that although I respected tenure,

I did not want it so badly that I would sacrifice my integrity over issues of equality and equity. She agreed and supported me. I felt empowered by her support and as a result, I was probably much more outspoken than most of my junior colleagues at the time, regardless of race. That said – I do realize that there is a certain safety in Whiteness and my femaleness and I typically recommend that all faculty members choose their battles when standing up against faculty colleagues. I did not fight back against every little thing but chose which incidents and topics I wanted to speak out on – these typically involved race, gender, class, and sexuality, and every so often religion. My motto as an untenured professor was always this: "If you are productive, it is hard for someone to take your voice away." Productivity was a protective shield for me as it is harder to get rid of someone who publishes a lot and brings in substantial grant funding.

Upon receiving tenure, I did feel slightly more empowered and I have to admit that tenured professors who remain tight-lipped frustrate me. I did not work extremely hard to get tenure only to be silent about that which I feel strongly. On one particular occasion, I was happy to have the security of tenure. Our school had just finished selecting the year's round of Ph.D. students and the administration distributed a list of the students, noting their race, gender, and other particulars. I noticed that the percentage of students of color was down significantly from the year before and after studying the list, I realized what had happened. Without oversight from a higher level, each of the divisions in the school had relied on the other divisions to bring in the students of color – the result: very few students of color. I wrote an e-mail to our dean and he agreed, stating that he had noticed the same thing when he saw the list of students. When we had our school-wide faculty meeting that month, the dean raised the lack of diversity in the Ph.D. cohort for discussion and I decided it was an opportune moment to speak up. After listening to faculty members make statements such as "I want to recruit students that I feel comfortable mentoring" and "I want to advise students who do research that is similar to mine," I spoke up. I asked how we could in good conscience keep what Penn had to offer for Whites only, and for that matter only affluent Whites. I explained that if we only mentored people who were "like us" then the academy would remain exactly the same (realizing that some people would like the academy to stay the same). I said that I was ashamed that our Ph.D. cohort lacked diversity and that based on the few years prior, I thought we had reached an understanding as a faculty that there was great value in having a diverse Ph.D. cohort and, in essence, preparing a diverse professoriate. When I made these comments, I saw a few eyes rolling but interestingly, afterwards I received quite a few supportive e-mails from faculty members. I wish that they had spoken up in the actual meeting; however, some people will never do this even if their research is related to race or social justice.

Another incident that took place after I received tenure pertained to the recruitment of faculty of color. While serving on several search committees for faculty positions, I began to notice that there was not a systemic approach to recruiting faculty of color; it was haphazard at best. Curious, as usual, I secured funding from the dean's office to conduct a study on our institution's policies and practices for recruiting faculty of color. I met with all of the faculty members who had served as chairs of search committees as well as members of the administration and faculty of color who had come through the recruitment process in the past five years. If I had been untenured, I might have been uncomfortable conducting the interviews as some of my colleagues were hostile in their views on race-based recruiting (most colleagues were supportive even if they didn't quite understand how to recruit a diverse faculty). I learned an incredible amount about what we do and don't do at Penn to ensure a diverse faculty. In addition to writing several peer reviewed articles, an op-ed, and a scholarly essay with the data from the study, I also talked with my dean. I told him about my findings and my concerns that we had no system in place – save an unwritten rule: "no more than two white men on a search committee." To my surprise, he was incredibly supportive and in the subsequent year, he continued to ask my perspective on faculty recruitment. Of note, he purchased books on faculty recruitment for search committee chairs, wrote letters to them stressing the importance of recruiting a diverse faculty, and made sure that they received training to help them reach candidates of color. With the efforts of our faculty of color and supportive White allies, we have been able to make slow, yet substantive change within our school.

## CONCLUDING THOUGHTS

My race, class, and gender have shaped the way that I approach scholarship, teaching, and service within the academy. Rather than merely pushing paper and pencil, I aim to push students, my colleagues, and the policies of the academy that exclude, oppress, and discriminate. I aim to push for change and progress regardless of the "sage" advice from older colleagues that researchers should be just that – researchers, keeping their noses out of activism. I urge future scholars to consider pushing back against the status quo. When you use empirical research to back up your opinions and perspectives, you can rest assured and feel confident that your actions are justified. Those who have tenure, regardless of race, need to work together to make the academy a better place for all faculty and students.

# REFERENCES

Branch, T. (1989). *Parting the waters: America in the King years, 1954–1963*. New York, NY: Simon & Schuster.
Peterkin, D. (2008). *Entry made on Teagle Foundation Blog*.

# CHAPTER 4

# ADVOCATING FOR CHANGE: A REFLECTION ON MY JOURNEY TO SOCIAL JUSTICE EDUCATION

Bonita K. Butner

## ABSTRACT

*It takes a deep commitment to change and an even deeper commitment to grow.*

— Ralph Ellison

*This quote from Ralph Ellison highlights the complexity of the concepts of change and growth. As faculty, we are constantly called on to facilitate the growth and change of our students through their academic work. This chapter provides a narrative of one faculty member's growth toward understanding and the incorporation of social justice concepts and structures into her classroom.*

*I had my first microbiology test last week and as the professor returned the papers, he made a point to acknowledge the work of one student who received a perfect score. When he called my name and I stood up, I saw confusion on his face ... and a look of disappointment.... I guess he didn't expect a Black female to do well on the test.*

— Anonymous student

Social Justice Issues and Racism in the College Classroom: Perspectives from Different Voices
International Perspectives on Higher Education Research, Volume 8, 45–53
Copyright © 2013 by Emerald Group Publishing Limited
All rights of reproduction in any form reserved
ISSN: 1479-3628/doi:10.1108/S1479-3628(2013)0000008006

Faculty expectations can energize students to achieve at levels they may not
have thought possible. Faculty expectations can also demoralize students
and leave them with diminished views of their capabilities. For faculty
teaching on college campuses, it is imperative that we expect the best from
all students and that we gain the knowledge and skills to ensure a socially
just education for all.

Social justice has been defined in a number of ways. In a foreword to
Ladson-Billings and Tate's (2006) *Education Research in the Public Interest*,
James Banks defines social justice as the promotion of educational equality
for marginalized groups (p. xi). In this view, the examination of marginalization requires the study of oppression and the implications to the
oppressed group and society at large. Bell (2007) further defines social
justice as both a process and a goal. We understand that the goal of social
justice is, as banks describe, equal participation by all groups. Bell states
that educational processes must be developed in order to reach the goal of
equal participation. The processes are the ways that curriculum is developed
and the pedagogical approach to infusing the principles of social justice in
our classes. Ultimately, our classes should prepare individuals to become
agents of change in an oppressive society.

I find that the concepts of social justice permeate various spheres of my
life. These spheres include my religious sphere, my professional administrative sphere, and my current academic sphere. For instance, I am rooted in
the teachings of the Methodist Church and my beliefs are grounded in the
major tenets of the Church. Most notable among the tenets is the social
principle of justice. Supported by Christian principles, the United Methodist
Church espouses the rights of all people to equal access to areas such
as housing, education, and health care (United Methodist Church, p. 1).
Within the structure of the United Methodist Church is the United
Methodist Women. The mission of this group is to support spiritual growth,
develop leaders, and most important, advocate for social justice. At a recent
national meeting the group focused on social justice within the context of
immigration. As an example of agents of social change, women marched in
support of just immigration laws and lobbied legislators to implement laws
that provided humane paths to citizenship.

My professional background is in the field of student affairs administration. I served for a number of years on college campuses in positions such as
academic advisors, admissions coordinator, and multicultural affairs
director. The American College Personnel Association (ACPA), one of the
umbrella organizations for those who work in nonacademic positions on
college campuses, includes the term "advocacy" in their both mission and

core values. Advocacy is centered on the development of all students, respect for diversity and human dignity, and on the implementation of just policies that are vital to the higher education community including Affirmative Action (ACPA). Professionals working in the field of student affairs are expected to be advocates for their students and for the principles the organization promotes. Finally, my current academic life is as a faculty member teaching in a Higher Education Administration graduate program. We, too, have a professional organization with ethical principles that guide behavior. Key among the principles are respect and fairness (ASHE). Members of the organization are called on to be respectful in relationships and to judge without discrimination or prejudice. An event that demonstrated the organization's commitment to a just society was the relocation of our national meeting in 2002. The leadership placed the organization in financial jeopardy by announcing the move several months prior to the meeting, but felt the principles of social justice espoused by the organization superseded potential financial loss. Fortunately, the organization held firm in their principles and did not suffer financially.

While all individuals who share these various "spheres" of my life may not fully ascribe to the principles listed above, I have chosen to embrace these principles and to hold the organizations and my discipline accountable to these principles. Friere (1970) has suggested that teaching is a political act that is never neutral. College faculty can chose to support the principles of social justice through the structure of the curriculum, the required readings, and their pedagogical approach. So, how do I implement these principles in the classes I teach? How have I made sure the environment in my classes will not illicit comments such as the one above that left a student dispirited and questioning her worth?

## MY JOURNEY BEGINS

In an article titled "Coping with the Unexpected" (Butner, Burley, & Marbley, 2000), I recounted an incident in my first academic position that led to a teachable moment. Visiting coaches from a Historically Black Institution (HBI) were picking up items at the local Walmart. Upon leaving the store they were confronted by police who indicated they had been identified as operating a scam and on the statement of one witness, the coaches were taken into custody. The coaches provided identification, but the questioning continued for several hours. In spite of their education and their status as coaches at a nationally known institution, their declaration of innocence was not heeded. Needless to say, the incident made the local and national news.

I taught a graduate class on the evening following this incident. It seemed like the perfect time to talk about inequality in society and how we view various groups. Students in the class were at the master's and doctoral level and all were Anglo. I started the conversation asking if they knew about the situation and what were their thoughts. They all agreed that it was an "unfortunate" situation, but that the police had acted appropriately. They suggested that if someone is accused of a crime, no matter who they are, they should be taken into custody. In an attempt to extend this line of thinking, I asked if the situation would be the same if the institution's nationally known Women's basketball coach (who is Anglo) were accused of a crime, should police automatically take her into custody. After some thought, the students suggested that the police knew the local coach so would probably need to question her before taking her into custody. I pushed further by asking if there were a positive identification, would the coach be taken into custody. The final analysis was that even with a positive identification, the police should be sure of the charges before taking the local coach into custody.

This incident pushed me as an instructor to think about how I could organize my classes to infuse issues of social justice and to be prepared to discuss current newsworthy issues that might come up during the semester. I wanted to move away from the "accidental" method of infusing social justice principles and work to ensure that students left my class with the knowledge and skills to address issues of inequity. While I do not teach courses that specifically examine issues of oppression, I find that I can work to ensure that my students

> ... develop the critical analytical tools necessary to understand oppression and their own socialization within oppressive systems ... and to [develop] the capacity to interrupt and change oppressive patterns and behaviors in themselves and in the institutions and communities of which they are a part. (Bell, p. 2)

## A SOCIAL JUSTICE PEDAGOGICAL APPROACH

Since that incident at my former institution, I have purposefully looked for ways to incorporate the principles of social justice in all of the classes I teach. My major consideration is to make issues real to students and to be sure not only that they have information, but also that they become critical consumers of the information which will in turn help them make decisions that are grounded in the social justice paradigm. For example, my organization and administration class examines the typical topics of organizational structure, governance, and institutional change. In addition to the seminal text "How Colleges Work (Birnbaum, 1988)," I use current articles and information from various Web sites to support and generate discussion around the basic principles. An example might be using an article that highlights an urban institution's decision to use eminent domain to expand their campus. This allows the conversation to move from the abstract to the concrete. Students read the seminal text and articles that discuss governance while juxtaposing it with the real-life decision of institutions. How are these decisions made? What is the governance structure at the institution? Who has final authority to make these decisions? In addition, students can examine the issue from the standpoint of the neighborhood. Students could research the demographics of the neighborhood. They can examine other institutions and neighborhoods that have gone through similar processes. What was the conversation surrounding the change? What was the perspective of the community? How do power relationships mediate decisions? By looking at a situation through various lenses, students are challenged to think about decisions that are made and the implications of those decisions.

The field of higher education administration draws its theoretical grounding from multiple disciplines. Critical Race Theory, social identity theories, and cognitive development theories are just a few of the theoretical perspectives that guide our understanding of the college setting and the groups that operate within those settings. The program curriculum is designed to prepare administrators who understand the postsecondary environment and its constituents within the context of the larger society. Beyond a basic procedural understanding of how a campus operates, our students must understand the dynamics of group relations and how societal norms can produce inequality. To assist me in understanding how to incorporate social justice and diversity issues in my classes, I participated in my institution-sponsored Diversity Curriculum Infusion Institute. The intent of the Institute is to help faculty develop the skills to incorporate social justice issues and reading into their classes. The Institute accepts applications for the year-long program and faculty representing the myriad divisions and departments of the institution are selected. We benefit from the introduction of resource material and the various perspectives of the participants. Faculty from diverse disciplines such as pharmacy, English, and education came together the year I participated in the Institute.

I teach a variety of courses throughout the academic year. They range from an introductory course in organization and administration of higher education to a capstone class that is taken at the end of the master's program. Given the wide range of topics and times that I encounter the student, I decided that in addition to the skills learned in the Diversity Curriculum Infusion Institute, a framework for my classes would best position me to infuse social justice into my classes. I utilized the framework suggested by Adams (2007) that puts forword the following educational principles of practice:

1. *Balance the emotional and cognitive components of the learning process*: facilitation that pays attention to personal safety, classroom norms, and guidelines for group behavior.
2. *Acknowledge and support the person (the individual student's experience) while illuminating the systemic (the interactions among social groups)*: facilitation that calls attention to the here and now of the classroom setting and grounds the systemic or abstract in an accumulation of concrete, real-life examples.
3. *Attend to social relations within the classroom*: facilitation that helps participants name behaviors that emerge in group dynamics, understand group process, and improve interpersonal communications, without blaming or judging each other.
4. *Utilize reflection and experience as tools for student-centered learning*: facilitation that begins from the student's worldview and experience as the starting point for dialogue or problem posing.
5. *Value awareness, personal growth, and change as outcomes of the learning process*: facilitation that balances different learning styles and is explicitly organized around goals of social awareness, knowledge, and social action, although proportions of these three goals change in relation to student interest and readiness. (pp. 32–33)

These principles guide my pedagogical approach to teaching my classes. As with any framework, obstacles will be encountered. Principle 1 states that we must pay attention to a student's personal safety. We do this by developing norms for behavior. As previously indicated, norms for behavior and interaction must be developed by the students. Students are more likely to adhere to norms that they have helped to develop. I find that students also hold each other accountable if the group has agreed to certain standards of behavior. Principle 2 asks us to support students by recognizing their life experiences. When discussing issues of social justice, a student's understanding will be grounded in their life experiences. We must recognize that the student's experience is their own and is valid. In classroom discussions, we should not challenge the experience, but should structure discussion to expand the student's worldview. Principle 3 highlights relations in the classroom. This is a challenging principle. Group dynamics are impacted by course content. Faculty must help students to understand the importance of interpersonal communication as the classroom norms are established. Principle 4 calls for allowing time for reflection. There are numerous examples of reflective strategies that faculty can use in their classroom. From probing questions that engender reflection to stories that create a framework for reflection, faculty must be creative in allowing student time and space for reflection. An example of a story that has been used to encourage reflection might be appropriate for faculty in higher education programs. This story aligns very well with the aforementioned scenario on eminent domain. It is cited in a book byLathrop (1977) that tells the story of a woman who has been displaced. As her original home is being burned, she comes out of her new home and states "You may have built me a new house, but you're burning my home." This type of story can be used to create a framework for reflection on decisions that administrators make. Are we examining issues and the impact of our decisions from various perspectives? Finally, Principle 5 exhorts us to value those areas that have not always been valued. Difficulties may arise in faculty ability to incorporate social awareness into their learning outcomes, and also developing ways to assess these outcomes that are affective in nature.

## CONCLUSION

While I do not teach courses that specifically address diversity, oppression, or social justice, I find that all of these issues are critically important for future administrators to understand. Therefore, I place course topics such as understanding organizational structure or college administration within a social justice context. The five principles proposed by Adams create the environment that supports readings and discussion in a social justice context. For example, in my capstone class, students develop a set of norms for classroom behavior and interaction. We anticipate that difficult dialogues may occur during the semester and we want to establish a group understanding of how we will engage in those discussions. In other classes, I try to provide real-life examples for students when discussing various classroom issues. In my college student class, we examine how policy might impact different student groups. A favorite scenario I provide addresses inequitable policies in campus housing for White and African American Greek letter organizations. The scenario goes like this: A predominantly White campus has a sorority house with 40 beds on each of eight wings. The housing policy states that a sorority must fill 80% of the beds in order for the chapter to remain in the house. This equates to a minimum of 32 women who need to be willing to live in the sorority house. Students are asked to examine the policy and the campus statistics and to respond to the question: "Does this policy privilege one group of sororities over others? Why or why not?"

In addition to the examples provided above, I utilize reflective exercises that allow the student to share their understanding of issues as a way to begin conversations that lead to an understanding grounded in the literature and an expansion of the student's worldview. As the five principles suggest, I see myself as a facilitator of student growth as they gain the content knowledge and contextual understanding of societal issues.

Social justice is a central concept at my institution. Our urban setting makes issues of social justice a natural fit as we prepare teachers, counselors, and administrators to work in urban institutions. In my program, preparing individuals for college-level positions that will work with students requires that they have the practical knowledge of campus administration as well as a deep understanding of the context in which colleges and universities operate. If we are to live out the principles of our professional organizations, we must structure our classrooms to ensure we produce professionals that understand the social justice context of the work we do and who become advocates for change.

# REFERENCES


Adams, M. (2007). Pedagogical frameworks for social justice education. In M. Adams, L. Bell & P. Griffin (Eds.), *Teaching for diversity and social justice*. New York, NY: Routledge Press.

American College Personnel Association-College Student Educators International (ACPA). Retrieved from http://www2.myacpa.org/

Association for the Study of Higher Education (ASHE). Retrieved from http://www.ashe.ws/

Bell, L. A. (2007). Theoretical foundations for social justice education. In M. Adams, L. Bell & P. Griffin (Eds.), *Teaching for diversity and social justice* (pp. 1–14). New York, NY: Routledge Press.

Birnbaum, R. (1988). *How colleges work*. San Francisco, CA: Jossey-Bass.

Butner, B., Burley, H., & Marbley, A. (2000). Coping with the unexpected: Blacks at predominately white institutions. *Journal of Black Studies, 30*(3), 453–462.

Friere, P. (1970). *Pedagogy of the oppressed* (2nd ed.). New York, NY: Penguin Press.

Ladson-Billings, G., & Tate, W. (Eds.). (2006). *Education research in the public interest. Social justice, action and policy* (pp. xi–xvi). New York, NY: Teachers College Press.

Lathrop, C. (1977). A gentle presence. Appalachian Documentation (ADOC).

*United Methodist Church.* Retrieved from http://www.umc.org/

# CHAPTER 5

# CONFESSIONS OF A *BORDER-CROSSING BROTHA-SCHOLAR*: TEACHING RACE WITH ALL OF ME

Ty-Ron M. O. Douglas

## ABSTRACT

*In this chapter, Douglas draws on his experiences in various educative spaces to share how he utilizes his positionality as a* border-crossing brotha-scholar *to teach about social justice and racism in university classrooms. In sharing how he employs his unique identity to help students negotiate various ideological borders in his courses, Douglas also models how socially just pedagogical practices can emerge out of who we are.*

I teach with all of me, and as an international scholar whose work is undergirded by a social justice ethos, I am always in *teacher mode*. From passionate conversations at the dinner table with my teenage son about the insidious nature of racism to impromptu exchanges with inquisitive airplane passengers who – after peeking at a PowerPoint slide on my laptop – want to know more about White privilege, class is always in session. Ironically though, as a *border-crossing brotha-scholar*, a Black male academician who has traversed many geopolitical, cultural, and physical borders between Bermuda – my country of birth and rearing – and the university classroom,

Social Justice Issues and Racism in the College Classroom: Perspectives from Different Voices
International Perspectives on Higher Education Research, Volume 8, 55–67
Copyright © 2013 by Emerald Group Publishing Limited
All rights of reproduction in any form reserved
ISSN: 1479-3628/doi:10.1108/S1479-3628(2013)0000008007

I draw on various aspects of my identity to forward the work of teaching about social justice and racism. As I do this work, I also recognize that I am often being (mis)*read* even as I constantly read the world through the unique lens of my identity.

Teachable moments arise at the oddest times. During a recent visit to the playground with my 4-year old son, I had an unusual exchange with two African American women whose probing questions reminded me of the complexities of teaching about race and identity inside and outside the academy.

> "Is he your son?" one of the ladies inquired from the bench they shared. "Yes," I replied, as I walked beside my son who was eagerly riding his tricycle. "What's his name?" the other questioned as we passed by them for the second time. "Essien," I responded, to which she quickly retorted: "Are you African?" I replied, "no, but his name is African." Though I knew she was inquiring about my nationality, I was beginning to feel slightly conflicted about my last answer as I circled the playground a third time. "Certainly, I am African," I thought, as I reflected on my reading, writing, and teaching about Black identities. Before I could decide whether I would continue to subject myself to another round of the *Spanish Inquisition*, my son and I were already approaching their bench again and the look on their faces suggested they were enjoying this exercise. "So you're not African?" one of the ladies inquired again. Taking the bait and accepting the reality that my walk with my son would be less peaceful than I had hoped, I responded: "yes, I'm African, just like you. We're all African, right?"
>
> "No, I am not African! But you must be African because you have an accent," the most inquisitive of the two retorted. "I am European," she continued, before the other asserted that there was no way she was African because she was from Virginia. Slightly perplexed by their answers and facetious attempts to make fun of my accent, I responded, "Well even Europeans are African if you believe scholars who suggest that the Garden of Eden and the first humans were in Africa."

Feeling tired and uncharacteristically impatient, I led my son to another section of the playground in order to give him my undivided attention and, in truth, to escape a conversation that I was not particularly enjoying on that day or at that time. Still, there was no escaping my thoughts about the brief exchange and its implications for my understandings and teaching about racial identity in general and Black identities in particular. "Surely," I thought, "these two ladies had ticked a box on a survey that said African-American and yet when I suggested that they were African they baulked at the idea." "What does it mean to be both African *and* American?" I wondered. This playground encounter reminded me of the complexities of teaching about race and racism in light of the nuanced histories and ideologies that complicate perceptions of self and understandings of others. Always the reflective pedagogue, I also felt a bit disappointed that I did not have the energy to more effectively use the pedagogical space of the playground to further engage the two ladies. So much for always being in *teacher mode*.

Drawing on my experiences in various educative spaces, the purpose of this chapter is to share how I utilize my positionality as a *border-crossing brotha-scholar* to teach about social justice and racism in university classrooms. In sharing how I employ my identity to help students negotiate various ideological borders in my courses, I also model how socially just pedagogical practices can emerge out of who we are. To ground this discussion, I begin by detailing some of the nuances of identity construction and border-crossing theory in order to situate how they undergird my positionality and practices as a *border-crossing brotha-scholar*.

## MORE THAN THEORY: BORDER-CROSSING AS EMBODIMENT

Identity construction is a complex and contested process that involves an amalgamation of difference across and within a continuum of races, ethnicities, genders, social classes, sexual orientations, religions, (dis)abilities, languages, political allegiances, and other culturally and historically contextualized markers (Gresson, 2008; Johnson, 2006; Omi & Winant, 1993; Schwalbe, 2005; Villaverde, 2008; West, 1993). Indeed, Leonardo (2000) explains, "identity is only achieved in the context of difference;" thus, identity is relational and one typically constructs themselves as "I" and those different from them as the "other" (p. 113). Various identity dimensions and markers can function distinctly from, in concert with, or in conflict with each other, thereby embodying conceptual borders that are encroached, pushed, redefined, and reestablished within individuals, communities, institutions, and in society at large (Hal, 1993; Johnson, 2006; Omi & Winant, 1993). The extent to which identity markers and the borders they designate are affirming or oppressive usually rests on the extent to which the differences of others are perceived as positive, neutral, negative, or threatening.

As a professor teaching critically about race and racism, I have come to understand that personal and community identities are the tenants that ground the intersections between race, epistemology, and positionality in my praxis. I also recognize that identities are not static, "essential (whether in the biological or even cultural sense)...[or] benign" (Wright, 2003, p. 207). Identities, like positionality, are complex, contextual, and constantly in flux. This means that *ways of knowing*, both for me and for my students, can be contested since all of these dynamics intersect at the point of identity. As a responsible pedagogue, I try to balance and respect the individual and communal *readings* of reality, even as I remain open to the fact that the best courses and classroom discourses are always partial, situated, and always needing to be problematized.

## BORDER THEORY: DEFINED, SITUATED, AND EXPLAINED

Finding a universally accepted definition of border theory is a daunting task. In fact, it can be argued that a single definition cannot fully capture the fluidity, breadth, and transience of border theory. Metaphorically and literally, border theory is a theory on the edge (Hicks, 1991) – on the borders or boundaries – that must remain flexible in order for theorists to recognize and rupture the "epistemological, political, cultural, and social margins that structure the language of history, power, and difference" (Giroux, 2005, p. 20). But this is not all.

While border theory has come to describe studies that are philosophical and cultural in nature, there are more specific branches of border theory that attempt to capture the multidimensionality of perspective, experience, and otherness (Larson, as cited in Hicks, 1991). Moreover, border theory encompasses the multifaceted approaches that use hybrid positionalities to problematize and reconfigure how power is distributed within and across difference. The capacity to use hybridity to rupture the distribution of power is vitally important for me as a scholar who embodies a hybrid positionality as a Black man with African Bermudian and African American lineage. Through the embodiment and expression of my identity, I am able to problematize essentialist understandings of Black identities while also leveraging the pedagogical power present in liminal spaces: the "gaps created by the juxtaposition of binary terms" (Villaverde, 2008, p. 52). At stake in my classroom, then, are not just the individual and ideological identities of my students (usually preservice educators and school leaders) who are often experiencing their first constructive dialogue about race and racism in a classroom setting, but also their perceptions of the cultural and collective identities of peoples whose national and native histories have come under the onslaught of racism. In the next section, I share how my personal identity undergirds my perspective on *space* and my positionality as a *border-crossing brotha-scholar*.

## PEDAGOGUE AS BORDER-CROSSING BROTHA-SCHOLAR: POSITIONING MY POSITIONALITY

Being born and raised on a 21 square mile island in the middle of the Atlantic Ocean does something to one's understanding of space and border-crossing. While a discussion of Bermuda's past and present is beyond the scope of this chapter,[1] to narrowly think of space and border-crossing as merely geographically significant is to miss how racism and colonialism have functioned as global and geopolitical imperatives in Bermuda and beyond. Plus, my identity transcends my national affiliations. In addition to being a Black (African Bermudian/American) man, I am also a Christian who is sensitive to the fact that I can be viewed with some degree of suspicion by those who may have had a distasteful experience with institutions and individuals who utilize similar labels, or those who simply subscribe to a different belief system. For example, I recognize that more people have been killed in the name of God than any other name; and as a Black man, I also understand that despite the accomplishments of inspirational Black men like President Obama and Dr. Martin Luther King, Jr. Black men are still, by in large, expected to emulate the characteristics espoused by the media – criminals, athletes, and dead-beats (Douglas, 2012b; Gause, 2008).

The pervasive ideologies of men as egotistical, unfaithful brutes all affect my role as a *border-crossing brotha-scholar* because they influence how I *know* reality and also influence the ideologies of my students who often confess that I am their first Black male teacher at any level. As a Black Bermudian/American male who has been afforded the opportunity to prepare future educators and leaders in the United States, I am both an insider and an outsider on multiple levels – a border crosser. Certainly, I believe that to transcend borders, an educator must be fully aware of his/her limits. Drawing from the work of West (1993), it is also clear that for academicians, researchers, and scholar-practitioners who see their work as part of a larger emancipatory project and/or a fulfillment of their "prophetic-socratic" calling, it is essential that they are first emancipated. I see my work in this vein.

The next section of this chapter will share how my positionality informs my classroom practices when teaching about race and racism. Each strategy – or confession – could be useful in informing the work of other critical scholars who are teaching about social justice and racism.

## FROM POSITIONALITY TO PRACTICE

It has been said that "confession is good for the soul.[2]" In this section, I confess some of the strategies I employ in order to leverage my positionality as a *border-crossing brotha-scholar* for socially just ends. Some of my approaches are more traditional than others, but all of them are grounded in an understanding of my identity and the sharing of who I am with my students. I agree with hooks (1994) who suggests that we cannot lead our students any further than we ourselves have gone; thus, I am intentional about sharing relevant elements of my identity and journey as an African Bermudian/American border-crossing scholar negotiating various terrains.

## CONFESSION 1: CREATING REQUISITE DISEQUILIBRIUM[3]

For me, effectively teaching about racism and social justice requires that I destabilize taken-for-granted notions as swiftly as possible. One of the chief means I use to create this requisite disequilibrium is to intentionally allow the first class session of a new course to begin a few minutes late, so I can disguise myself as a student,[4] sit toward the back of the classroom, and engage in my "where's the professor" routine. Dressed down in somewhat casual clothes and dubbing as one of many students waiting for the late professor to arrive, I instigate questions to students sitting near me about the identity of the professor, whether they have read the syllabus, or if we have to wait 10 or 15 minutes based on the seniority of the professor. Student responses vary but there are always those who admit they have not read the syllabus, ordered the required texts, or taken a course from this "Ty Douglas guy." After approximately seven minutes or so and numerous exaggerated glances at my watch, I employ the persona of a frustrated student who is about to leave if the professor does not arrive within ten minutes of the scheduled start time. I usually initiate a sign in sheet for those of *us* who are about to leave (since there is usually one or two others who are considering leaving with me), march toward the door in *disgust*, and then turn around and welcome my students to the new course: "Hi, I'm Ty Douglas."

Most students find this exercise funny, engaging, and thought-provoking as they pursue my subsequent line of questioning: "So, why didn't you all think that I was the professor…and why didn't you consider that the professor may have been in the room?" An enthusiastic discussion usually ensues that unveils key tenets to any course that seeks to explore racism: "To see what is in front of one's nose needs a constant struggle" (Orwell, 1968, p. 125). Students often note my location in the classroom, my young appearance, and my casual clothing as culprits of my successful disguise. Of course, I push them to consider how my identity as a Black man may have been a factor as well, and inquire how many of them had been taught by a Black man in the past. Typically, with the exception of three or four students, the vast majority note that I am the first Black male instructor they have had in their entire educational journey. In light of my name "Ty-Ron," I also inquire whether they had any suspicions about my identity prior to our first face-to-face encounter. "After all," I confess to them, "I have never met a White male with my name, or with a hyphen and capital 'R' in the middle of his name, for that matter." My humor and frankness disarm the students and provide a platform for them to not only talk about race and racism, but many White students also admit that they are not sure when or if they should use labels like "Black" or "African-American." I broach these topics head on and encourage students to reflect on the questions they have been thinking about but are afraid to say. We also explore the question: "What's in a name?" and I push them to consider what hyphenated identities like "African-American, Latin-American, Asian-American" mean for how others are perceived and treated. These questions create dissonance and teachable terrain to begin to unpack racism, which I define in my classes as "race prejudice + social and institutional power" (Okun & Jones, 2000). A few brave students will admit that they thought the professor was African American when they saw the name "Ty-Ron," which then provides context for me to share what my Bermudian accent has already suggested: the label "African-American" does not capture the totality of who I am. This, too, is an important realization for many students – of varying ethnic and cultural backgrounds – who have never considered that Black identities, as a Diasporic reality, transcend the borders of the United States.


## CONFESSION 2: ACCENTS AS TEACHABLE TERRAIN

How scholars experience and navigate international identities (and specifically, blackness) in educative settings is not monolythic. In classroom settings and nonschool-based settings, like my encounter at the playground, my accent often creates opportunities for dialogue and the destabilization of stereotypes. For example, I have found that my Bermudian accent – which much like Bermuda's geopolitical history, is a unique blend of English, Caribbean, and American culture – is often privileged over many other Caribbean and African accents. I share stories with my students of how I am treated differently – usually by White people – when they learn that I am from Bermuda. Warm memories about honeymoons spent on the pink sands of Bermuda's beaches and references to anniversary getaways by the "in-laws" become conversation pieces that seem to position me differently than if I had been read as *just* an African-American man. I unpack and problematize these dynamics to my students. I suggest to them that the privileging of my accent may be rooted in the fact that the Bermudian accent sounds more British than African, and is thus more aligned with a Eurocentric paradigm. Raising this point in our class discussions gives my students the opportunity to unpack how we stereotype and judge others based on the accoutrements of appearance and accents. As a result, students from the South often confess their own prejudices about Northern accents and Northerners often speak about common perceptions of the "southern drawl." Ultimately, these confessions and discussions give students opportunities to interrogate *who* is perceived as intelligent, who are the insiders, who are the marginalized, and what/whose *standards* or *norms* are used to make these determinations. It is often at this point that my students begin to become ideological border crossers.

## CONFESSION 3: TIPTOEING ON SACRED TERRAIN

Leading discussions and facilitating assignments that cross into the realm of religion/spirituality are risqué but necessary work I engage in to help students uncover ways that racism continues to function today. As I engage in this work, I am encouraged by the scholarship of intellectuals like Freire (1970), Dillard (2000), West (1982, 1993), Dantley (2005), and hooks (1994), who (in their own ways) name how spirituality undergirds who they are and the risks they take for the sake of the educational advancement of their students. Even now, as an emerging scholar who sees spirituality as central to my work in the academy, I can relate to the "spiritual crisis" and tensions Cozart (2010) experienced as a result of her "belief that spirituality was a separate layer of marginalization, separate from race and gender…[which caused her to act] as if spirituality was a third consciousness, rather than part of my merging double-consciousness into a better truer self" (p. 253).

Like Cozart, I have no desire to live or teach from such an oppressive paradigm, even as I embrace the inherent risks that emerge anytime one names her/his positionality. Frankly, to encourage dialogue and investigations around issues of spirituality exemplifies my commitment to teaching *with all of me* and my belief that "there is an aspect of our vocation that is sacred [and]…our work is not merely to share information but to share in the intellectual and spiritual growth of our students" (hooks, 1994, p. 13). I understand and embrace that there are tensions around topics of spirituality that I carefully navigate, including the tendency to conflate spirituality with religion and religious experiences (Cozart, 2010; Dantley, 2005), and respect for separation of church and state legislation.

### Going beyond "Middle People"

Many of my students have expressed their discomfort and fear of discussing topics like religion and spirituality in their other course experiences. Graduate students and colleagues who embrace various religious/spiritual traditions have expressed similar sentiments to me. Yet, I use discussions on religion and spirituality to broach discourses on aspects of race and racism, since most of my students enter my classroom with prior knowledge and experiences with some form of religion.

In my classroom, I emphasize the importance of dialogue, recognizing that it is a means through which transformation can begin, relationships are developed, and mutual respect is forged. I also emphasize the importance of reading and researching primary documents for ourselves. For example, we discuss how religion – particularly Christianity in the United States – has been abused and used as a means of forwarding racist agendas. My students are usually astounded by what they learn about Christopher Columbus and his disturbing exploits in the name of God (Loewen, 2007). As students try to reconcile the purpose for and means by which they would teach their students about Columbus (in light of their new knowledge), they are also challenged with the reality that most school textbooks herald Christopher Columbus as a brilliant hero. These revelations and discussions often propel students to declare: "what else haven't we been told and why have these truths been kept from us?" Through various exercises and activities, I challenge students to research and consider contemporary manifestations of these dynamics – particularly as it relates to *textbooks*. In this context, spiritual/biblical texts are textbooks. Students are encouraged to bypass the "middle people" (my gender-sensitive adaption of "the middle men") – teachers, pastors, rabbis, bishops, priests – in order to engage in their own study of primary and secondary documents. Students are encouraged to dialogue with the documents in whatever manner they deem appropriate: listening, responding, contesting, interrogating, meditating, and praying are options some students utilize to dialogue with the documents. I give no parameters for how students should engage in this *re*-search, except that they look at the documents for themselves and allow their previously held perspectives to be challenged. For me, this exercise is about encouraging future teachers and school leaders to develop the agency to question the taken-for-granted and challenge institutions, understanding that the schoolhouse is not the only institution of education.

Students often research common assumptions that are grounded in historical, political, and religious traditions. For example, we unpack how racism is institutionally perpetuated in religious settings today, question what Black church/White church dichotomies reveal about humanity and the Christian church, and analyze children's literature and film clips that portray angels as exclusively White and male. These activities push students to reflect on and account for how racism (race prejudice + social and institutional power) impacts their positionalities, praxis, and blind spots.

## CONFESSION 4: TRADING SPACES

Having been raised in Bermuda, the significance of *space* to me is likely more pronounced than to those raised in larger contexts. This aspect of my identity informs my praxis and intentional efforts to trumpet the significance of spaces outside of the schoolhouse as being powerful educative locales. Sadly, far too many teachers, administrators, and policy makers continue to ignore the impact of non-school based educative spaces on students. Community-based pedagogical spaces are "non-school based locales, institutions, forces, or methods that have been/ are utilized for educational purposes," such as the media, music, churches, barbershops, hair salons, sports clubs/fields, and theaters (Douglas & Gause, 2009; Douglas & Peck, 2013). Drawing on the tradition of historical scholarship and the works of Freire (1970) and Cremin (1970, 1980, 1988), scholars who embrace the breadth of what it means to educate, I utilize a community-based pedagogical space assignment to encourage students to cross over into community-based pedagogical spaces (i.e. barbershops and neighborhood basketball courts) in order to learn from the pedagogues in spaces outside of traditional classrooms. In so doing, preservice teachers and school leaders are challenged to (re)consider where and how learning takes place – particularly for students of color. Moreover, by challenging and unpacking the realities of *spaces*, I also create terrain where narrow Western and American-centered conceptualizations can be challenged. People of color have always had to buttress their education outside of traditional schoolhouses (Anderson, 1988; Douglas, 2012a; Douglas & Peck, 2013; Williams, 2005), and to ignore this reality is to reify and privilege Eurocentric paradigms that disadvantage students of color. Similarly, as educators are challenged to consider the learning that takes place outside the schoolhouse, they also become more open to the lessons that can be learned from communities beyond the borders of the United States.

## CONCLUSION

As I challenge educators to investigate and reflect on racism and social justice inside and outside of classroom spaces, I simultaneously challenge them to reflect on the risks that will be necessary if they are to share a sense of hope through their pedagogy and leadership. I push them to consider and cross many ideological and – in the case of their assigned visits to community-based pedagogical spaces – physical borders. The outcomes of these processes are not always fully apparent to me. I often remind my students that *the process is more important than the product; in fact, the process is the product.* At times, the fruits of the process are readily apparent in educators who exit the course more committed to a social justice agenda. Ultimately though, this process-based approach is rooted in the hope and faith that I have in my students to continue the inquiry processes that is promoted in my courses. Where the journey leads them is beyond my influence and jurisdiction. My responsibility is to give them tools and opportunities to challenge oppressive systems, ideals, and borders. It is a process I continue to engage in personally. Even as I name and identify with particular positionalities, systems, and ideologies, my position as a *border-crossing brotha-scholar* is not a passive one: I draw on a broad set of experiences, identities, and spaces to name and teach about racism and social justice with *all of me.*

## NOTES

1. For a fuller discussion of some of the geopolitical factors in Bermuda, see Douglas and Peck (2013). Education by any means necessary: An historical

exploration of community-based pedagogical spaces for peoples of African descent. *Educational Studies*.

2. This Scottish proverb, which is attributed to the pen of J. Kelly, is believed to have been written in 1721.

3. This phraseology of "requisite disequilibrium" was inspired by, but distinct from, Ron Heifetz's notion of "productive disequilibrium" as expressed in his book, *Leadership Without Easy Answers*.

4. My *disguise* is usually nothing more than dressing a bit more casually than I usually would or wearing a hat or hoodie. Frankly, my identity serves as an *adequate disguise* to most students who unquestionably expect their professor to be a White, older male. As a Black man who many mistakenly read as being in my 20s, I am able to use my identity and this "where's the professor" exercise to cross over into conversations about race, expectations, and stereotypes from the first class meeting.

# REFERENCES

Anderson, J. D. (1988). *Education of Blacks in the South: 1860–1935*. Chapel Hill, NC: University of North Carolina Press.

Cozart, S. C. (2010). When the Spirit shows up: An autoethnography of spiritual reconciliation with the academy. *Educational Studies, 46*(2), 250–269.

Cremin, L. A. (1970). *American education: The colonial experience, 1607–1783*. New York, NY: Harper and Row.

Cremin, L. A. (1980). *American education: The national experience, 1783–1876*. New York, NY: Harper and Row.

Cremin, L. A. (1988). *American education: The metropolitan experience, 1876–1980*. New York, NY: Harper and Row.

Dantley, M. E. (2005). African American spirituality and Cornell West's notions of prophetic pragmatism: Restructuring educational leadership in American urban schools. *Educational Administration Quarterly, 41*, 651–674.

Dillard, C. B. (2000). The substance of things hoped for, the evidence of things not seen: Examining an endarkened feminist epistemology in educational research and leadership. *International Journal of Qualitative Studies in Education, 13*(6), 661–681.

Douglas, T. M. O. (2012a). *Border crossing* brothas: *A study of Black Bermudian masculinity, success, and the role of community-based pedagogical spaces*. Unpublished doctoral dissertation, The University of North Carolina at Greensboro, Greensboro, NC.

Douglas, T. M. O. (2012b). Resisting idol worship at HBCUS: The malignity of materialism, Western masculinity, and spiritual malefaction. *The Urban Review, 44*(3), 378–400.

Douglas, T. M. O., & Gause, C. P. (2009). Beacons of light in oceans of darkness: Exploring black Bermudian masculinity. *Learning for Democracy, 3*(2).

Douglas, T. M. O. & Peck, C. M. (2013). Education by any means necessary: Peoples of African Descent and community-based pedagogical spaces. *Educational Studies, 49*(1), 1–24.

Freire, P. (1970). *Pedagogy of the oppressed*. New York, NY: Seabury Press.

Gause, C. P. (2008). *Integration matters: Navigating identity, culture, and resistance*. New York: Peter Lang Publishing.

Giroux, H. A. (2005). *Border crossings* (2nd ed.). New York, NY: Routledge Taylor & Francis Group.

Gresson, A. D., III. (2008). *Race and education primer*. New York, NY: Peter Lang.

Hall, S. (1993). New ethnicities. In J. Donald & A. Rattansi (Eds.), *Race, culture and difference* (pp. 252–259). London: Sage Publications and Open University.

Hicks, D. E. (1991). *Border writing: The multidimensional text*. Minneapolis, MN: University of Minnesota Press.

hooks, b. (1994). *Teaching to transgress: Education as the practice of freedom*. New York, NY: Routledge.

Johnson, A. G. (2006). *Privilege, power, and difference* (2nd ed.). Boston, MA: McGraw-Hill.

Leonardo, Z. (2000). Betwixt and between: An introduction to the politics of identity. In C. Martinez, Z. Leonardo & C. Tejeda (Eds.), *Charting new terrains of Chicana(o)/ Latina(o) education* (pp. 107–129). Cresskill, NJ: Hampton Press.

Loewen, J. W. (2007). *Lies my teacher told me: Everything your American history textbook got wrong*. New York, NY: Touchstone.

Okun, T., & Jones, K. (2000). *Dismantling racism: A workbook for social change groups*. Atlanta, GA: dRworks.

Omi, M., & Winant, H. (1993). On the theoretical status of the concept of race. In C. McCarthy & W. Crichlow (Eds.), *Race, identity, and representation in education* (pp. 3–10). New York, NY: Routledge.

Orwell, G. (1968). To see what is in front of one's nose takes constant effort. In S. Orwell & I. Angus (Eds.), *The collected essays, journalism and letters of George Orwell: In front of your nose, 1945–1950* (p. 125). London: Harcourt Brace Jovanovich.

Schwalbe, M. (2005). *The sociologically examined life: Pieces of the conversation*. Boston, MA: McGraw-Hill.

Villaverde, L. E. (2008). *Feminist theories and education primer*. New York, NY: Peter Lang.

West, C. (1993). *Race matters*. Boston, MA: Beacon Press.

Williams, H. A. (2005). *Self-taught: African American education in slavery and freedom*. Chapel Hill, NC: University of North Carolina Press.

Wright, H. K. (2003). An endarkened feminist epistemology? Identity, difference and politics of representation in educational research. *International Journal of Qualitative Studies in Education, 16*(2), 197–214.

# SECTION III
# VOICES FROM FACULTY AND STUDENTS: FOCUS UPON STUDENTS

# CHAPTER 6

# THE EXPERIENCES OF MARGINALIZED ACADEMICS AND UNDERSTANDING THE MAJORITY: IMPLICATIONS FOR INSTITUTIONAL POLICY AND PRACTICE

Dannielle Joy Davis

## ABSTRACT

*This study features interactions with White students and female colleagues from two regions in the United States. Helm's Racial Identity Model for Whites offers a conceptual lens to understand classroom and workplace dynamics between Blacks and Whites in predominantly White postsecondary settings, regardless of national context. Findings suggest that the quality of experiences with White colleagues and students often reflected the status individuals held in terms of their own racial identity development. These findings promise to inform institutional policy and faculty evaluation practices.*

Social Justice Issues and Racism in the College Classroom: Perspectives from Different Voices
International Perspectives on Higher Education Research, Volume 8, 71–83

ISSN: 1479-3628/doi:10.1108/S1479-3628(2013)0000008008

Contrary to claims of the nation's expedited evolution into a postracial society, the gross underrepresentation and marginalization of Black faculty in predominantly White U.S. postsecondary institutions persists. Culprits to marginalization include the behaviors and attitudes of not only White faculty and administrators, but also students (Thompson & Louque, 2005). Thompson and Louque's (2005) "Exposing the 'Culture of Arrogance' in the Academy: A Blueprint for Increasing Black Faculty Satisfaction in Higher Education," found that 82% of study participants experienced direct and indirect cultural insensitivity from students. Seventy-four percent perceived these student insensitivities as racist. Cultural insensitivities included rude, disrespectful behavior; prejudiced perceptions based on bigoted stereotypes; and addressing Black faculty informally as compared to non-Black peers. Forty-five percent of respondents also agreed that "African American faculty [were] less respected than other faculty" (p. 61). Picca and Feagin's (2007) analysis of 626 White college students' journals revealed that 75% of racist commentary centered upon African Americans. This illustrates the gravity of the issue as it pertains to student perception of and interaction with Black faculty. Research also suggests that students evaluate minority professors less favorably than White counterparts in academe (Carle, 2009).

Leonardo (2009) argues that Whites who "consistently evad[e] a racial analysis of education should not be represented as [not participating] in a racialized order, [but that they showcase] precisely how they ... perpetuate the racial order by turning the other cheek to it or pretending that it does not exist" (Ayers et al., 2009, p. 231). The evasion of racial analysis, particularly regarding challenges faced by African Americans teaching in predominantly White institutions, also emerges upon review of racial minority faculty members' student evaluations by White European colleagues. One member of the professoriate describes this challenge:

> During my first year of teaching, an African American man ... at another institution received some negative student evaluations. A senior White male professor ... gave him some advice on how to maintain discipline in this classroom. [The African American professor] responded: "With all due respect, Sir, when you try to take control of your class, the students accept it. Maybe they're grateful for it. When I try to take control of my classes, I get student evaluations that say "I'm mean," "I'm intimidating," "I make them uncomfortable," "I force my opinions on them," or "I'm racist." With this type of resistance, many students avoid all challenges to some of their core values and assumptions. Consequently, African American faculty are marginalized by both their colleagues and by students resistant to having racist views challenged in the classroom. (King & Watts, 2004, p. 117)

Even minority faculty who receive positive evaluations report students initially not giving them "the benefit of the doubt" as compared to their White peers, whose credentials were not questioned and were deemed respectable (Sekayi, 2004). In essence, a double standard exists for Black and White faculty. While discussing her strategy to address students' negative perceptions of her Black race, gender, and youth, one faculty member shared:

> At some point I began to realize that there was very little I could do about students' negative perceptions of me based on that combination of race, gender, and age. I was not willing or even interested in "proving myself" to people, students included. That was a new discovery for me. After tirelessly seeking the approval of students to "make up for" being younger than the average professor, I decided that this was an exercise in futility. I will teach. I will tell them what I know, I will tell them what I think, I will encourage them to express their knowledge and thoughts, and I will attempt to create an environment where we can all be learners and feel comfortable in that role. I came to this philosophy as I moved further into my own personal process of transformation and away from my lifetime of miseducation [Woodson, 1933]. (Sekayi, 2004)

Racist and sexist micro-aggressions from students, members of the professoriate, or administration; racial battle fatigue; and lacking a "protective network of sympathetic senior faculty" (Davis, 2004, p. 136) can result in toxic work environments for Black academics. Such inequities suggest an unequal playing field between Black faculty and their more supported White peers that remains overlooked. In her work, "The Slippery Slope of Student Evaluations for Black Women Faculty," Beverly Davis notes how the intersectionality of race and gender contributes to fewer genuine relationships with senior faculty and less opportunities for research collaboration and professional development for Black female academics (2004).

White racial identity development and subsequent student processing of both race-related course material and having a racial minority instructor counter the perception of student evaluations as "authoritative and unappealable" (Coren, 1998, p. 203). It further questions the assumption of students' perceptions of faculty as equals (Davis, 2004; Thompson & Louque, 2005). A faculty member in Krenzin's (1995) study held:

> Some of my students have never had a Black professor, never even knew a Black adult that did anything. So they look at me like, "How'd you do this?" (p. 124)

For a surprising number of undergraduate and graduate students, not studying under a Black professor continues as the norm throughout the nation due to the group's low numbers in academe (Blacks comprise only 5.5% of the professoriate (Cataldi, Bradburn, Fahimi, & Zimbler, 2005)). The challenge of insufficient diversity in the professoriate reflects research suggesting that course material taught by White men "was perceived as more controversial when taught by women and Black faculty" (Ludwig & Meacham, 1997 in Davis (2004, p. 134)). Students' double standard in their perceptions of faculty suggests the importance of addressing the lack of racial parity within academe.

While the election of Barack Obama as the 44th President of the United States indicates a degree of racial progress, this is only the beginning of the end for what Cornell West calls the "Ice Age," or the age of indifference to the marginalized and suffering in our society (West, 2009). The long history of the country's use of race as a basis to exploit and dehumanize (as with the institution of slavery), coupled with the lower frequencies of spirit that promote such actions, cannot be erased by the election of one man. Such racism is not unique to the U.S., but poses a problem throughout the Western world (Chakraborti, 2010; Stevens, 2009; Velisek, 2010). Helms (1990) suggests that racism, or lack thereof, may be understood through examining specific psychological stages of White racial identity development. Her work inspired me to view some of the racial micro- and macro-aggressions of White students and colleagues I have encountered along my academic journey in a new light.

Why is understanding White racial identity development important? How does the model assist in moving beyond merely illustrating the known: that racism exists and that people are racist to varying degrees? This work seeks to address these questions as they pertain to teaching and working in postsecondary settings.

As a new scholar, I have had the opportunity of co-teaching two courses in different sociopolitical, predominantly White contexts. The first course was on race, class, and gender at a Northern institution. The second was an educational policy course taught at a Southern university. As the United States continues to struggle with overt and covert racism, the history of America's enslavement of Africans and legal segregation makes the South particularly interesting in the study of prevailing racist attitudes and their influence upon teaching and learning. This study centers upon my interactions with White students and female colleagues from these two regions. Because society tends to portray Whiteness as "normal" and thus invisible, White majority students and faculty rarely reflect upon their experiences as Whites or these experiences in regards to racial minorities (Brion-Meisels in Ayers, Quinn, & Stovall, 2009).

Helm's Racial Identity Model for Whites (1990) provides a framework to understand classroom and workplace dynamics between diverse groups. The intent of this work is to understand White racial identity development and how it manifests in the postsecondary learning environment. While I am particularly interested in how Helms' work helps me interpret interactions with White students and faculty as a Black woman, the experiences herein might reflect those of non-Black minority peers in other academic settings as well.

## METHODS

Using an auto-ethnographic approach, with myself as the "autobiographical subject" (Reed-Danahay, 1997, p. 6), this research features two classrooms or units of study which individually represent bounded systems (Merriam, 2009; Yin, 2009) within the general context of American higher education, particularly predominantly White institutions. As co-instructor for the featured courses, I used journaling to record my experiences and reflections following each class session. Journaling allows researchers to be more reflexive (Janesick, 1999; Mertens, 2009) and facilitates "deepening knowledge of whatever subject matter the researcher takes part in," while serving as a member check for one's thoughts (Janesick, 1999, p. 522).

Through journal writing "individuals become connoisseurs of their own thinking and reflection patterns, and indeed their own understanding of their work ... " (1999, p. 506). Triangulation of data through location and time (Denzin, 1978) takes place via study of two regions and settings at different points of my career. Triangulation also occurred in regards to demographics of students in terms of age, as one class comprised traditional aged students from 18 to 21 years and the other graduate students. This work employs Helms' White Racial Development Model to analyze and understand the journal data. Specifically, journal entries were sorted based upon their applicability to Helms' stages.

## LIMITATIONS

Limitations of this work include truncated variation in data collection, differing subject matter of the courses taught, as well as student age differences between classes. Also, the study yields little generalizability. However, the experiences described herein may mirror those of others and inform academics of similar backgrounds or White allies, therefore yielding transferability. It likely will spark subsequent work on the topic. Future work in this area may further triangulate the data by incorporating interviewing and content analysis of student evaluations as additional data sources. Applying Helm's model to multiple cases promises to enhance transferability and further contribute to this new direction of inquiry.

# CONCEPTUAL MODEL: WHITE RACIAL IDENTITY STATUSES AND MENTAL PROCESSING

## *Strategies*

Janet Helms' White Racial Identity Model offers a framework to view the featured study. The first segment of the model, Contact Stage, comprises realization of the existence of Black individuals as those holding phenotypically African features. One lives with "either naïve curiosity or timidity and trepidation" (p. 55) regarding Blacks. While Contact Stage individuals may benefit from institutional racism, they may not be aware of their advantages, reflect upon their experiences in terms of race, nor have faced moral issues embedded within racist paradigms. Someone in Contact Stage approaches issues "with a color-blind or cultureless perspective and general naiveté about how race and racism impact herself and himself as well as other people" (p. 68). They have limited occupational and social interaction with Blacks unless that interaction is with Blacks who "seem" White to them, despite whether or not the individual has traditional African features. Generally, anxiety emerges when Contact individuals relate with Blacks. Should the Contact person begin to interact with Blacks and maintain that interaction, Whites may move on to Disintegration (1990).

The Disintegration Stage marks one's conscious, yet conflict-laden acknowledgement of his or her Whiteness, yielding moral challenges related to the White experience. Here the individual questions racist ideas previously taught and recognizes the social inequities between Blacks and Whites. Helms describes this as being caught between the acknowledgement of humanity and conflict of continued oppression (1990).

Following Disintegration, Whites move into the Reintegration Stage where Whiteness is idealized and Blackness is denigrated. Overt or covert anger characterize the dominant emotion at this point. In addition, Whites within the stage tend to distort information to favor their own racial group (1990). Reintegration may evolve into Pseudo-independence.

At the Pseudo-independence Stage, Whites hold the capacity to understand their individual roles in ameliorating the outcomes of racism. Whites at this juncture possess an intellectual understanding of the culture of Blacks and acknowledge their own White privilege in the U.S. context. Those dwelling within the phase tend to make life choices to "help" marginalized races (1990).

At the Immersion-Emersion Stage, individuals honestly acknowledge racism and the significance of their own Whiteness (1990). Understanding the benefits of Whiteness may spur racial activism (1990). Reeducation at this step involves a redefinition of Whiteness and acquiring more informed racial views.

In the final stage, Autonomy, Whites "internaliz(e) a positive, nonracist White identity, value cultural similarities and differences, feel a kinship with people regardless of race, and seek to acknowledge and abolish racial oppression" (p. 68). At this stage, individuals exhibit flexible analyses of race-related material (1990). Furthermore, they are willing to relinquish the privileges of racism via various life choices (1990).

Helm's Racial Identity Model for Whites, both the statuses and the mental processes utilized when responding to racial stimuli, serve as the framework for data analysis of the study. The next section illustrates examples of these stages in relation to the data.

## FINDINGS

The following briefly reviews one or more of Helms' stages as they relate to components of the journal data. Examples from my experiences exemplify components of Helms' model in the classroom and academic work setting. The work seeks to demonstrate how Helms' model may help us understand interactions within both the classroom and academic workplace between racial minority and majority groups.

Contact Status is indicated by satisfaction with the racial status quo, as well as one's, obliviousness to racism and participation in it. Racial factors may influence life decisions, only in a simplistic fashion (1990). The Mental Processing Strategies used include denial, obliviousness, or avoidance of anxiety evoking racial information (1990). This was demonstrated in a Southern graduate classroom through the incivilities of two White students, one who left the room loudly multiple times and another who talked throughout a film on Black men in education, despite disapproval from me and criticism from classmates. Physically removing themselves from the room in a disturbing fashion and talking during the documentary featuring race-related material may have served as forms of denial, avoidance, or resistance for these students.

Disintegration Status involves "conscious, though conflicted, acknowledgement of one's Whiteness" (1990, p. 58). In other words, the person feels disintegrated or caught between two conflicting worlds of Black and White. Confusion, dissonance, and avoidance of information which counter emerging realties on race inequities include the processing strategies employed (1990). Disintegration occurred in the North with White undergraduate students' expressions of discomfort learning about the past and present injustices suffered by racial minorities in the United States.

Reintegration Status refers to idealization of one's socio-racial group, yet expressing denigration and intolerance for other groups. At this stage, racial factors may strongly affect life decisions (1990). Distortion of information in an own group-enhancing manner serves as the strategy for processing information (1990). Reintegration behavior took place in the North when one undergraduate student likened the Black Panther Party to the Ku Klux Klan.

In response, I noted the historical genesis of both groups, the former rooted in self-defense against a racist social system (resistance to oppression) and the latter as terror and oppression toward the marginalized. An additional example includes a Southern colleague's reluctance to discuss student disrespect of me as an instructor, stating that she didn't see the offense, insinuating the occurrence did not happen. Another was when a Southern White male (graduate student) discussed a connection between Black males, baggy pants, and the style's prison origins. When I asked whether or not this was a function of race or class, he suggested it was a function of race. This was the same male who was disruptive during the documentary on African American males. Hence, individuals may utilize more than one processing strategy when taking in race-related material.

Immersion-Emersion Status entails the search for understanding personal meanings of racism, ways by which individuals benefit, and the redefinition of Whiteness (1990). Life choices may include racial activism (1990). Reeducation and searching for internally defined racial standards aid in processing information (1990). An example of this is a Northern colleague's openness to discussing and confronting differential treatment from White students of us as instructors during a specific class session. For instance, when I posed questions to students, some would only look at my White colleague when answering as opposed to me. She was the first to bring this up following the class and prompted our dialogue on the issue. This differed from the Southern colleague's response to disrespect toward me from students, which was abruptly claiming not to see the occurrence and avoiding the topic rather than discussing it further.

Those demonstrating Autonomy Status hold informed, positive socio-racial group commitments, use internal standards for self-definition, and are able to relinquish the privileges of racism (1990). These individuals hold flexible, less stringent responses and analyses to racial material (1990). A Northern colleague's willingness to split her salary with me as a co-teacher even though this was not required or requested of her illustrates Autonomy. She shared that this was her effort to actively counter economic exploitation of me as a then new instructor.

## SUMMARY

The majority of White students at the Southern university did not move beyond Reintegration Status. However, the Northern White students shared thoughts and demonstrated behaviors at almost every stage, including the final most advanced stage of Autonomy. This contrasts the findings of Brion-Meisels, who notes how despite having a diverse educational environment, her students dwelled at the initial Contact Stage of Helms' model (Ayers et al., 2009). In terms of interactions with colleagues, the Northern co-teacher at the Autonomy Status held strong communication and pedagological collaboration skills, and respectfully worked through challenges as an instructional partner. The Southern co-teacher at the less advanced Reintegration level was less willing to confront race issues directly and collaborated less in terms of teaching. The quality of experiences with White colleagues and students often reflected specific developmental stages. Examples of the Pseudo-independence Stage were not identified in the data.

Fig. 1 illustrates highlights from this journal-centered work as it relates to White racial identity development. Other's perception of and response to me as a Black professor, coupled with race-based material and the students' or colleagues' developmental stages, merged to influence interpersonal interactions and classroom experiences.

The illustration shows how racial identity development, the race of the professor, and race-based material can help us understand classroom and workplace dynamics regardless of national context. Understanding of these

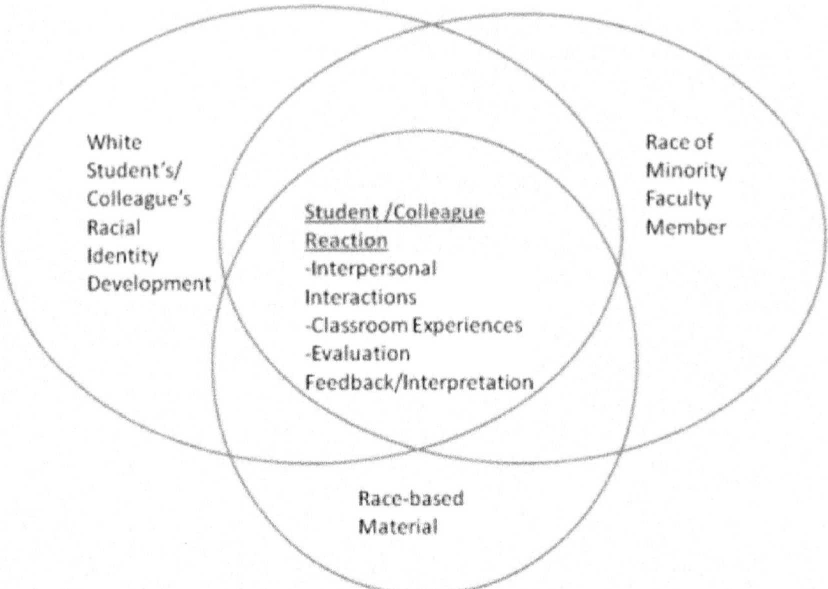


*Fig. 1.* White Racial Identity Development in the Postsecondary Setting.

dynamics may educate White colleagues who review the teaching evaluations and practices of minority peers. Unearthing the complexity of White perceptions and responses to minority professors promise to lead to more egalitarian evaluation processes, as well as tenure and promotion policy in postsecondary settings.

## CONCLUSION: IMPLICATIONS FOR INSTITUTIONAL POLICY

This work contributes to the field by illustrating continued challenges faculty of color face at predominantly White institutions, how we might understand racism in academic communities, and the interactions between people from different racial backgrounds. Minority challenges often take root in failure of postsecondary institutions to address both structural and curricular diversity. As Fred Bonner notes in his comparison of racism exhibited in the Bush administration's ill response to Hurricane Katrina survivors, with racism in the ivory tower, "merely occupying the same space does not constitute [an academic] community" (2006, p. 3).

Via sharing my story and applying Helm's model, I demonstrate the need for improving campus climate for diverse populations by unveiling challenges faced by White majority faculty and students that hinder capacity to understand and engage minority groups, their histories, and world views. Helms' model and the work herein suggest that education can play a key role in the development of an Autonomous, healthy White racial identity. It further exemplifies the importance of continued inclusion of race-based diversity-related material throughout university studies in moving toward Autonomy.

The work also informs academic promotion and tenure policies, where faculty are evaluated on their teaching via student evaluations and collegiality. Women and racial minority faculty tend to be rated more harshly than their White male peers (Carle, 2009; Davis, 2004). This, coupled with the likelihood of women and minorities teaching race- and gender-based material, which may cause discomfort for some White learners, contributes to the possibility of students expressing resistance to difficult classroom topics. Consideration of how students' individual racial identities influence the ratings of underrepresented faculty should be a component of both annual evaluations and promotion and tenure decisions. Such acknowledgment promises to increase the level of fairness within the review process and facilitate the retention of minority faculty. The information would also be valuable for hiring committees in their understanding of the past teaching performances of minority candidates.

Implications of such considerations in the review process are far reaching, as postsecondary institutions continue to lack democratic parity in terms of representation of faculty. Though they make up over one fourth of the U.S. population, underrepresented minorities comprise merely 9% of the professoriate, with Blacks comprising 5.5% and Hispanics representing 3.5% in tenure-track, tenured, and nontenure lines (These groups represented 12.3% and 12.5% of the population during the 2000 U.S. Census) (Cataldi et al., 2005; Grieco & Cassidy, 2001). Sparse numbers within the population for marginalized academics, coupled with the need to retain these members of our academic community for the depth and excellence offered from their diverse perspectives, suggests the importance of understanding White racial identity development as it affects their work.

Application of Helm's White Racial Identity Model promises to counter the effects of racial battle fatigue. By informing the pedagogy and evaluation of minority academics with courses holding high numbers of

White students, the model offers a fuller understanding of teaching and learning in racialized contexts.

Understanding that White students operate at varied developmental levels facilitates efforts to design curricula that meet students where they are, while not compromising course content. For instance, students at lower stages may require substantially more background or history pertaining to marginalized groups. Application of Helms' work in the classroom may therefore serve as a tool to understand and address racism in educational settings. While this work features a U.S. context, application of the framework may transfer to global educational arenas. Hence, employing Helms' work may be useful regardless of context, holding utility internationally as well.

## ACKNOWLEDGMENTS

The author thanks Linda M. Davis and Dave Harris for feedback on early drafts of this work. She also appreciates the outstanding scholarship of Dr. Janet Helms and thanks her for providing new ways of viewing race and racism.

## REFERENCES

Ayers, W., Quinn, T., & Stovall, D. (2009). *Handbook of social justice in education*. New York, NY: Routledge.

Bonner, F. (2006, February 3). *Wade in the water: Lessons learned from Katrina by one African American academic. Teachers College Record*. Retrieved from http://www.tcrecord.org/content.asp?contentid=12318

Carle, A. C. (2009). Evaluating college students' evaluations of a professor's teaching effectiveness across teaching and instruction mode (online vs. face-to-face) using a multilevel growth modeling application. *Computers and Education, 53*(2), 429–435.

Cataldi, E. F., Bradburn, E. M., Fahimi, M., & Zimbler, L. (2005). 2004 National study of postsecondary faculty (NSOPF: 04): Background characteristics, work activities, and compensation of instructional faculty and staff: Fall 2003 (NCES 2005–176). U.S. Department of Education. Washington, DC: Institute of Education Sciences.

Chakraborti, N. (2010). Beyond "passive apartheid?" Developing policy and research agendas on rural racism in Britain. *Journal of Ethnic and Migration Studies, 36*(3), 501–517.

Coren, S. (1998). Student evaluations of an instructor's racism and sexism: Truth or expedience? *Ethics and Behavior, 8*, 201–213.

Davis, B. A. (2004). The slippery slope of student evaluations for Black women faculty. In C. Y. Battle & C. M. Doswell (Eds.), *Building bridges for women of color in higher education: A practical guide for success*. Lanham, MD: University Press of America.

Denzin, N. K. (1978). *Sociological methods: A source book* (2nd ed.). New York, NY: McGraw-Hill.

Grieco, E. M., & Cassidy, R. C. (2001). *Overview of race and Hispanic origin: Census 2000 brief. United States Census 2000.* Washington, DC: U.S. Census Bureau.

Helms, J. (1990). Towards a model of White racial identity development. In J. Helms (Ed.), *Black and White racial identity: Theory, research, and practice* (pp. 49–66). New York, NY: Greenwood Press.

Janesick, V. J. (1999). A journal about journal writing as a qualitative research technique: History, issues and reflections. *Qualitative Inquiry, 5*(4), 505–524.

King, K. L., & Watts, I. E. (2004). Assertiveness or the drive to succeed?: Surviving at a predominantly White university. In D. Cleveland (Ed.), *A long way to go: Conversations about race by African American faculty and graduate students* (pp. 110–119). New York, NY: Peter Lang.

Krenzin, J. (1995). Factors influencing the retention of Black faculty on predominantly White campuses. *Research in Race and Ethnic Relations, 8*, 115–138.

Leonardo, Z. (2009). Reading whiteness: Antiracist pedagogy against White racial knowledge. In W. Ayers, T. Quinn & D. Stovall. (Eds.), *Handbook of social justice in education* (pp. 231–248). New York, NY: Routledge.

Ludwig, J., & Meacham, J. (1997). Teaching controversial courses: Student evaluations of instructors and content. *Educational Research Quarterly, 21*, 27–38.

Merriam, S. B. (2009). *Qualitative research: A guide to design and implementation.* San Francisco, CA: Jossey-Bass.

Mertens, D. M. (2009). *Transformative research and evaluation.* New York, NY: The Guilford Press.

Picca, L. H., & Feagin, J. R. (2007). *Two-faced racism: Whites in the backstage and frontstage.* New York, NY: Routledge.

Reed-Danahay, D. E. (Ed.). (1997). *Auto/Ethnography: Rewriting the self and the social.* Oxford: Berg.

Sekayi, D. (2004). From disbelief, presumption, and disrespect to membership in the legacy of competence: Teaching experiences at the HBCU and the PWI. In D. Cleveland (Ed.), *A long way to go: Conversations about race by African American faculty and graduate students* (pp. 110–119). New York, NY: Peter Lang.

Stevens, P. A. (2009). Pupils' perspectives on racism and differential treatment by teachers: On "stragglers," the "ill" and being "deviant". *British Educational Research Journal, 35*(3), 413–430.

Thompson, G. L., & Louque, A. C. (2005). *Exposing the "culture of arrogance" in the academy: A blueprint for increasing Black faculty satisfaction in higher education.* Sterling, VA: Stylus.

Velisek, Z. (2010). Different times in a different Europe. *New Presence: The Prague Journal of Central European Affairs, 13*(1), 12–14.

West, C. (2009). *State of the Black Union.* CSPAN Archives. Washington, DC: CSPAN.

Woodson, C. G. (1933). *The miseducation of the Negro.* Trenton, NJ: Africa World Press.

Yin, R. K. (2009). *Case study research design and methods.* Thousand Oaks, CA: Sage.

# CHAPTER 7

# CHICANOS TEACHING SOCIAL JUSTICE IN HIGHER EDUCATION/ CHICANOS ENSEÑANDO JUSTICIA SOCIAL EN LA UNIVERSIDAD: EXPERIENCES AT PREDOMINATELY WHITE AND HISPANIC SERVING INSTITUTIONS

Juan Carlos González and Edwardo L. Portillos

## ABSTRACT

*This chapter will provide examples of how Chicano faculty teach and practice social justice in the U.S. college classroom, where subtle forms of racism operate through White privilege, and influence faculty credibility and authority. From a Latino Critical Theory (LatCrit) perspective, the authors address the question,* What are the similarities and differences in classroom experiences of Chicano faculty in Predominately White Institutions (PWI) and Hispanic Serving Institutions (HSI)? *In addressing this question, the authors will provide examples from their teaching experiences at both PWIs and HSIs, and how a Chicana/o-centered social*

Social Justice Issues and Racism in the College Classroom: Perspectives from Different Voices
International Perspectives on Higher Education Research, Volume 8, 85–111
Copyright © 2013 by Emerald Group Publishing Limited
All rights of reproduction in any form reserved
ISSN: 1479-3628/doi:10.1108/S1479-3628(2013)0000008009

*justice perspective can help to mediate and overcome classroom challenges. The chapter will end with a discussion of how a social justice framework is necessary in college classrooms that are becoming increasingly diverse; and recommendations for how PWIs and HSIs can support Chicana/o faculty in endeavors to institutionalize a social justice framework in the college curriculum.*

> Education either functions as an instrument which is used to facilitate integration of the younger generation into the logic of the present system and bring about conformity to it, or it becomes "the practice of freedom," the means by which men and women deal critically and creatively with reality and discover how to participate in the transformation of their world.
> — (R. Shaull, 1988, p. 15, in P. Freire's *Pedagogy of the Oppressed*)

The above quote exemplifies the tension that makes being a university professor one of the most difficult and rewarding professions, as we are tasked with both integrating students into the system, and at the same time asking them to challenge and transform systems of oppression. One of the most fulfilling challenges of being a university professor is teaching, where students' expectations run the gamut from merely wanting to be treated fairly, to other students expecting advantageous treatment. What is and is not fair is sometimes easy if all students were merely doing mathematical problems that are either right or wrong, but this is rarely the case in higher education. Students are all different, with unique needs, and different life situations, and a range of skills and potential. And this is where how you teach, and how you assess learning, can become complicated. "Everything has been figured out, except how to live," said the French philosopher Jean Paul Sartre (1966). And college teaching and learning are so important to how to live and what we need to live in the 21st century where a college education is more of a prerequisite to entering the professional job market than it ever was in the U.S. society.

It is the university teaching profession, as a lifestyle, and as the method to transforming society into one that is more just and equitable, that lies at the core of what we will be addressing in this chapter. We see the teaching of social justice in the classroom as a process where students are at a different level in their understanding of issues – some are passive recipients of what we teach related to social justice, and others express hostility toward these issues. This latter group's ideals of social justice are generally rooted in beliefs that social injustice is an individual problem, not a systems issue; meaning that they fault individuals for being treated unfairly rather than critically evaluating the government and educational policies and legislation that created systematic social injustices. As university faculty, it is our responsibility to explore issues of social justice and injustice (coupled with how these issues intersect with race, class, and gender that we experience in the classroom) in ways that engage all students and help them understand the complexities of social problems in society.

To set the context for this chapter, first we will talk about social justice in the U.S. classroom as a framework. This will be done through juxtaposing LatCrit and social justice frameworks, which we use in tandem to guide us as Chicano faculty. In this section, we will also address how our social justice philosophy drives the way we teach. Second, we will talk about the history of our experiences as Chicano professors. This section is important because being Chicano redefines social justice in the classroom to naturally include a Chicana/o-centric pedagogy, which includes the use of Chicana/o-specific literature and methods. Third, we will talk about White privilege in the college classroom, and how this affects our pedagogy. Fourth, we will talk about our experiences, struggles, and successes, in both Predominately White Institutions (PWIs) and Hispanic Serving Institutions (HSI), and how we are advantaged as males, but disadvantaged as faculty of color. We will end this chapter with recommendations for both PWI and HSI institutions, and a conclusion.

## LATCRIT AND SOCIAL JUSTICE FRAMEWORKS

Over the last 8 years, we have been using Latino Critical Theory (LatCrit) to theoretically frame many of the research studies we have collaborated on (see González, 2007, 2008; González & Portillos, 2007, 2012; Portillos, González, & Peguero, 2011; Turner, González & Wong, 2011). LatCrit has been useful because it focuses on shedding light on societal injustice and inequity encountered by Latinas/os nationwide, particularly by institutions such as education and criminal justice (Johnson & Martínez, 2000; Solórzano & Delgado Bernal, 2001).

In this sense, it is important to articulate the similarities between a LatCrit and a social justice framework for looking at college classroom experiences and practices of Chicana/o faculty. While LatCrit operates on the foundation of five tenets, four are important due to their relationship and transferability to a social justice framework. First, LatCrit (Solórzano & Delgado Bernal, 2001) and social justice (Bell, 2010a) frameworks both take the analysis of institutional racism and sexism seriously. The nuanced difference between a LatCrit and a social justice framework is that the former is particularly interested in the analysis of institutionalized injustices, while the latter is more concerned with raising group consciousness about injustices and promoting advocacy to challenge them (Hays, Arredondo, Gladding, & Toporek, 2010). In the case of the college classroom, a social justice framework can help with how professors are treated based on their race/ethnicity and gender if professors help to problematize these issues with students. Sometimes, as a Chicano professor, you do not realize how students perceive you until they turn in their evaluations. We have had many experiences in where students have directly and indirectly mentioned our ethnicity for the reason they did not like our classes, but more often evaluations indirectly make mention to our ethnicity. Being male does provide certain privileges, and establishes us as particular authorities in the eyes of students, and we know this from the continued conversations we have had with our female colleagues over the years. From a social justice perspective, it is important to dissect the institutionalized practices that allow the ill-treatment of Chicana/o faculty to continue, but more so, it is important to understand the beliefs that students bring with them into the classroom that allow them to treat professors differently based on race/ethnicity and gender. In essence, LatCrit, working in conjunction with a social justice framework, can assist in addressing institutionalize discrimination – LatCrit can help in identifying and naming the problem, and social justice can help with problematizing and addressing it.

Another aspect of LatCrit that also applies to a social justice framework is the eradication of oppressive dominant ideology that has purported to explain the failures (e.g., economic and academic) of people of color (Solórzano & Delgado Bernal, 2001). This also requires that Chicana/o faculty teach Whites about Whites (See Leonardo, 2009), to build White allies that will ultimately challenge oppressive dominant ideologies that complicate the implementation of social justice in higher education. Some examples of how this ideology affects people of color include: (a) discrimination, (b) assumption of cultural inferiority, (c) ideas that non-English languages are inferior, (d) structural and legal inferiorizing of immigrant and undocumented peoples, and (e) racial/ethnic profiling by police, university leaders, and students. These ideologies are what Chicana/o faculty confront every time they enter the college classroom. I, Juan Carlos, once remember being called in by my dean to talk about my low teaching evaluation. "Do you have an explanation," I was asked. "Not one explanation, but I do see a trend. The more students of color I have in my classrooms, the higher the overall evaluations," I responded. "I think you have a good point, I have read literature on how faculty of color at PWIs are treated differently by students," said the dean. Why did both the dean and faculty, in this case, find merit in the idea that teaching evaluations of faculty of color can be improved by increasing the recruitment of students of color? In part, because many students of color have been negatively affected by these ideologies, they are more likely to speak against them when in the college classroom, particularly if they see faculty of color being treated what they perceive to be unfairly by White students. I have had many experiences where White students were challenging what I was saying, which is warranted and acceptable in the college classroom because you want students to learn to be critical thinkers, but students of color had challenged these White students before I even had the chance to respond to their concerns. A social justice framework in the college classroom is important because it provides the framework for presenting a pedagogy and structuring the classroom environment in a way where students learn to be both critical thinkers and respectful of the presentation of ideas that may not be part of how they see the world.

A third idea in LatCrit is the commitment to social justice in the presentation of alternative ideologies in the college classroom (Solórzano & Delgado Bernal, 2001). This is central to a social justice framework. Operating a college classroom from a social justice framework does not mean that students need to accept a liberal ideology of world, nor does it mean that students have to agree with the professor. It means that students need to be prepared as critical thinkers, and need to understand to completely remove blinders that only let them see the world through the eyes of who they are as racial/ethnic and gendered beings. The teaching of a social justice framework is successful when students: (a) learn to question unjust authority, (b) learn to have love and compassion for people regardless of their race/ethnicity, gender, nationality, religion, or ability, and (c) frame their futures (career or otherwise) as having something to do with improving the lives of all peoples, regardless of their differences.

The last idea where LatCrit and social justice frameworks coincide has to do with the valuing of experiential knowledge. Both LatCrit and social justice rely on storytelling to promote and value the knowledge of marginalized groups (see Bell, 2010b; Fernández, 2002; Rodriguez, 2010; Solinger, Fox, & Irani, 2008; Solórzano & Yosso, 2002; Stovall, 2006). In the college classroom, this means the valuing of all voices, and not giving preference to White, male, or even Latina/o voices. It means that the pedagogy is structured in a way that allows all students to make contributions of ideas. It means valuing and respecting students who are less easily understood because of foreign or regional accents. It involves group work in where all students are engaged and contributors to their own learning. It requires feedback from professors who understand students' academic levels and how to use these levels as a base for how to help students grow as critical thinkers. This pedagogy is more difficult to practice in classroom setting with over 30 students, but necessary even in large classrooms if a social justice framework is to be prioritized by college professors. This pedagogy also requires that professors see learning as happening beyond the classroom, and valuing students' voice outside the classroom, and this includes conversations that professors have with students during office hours, before and after class, and over e-mail. As professors are asked to further integrate technology into the classroom, or even teach online class, these nontraditional mediums of communication complicate the teaching of social justice in the classroom. But we argue that despite technology, social justice plays a central role if it serves as a primary framework for what professors feel students need to learn to be productive citizens.

## HISTORICAL PIECE ON OUR EXPERIENCES IN TEACHING AT THE UNIVERSITY

"The university should have a report card on how many faculty of color they hire because this year, of 20 new hires, only two were minority, and both were in education. And we need to do better" (Dean, West Coast University, 2012).[1] What this dean shared with one of the authors in a conversation at a recent education conference shows that despite the growth of students of color, the U.S. professoriate continues to be largely White. According to the National Center for Educational Statistics (2011), in the fall of 2009, 79% of U.S. college faculty were White, and only 4% were of Hispanic origin. Interestingly, this was not a dean of a PWI, but of an HSI, where the largest group of undergraduates is Latina/o. This context also shows that Chicanas/os who do make it to the professoriate have mixed feelings and experiences (see De Luca & Escoto, 2012; Garrison-Wade, Diggs, Estrada, & Galindo, 2012; González & Portillos, 2012). On the one hand, they are given the responsibility to teach, and help mold and transform the next generation of leaders, and also know that social justice ideals are not shared by all their colleagues, where some are politically against the hiring of more faculty of color who have the potential to transform higher education into a more just and equitable enterprise. With this said, we understand the privilege we do have as Chicano university faculty. But we also want to say that our path was not easy, and complicated by the injustices that we now fight against at the university. Before understanding our present positions as university faculty, it is important to understand a bit about our path.


*Juan Carlos*


I feel privileged to be a professor at a California State University (CSU) because I graduated from one. I attended CSU, San Bernardino because it was close to home and my friends were going there. I immediately fell in love with thinking, so I decided to major in philosophy. I finished in 7 years, but also got a second bachelor's in Spanish, and a minor in history. I had a high GPA, so I was encouraged to go to graduate school. I went to the Ohio State University because after one visit I had never seen a more beautiful university, complete with a lake right on the middle of campus. But the weather was too cold for a Southern Californian, so I decided to return west for my doctorate. I applied to Arizona State University because I received a scholarship. I did not know I was literally going to one of the hottest climates in the country.

As a doctoral student, I received teaching and research assistantships that were vital preparation for the professoriate. I also participated in a program entitled *Preparing Future Faculty*, where we learned the nuts and bolts of faculty life. I finished my doctorate in 5 years, and would have stayed another 5 if I had funding because it was one of the best experiences of my life. In every class, each professor was teaching the latest theory in their respective fields. I focused on qualitative methods and educational foundations.

As a teaching assistant in ASU, I was below average. I was basically thrown in the classroom to teach, and needed to figure out how to do this quickly. Graduate students often get these types of teaching responsibilities at research universities because professors are frequently tied up doing research with insufficient time to teach. Over time I improved, particularly because I had other graduate students of color who were also teaching assistants to dialogue with about university pedagogy. By the time I took my first job as a professor at the University of Missouri-Kansas City (UMKC), I thought I was ready. UMKC was predominately White, and I was asked to teach classes on diversity. Over the 4 years that I was at UMKC, I went from being an average teacher to better than average. My greatest impact was in teaching Chicana/o-centered topics to students who had little knowledge about Latinas/os in the United States Rarely did I have Latina/o students in my classes, and when I did most would say that I was their first ever Latino professor. I was also criticized for having expectations higher than what the students could accomplish, and soon learned to make assessments about where students are and how to push them to levels they were able to achieve.

When I left UMKC to come to California State University, Fresno (CSUF), I was coming to the type of campus that I had prepared to be at my whole academic life – an HSI. At CSUF, the majority of the undergraduates are Latina/o, and our master's programs and doctoral program have at least 20–30% Latinas/os. I am able to have an immediate impact on Latina/o students, in ways I have never been able to impact non-Latina/o students. Cammarota (2007) writes that Latina/o students who are taught a rigorous and relevant curriculum grounded in social justice can go from being labeled "at-risk" to excelling academically.

At CSUF, my Latina/o students treat me like family –like a lifelong mentor, a father, or even a brother. We are bonded by culture and language, and I am able to speak frankly with them about their abilities and my expectations for their scholarship. I am able to be highly critical of their scholarship without them taking it personal. Many become interested in my research on Latinas/os, and many take on similar topics for their research. Last year, I had a group of Latina/o students meet me after class to talk with me about their struggles, and how they were thinking about dropping out. "But we're still here because you're here, and we know you want us to succeed," they said. It is moments like this that reaffirm for me the importance of Latina/o faculty for Latina/o students. I have now completed 3 years of teaching at CSUF, and I know this is where I belong every time a student decides to write their thesis on topics that are related to and important for the Latina/o community.

One of the greatest lessons I have learned thus far as a Latino professor at an HSI is that when you are the majority group, you have different responsibilities and expectations. At UMKC, it was okay to focus more time on my Latina/o students because they were so few. And it was also okay to spend more time teaching on Latina/o issues because there was such ignorance about them. But here, at CSUF, I have learned to be the model professor for my Latina/o students as well as all my students. I teach Latina/o issues not because everyone is so ignorant about them, but because they are central to the future of the state of California. I am now a university professor that happens to be Latino, as opposed to a Latino who happens to be a university professor. I expect to excel across the university, not only on issues related to Latinas/os and/or faculty of color. I teach social justice issues not because they are important to people of color, but because they are important to the nation as a whole.

## *Edwardo*

I was born and raised in Colorado, and my road to academia was one of finding my voice and place in society. I grew up in Colorado Springs, in the same city where I now teach as a university professor. In my community Whites were in the minority, except for the teachers in our schools, but I grew up having friends of all ethnic/racial groups and not really knowing my own ethnic identity. In school I was the quiet student who found success by always doing my homework and quietly sitting and listening to the teachers. I graduated from high school with a very good GPA but I only applied to the University of Colorado (UC) at Boulder and with one $500 scholarship, the Pell Grant and school loans I was on my way to college. In Boulder I experienced culture shock and that first year was the toughest of my life. I managed to survive and graduate from UC, Boulder, by finding other students of color in various student groups and together with ethnic studies classes I took on campus; I finally found a place but not quite my voice. At CU Boulder, I also took sociology and criminology classes which further helped me develop a critical lens and helped me understand my negative experiences with law enforcement. I graduated from the university with a sociology degree with an emphasis in criminology and wanted to use my degree to work with youth of color due largely to my studies that showed they were disproportionately incarcerated. I wanted to help these youth transition back into society. In a matter of 5 years I had gone from having no social conscious about race to clearly recognizing how race operates in our society and desiring to do something meaningful about the ways in which our society criminalizes youth of color. Upon graduating from the university I applied for various probation officer jobs but given I had no experience and with over 100 applicants for each job, I was quickly passed over. Therefore, for the next year I worked at the Headstart program as a family service specialist. Although I loved working with the families and the children, after a year I decided to leave for graduate school, which I hoped would make me more marketable for a probation officer job.

When I applied for graduate school, I decided I would apply to a variety of schools throughout the southwest and surprisingly I was accepted to all the schools I applied. I decided to go to Arizona State University partly because I was offered the better financial aid package and also the professors there were doing the kind work with youth of color that interested me. Pursuing my master's degree was stimulating academically and at this time I was exposed to the academic literature on a variety of social justice issues from a multi-disciplinary perspective. For the first time in my life I was taught by feminist and began to analyze my life in a whole new way. For instance, not only was I oppressed because of my race/ethnicity, but through a self-reflective critical lens I also learned I was part of a male-dominated system that oppressed women. For example, in high school, I never made my bed nor did I ever clean inside the home. This was something that was always done by my mother and sisters. The feminist literature helped me to better understand the complexity of social justice issues and led to the realization that there are multiple spheres of oppression and these can and do vary by gender, race, and class. As a result when I studied gangs in Arizona I studied the way in which gender is socially constructed in poor urban communities for Chicana/o and Mexicana/o youth. During this time, I still had not found my voice. I remember doing presentations on campus and my hands literally shaking as I gave my talk. I would ultimately graduate with my masters and by the time I started my Ph.D. program I already had two publications and another that would eventually be published in the top rated journal in my discipline. At this point, due largely to excellent mentorship, my career aspirations changed from wanting to work in probation to realizing that I can help bring social change through research, and ultimately through teaching.

It was in the Ph.D. program at Arizona State University where I finally found my voice but it was not easy. It was not easy because as a Ph.D. student I remember having to do presentations and still feeling nervous but it was teaching my first class where I finally felt the confidence to go in front of a group of people and to teach critically about the criminal justice system. However, teaching was not easy because as a graduate student I received mediocre student evaluations. Also, a group of students from one class requested that the chair of the department no longer allow me to teach in the department. At that time I realized I could not teach the way in which I had been taught when I was an undergraduate by mostly White male professors, especially since I was a graduate student of color who virtually had no academic credentials. I was accustomed to professors lecturing for the entire class periods and I never once, either as an undergraduate or graduate student, questioned the grades that were given to me on papers or exams. The student revolt left me weary of teaching but at the same time I realized I had something to teach students, and despite the one bad experience, there were still many students, especially students of color, who valued having an instructor of color and also one who shared similar experiences with the police and racism growing up in the U.S. society. At this point, I knew I would never work in the criminal justice system, but instead I would use my voice to help students understand the complexities of social problems, especially those related to the criminal justice system.

In 2002, I went on the job market and was hired as an assistant professor at California State University, San Marcos (CSUSM). This university was working toward HSI status and today they are an HSI. Here I was able to hone my teaching skills in such courses as juvenile delinquency, youth gangs, and immigration and justice. My teaching experiences here were much different than at ASU where students of color composed a smaller percentage of my classes. At CSUSM I had classes where 50–75% of the students were Latinas/os. At the same time, my office hours were frequently filled with students visiting and asking for assistance. My evaluations were overwhelmingly positive as well. It seemed moving to a new institution, where my title included a Ph.D., I was now seen as a legitimate expert in the field. The only real difference in my teaching approach was that there was now more discussion than traditional lecture for the entire class and also on the first day of class I had legitimatized my presence by announcing my Ph.D. and my publications. Occasionally students would question their grades, but challenging of my grades by Latina/o students was very rare, if they were challenged it was by White students. After my first year at CSUSM, I applied for various academic jobs in Colorado. At this point, I missed my family and I wanted my children to grow up near family. Therefore, I considered and accepted a job offer from the University of Colorado at Colorado Springs (UCCS). I knew when I accepted the position that I would be leaving a campus with a large Latina/o population and move to a predominantly White institution, which I considered challenging given my negative experiences at ASU.

I started my second job as an assistant professor at UCCS in the fall of 2004. At UCCS, I was able to teach similar classes that I had taught at San Marcos but now I would also teach criminology and ethnic/racial relations at the graduate level and at the undergraduate level I would teach criminology, The Chicano Community, and a Freshmen Seminar course. At UCCS, I continued to love teaching and my evaluations remained high except for when I taught online courses. I think my current high teaching evaluations is a result of gender privilege which we discuss later in this chapter. Teaching at a predominantly White university has been different for me than teaching at San Marcos. First, I have noticed that students do not visit my office hours the way they did at San Marcos. Occasionally students will visit my office hours but most frequently my hours are spent doing other work, despite my plea to students to visit me when I am in my office. Second, I have noticed that White students are much more willing to challenge their grades on papers and exams. At least five to six times a semester I have to deal with students who are unhappy with their grade and who require further explanation for why they received a particular grade. Although I provide the explanation, I wonder if my White male colleagues are dealing with students who challenge their grading. Nevertheless, I am happy to be teaching using a critical pedagogy approach. In my classes I do not have to use this approach and sometimes I will hear from students why do we always have to talk about race, class, and gender but I feel in the study of crime and justice, these issues cannot be ignored. Surely I could teach my courses in a way where these issues are discussed in one or two classes but I want students to understand how systems of oppressions are an everyday production and reproduction. Today, I am now an associate professor of sociology and firmly believe I have found my place and my voice, and part of my pedagogical approach is to help students make a similar transformation in their own lives.

## WHITE PRIVILEGE IN THE CLASSROOM, AND OUR EXPERIENCES

In teaching social justice, it is important to understand the effect of the instructor in the college classroom setting (see Dolby, 2012; Holsinger, 2012; Stinson, Bidwell, & Powell, 2012). "If I have learned one thing over the years, is that students need to be taught by people that look like them, and people they can relate to," said one White dean of an HSI at a recent education conference. This has been clear and apparent to us over the years we have been college professors. But universities and university faculty are still largely the domain of Whites, and White privilege affects how the few faculty of color are treated by students, namely White students (Case, 2012; Messner, 2011; Nichols, 2010). To understand some of our classroom experiences, it is important to understand how White privilege has affected us over the years in various institutional settings.

It is also important to understand how race and gender operate in the classroom. Scholars who practice a feminist or critical pedagogy have recognized the classroom is not a socially neutral site in the production of knowledge (Rakow, 1991; Weiler, 1988). Larger structural inequalities related to race, sexuality, and gender are produced and reproduced in classrooms every day and identities are directly related to how the students view our social position, which influences how they rate our courses (Highberg, 2010; Rakow, 1991; Weiler, 1988). Unconsciously, students share the traditional perception that White males have the authority and legitimacy to teach in an unbiased way in the classroom. The literature shows giving low grades to students is viewed by students as a punitive action if the instructor is not a White male. This is especially true for women who are seen as violating the nurturing and mothering role that faculty are expected to hold for students in the classroom (Rakow, 1991; Weiler, 1988). Research also shows women who use a feminist pedagogy are more likely to have their authority challenged (Duncan & Stasio, 2001). In our experiences we have certainly observed the way in which gender and race privilege operate in the classroom especially by faculty who use a critical pedagogical approach.

*Juan Carlos*

I namely want to talk about three experiences, one dealing with a White student, and two dealing with co-teaching courses with White colleagues. In the first experience, I was teaching a course in sociological foundations at a PWI with a significant population of African American students. I am not sure how we got into a discussion about the confederate flag, but a White male student stated that the flag was not an issue as many people in his neighborhood have one on their porches, and no one in his neighborhood thought this was a big deal. An African American female then stated, "My momma told me that when I see that flag, to walk the other way." After class, the White student stayed to talk with me, he said he was attacked by the African American student, and that I had done nothing to stop her. I explained that this was a college classroom, where we have the liberty to express ourselves and talk about these types of issues openly and respectfully. He did not agree and wanted to file a complaint. So I told him that the next step was to meet with my department chair and explain the situation to her. The student later said that this was no longer an issue. I feel this had something to do with the fact that my chair was an African

American woman. I am not sure if she diffused the situation, or her mere presence in a position of power dissuaded him from pursuing his complaint. His being offended by the African American student challenging him was definitely based on his White privilege, and his believing that his position was right because he had an entire community to support him was also based in the institutionalization of White privilege. My mere presence in the classroom, even though I was not African American, was a symbolic challenge to this White privilege.

In the second example, I was invited to teach a diversity course with a White female professor. This was supposed to be a mutually beneficial arrangement, as I would learn from her given she had been a professor for over 20 years, and she would learn from my perspective on educational diversity. As most university professors can attest, co-teaching is not usually easier just because there are two professors in the class – it usually takes more work, planning, and coordination. Mostly, our co-teaching experience was a struggle because of our different pedagogy. My White colleague mainly wanted to feed students information, and I primarily wanted to present enough ideas for them to figure it out for themselves. She knew a bit more about the students and their abilities for reflective critical thinking, and I had higher expectations. But from the students' point-of-view, she was the professor and I was the sidekick. "You were a great teacher when you were able to talk," stated one student in the course evaluations. "I personally think there could have been a better partner for [White female professor]," stated another. Part of it was because she was a more experienced professor, but part of it also had to do with what students expect from their professors. Our students were all future teachers, mostly White females, and my colleague was a White female. I was a brown male in a city where few Latino males enter teaching as a profession. My colleague and I also dissected some important theories on diversity, on how the United States should integrate future citizens into the fabric of the nation. But because of our history and backgrounds, we obviously had different models, and the students did not want to think about complexity, they mainly wanted facts. Mostly they wanted to be fed a model that resonated with what they already knew, and my challenge to think was viewed as a challenge to the White professor, even though we were both the professors.

The last example involves another co-teaching experience, this time with a White male colleague, and we teamed up to teach a graduate research course at an HSI. At this institution, most students are afraid of the research courses, considered some of the most difficult courses in the curriculum. While this was an online course, and students did not see us, our names give away who we are, plus they are able to see videos of my colleague as part of the course. I particularly remember a Latino student who was having problems with one aspect of the course, and he decided to personally contact me only, even though the class instructions were that problems needed to be addressed to both professors. My colleague and I had agreed that we would both solve all problems together, but in this case, we had different perspectives. I was more understanding, and my colleague was not. Could it have been because I was Latino and I subconsciously try to help Latinas/os? Perhaps, but I also have a social justice pedagogy that I try to be understanding and accommodating to all my students. Part of my colleague's position, in this and other similar situations, had been due to his conditioning as someone from a working-class background that did not have anything handed to him. But students do not know this, all they see is a White male, the prototypical college professor, and so some might be less willing to challenge him and instead bring concerns to me. One aspect in where I clearly saw White male privilege was when several students wanted to challenge their grade at the end of the semester. My colleague basically said, "grades are not given, they are earned. Period." I believe I could never get away with responding to a student in this type of fashion, but I learned from my colleague about how White males communicate with students, and how this communication style commands respect.

### Edwardo

The only opportunity that I have had to co-teach with White colleagues has been in a freshmen seminar course. At the University of Colorado at Colorado Springs the campus offers a variety of freshmen seminar courses and I was asked by a colleague to participate in one geared toward students interested in teaching at the K-12 level. The courses are meant to ensure the students learn the skills, resources, and establish the kinds of relationships that would lead to academic success. In the freshmen seminar courses is where I have experienced the most resistance from students but it has never been directly expressed to me, in fact, in all cases students unhappiness were expressed to my colleagues or overheard during a presentation. One topic I discuss is how K-12 schools socially construct criminality and tend to penalize students of color more frequently than White students. A few of the students were talking quietly among themselves during my lecture and one of them mentioned the topic I was discussing was "so retarded." My White colleague overheard the comment and she asked me if she could quickly intervene to address something she overheard. I agreed, and this turned out to be a wonderful teaching moment where my colleague demonstrated how the words we use, although we may not intend, reproduce larger structural inequalities. She asked the students to think about why they used that specific word to refer to a concept I was teaching and look critically at how their use of a specific language reproduces the inequality. This teacher was essentially teaching the same concept, but through her own whiteness, she was able to further legitimize a concept I was teaching.

Eight years earlier in graduate school, I taught a similar concept but the focus was more demonstrating how the urban street gangs and fraternities could both be categorized as a criminal gang using existing state statutes. I had been asked by one of my peers in graduate school to guest lecture in her class on Arizona gangs. During the lecture students were frequently questioning how I could view fraternities and urban street gangs as similar. They could not get past the fact that White college students could be defined as criminals in the same way that urban street youth are perceived. They viewed the youth on two extremes of a social hierarchy, which led to some interesting discussion in the class. I thought that was the end of it but I would later learn from my colleague that several students in class sent her nasty e-mails to complain about my lecture and they also expressed their discontent with the entire class. What is interesting is that we were both graduate students of color and my colleague was a woman. In class, their level of discontent was not expressed but via e-mail and in the following class after my presentation, they had no problem expressing their concerns. I think the content of the lecture was thought provoking and today I still use the lecture, but it is interesting that the students were able to express their unhappiness about the lecture to my female colleague but they never did so to me, which has a lot to do with the gender privilege I hold. A similar example can be found in a recent discussion with my colleagues.

This past semester I was at a dinner held by the administration to celebrate the awarding of tenure. At the dinner, I had an opportunity to speak with two women colleagues and they were asking about the courses I teach and how I teach them. I explained I use a critical approach in all my crime-related courses and that I expose students to topics and ideas they may not completely agree with. For example, I told them I lecture on the violence in Mexico and the way in which this violence is gendered. I explain that many of the problems we see in Mexico can be directly and indirectly attributed to the United States. An idea that certainly is not popular with many students. I told them I talk about how racism operates in our society today through racial profiling and the criminal justice system. They asked if

I experienced any resistance from the students and they were amazed to find out that I did not and that in fact I have high student evaluations. They were dismayed because they also teach using a critical approach, including how racism operates in society but they receive a lot more resistance from students, and we all quickly realized that the reasons for these differences can be attributed to the way in which gender operates in the classroom.

## EXPERIENCES AT PWI AND HSI COLLEGE CLASSROOMS

We have both worked as professors in PWIs, an HSI, and a predominately Latina/o university, and have experienced the differences in students with regard to their receptivity to social justice. Our experiences are from faculty in education and sociology.

### *Juan Carlos*

I began as a college professor at UMKC, a PWI. I was hired to teach courses in cultural and sociological foundations, and I was also relatively new at teaching. In the courses I taught, I was expected to expose students to social justice in education, and help them develop the sensitivities to be able to operate in diverse urban schools. The majority of my students were White, and when I was hired I was the only Chicano faculty at the university. Being straight out of my doctoral program, I made the typical rookie mistakes, such as lacking understanding of students' abilities and having expectations few could reach. I remember in an undergraduate course I taught, I assigned students two 15-page papers, when few had even written one paper of this length. But my expectations were not the only problem. Most students also had never seen a Latino professor, let alone one talking about justice and equity for people of color in education. The more progressive students thought I was the best professor they'd ever had, but the majority thought my classes were a waste of their time. "I already took a diversity course," many would say at the first mention of people of color in my class. I struggled with students understanding what I was talking about or the purpose of what I was saying through my 4 years at UMKC.

By the second year at UMKC, I realized that: (a) the classroom cannot be the only place where I can influence students, (b) social justice needs to be taught in sections and tailored for White audience who are in different levels of social, emotional, and intellectual development, and (c) students of color will always be more receptive to learning about social justice because they feel it involves them. I then teamed up with a colleague in political science to organize a conference to empower men of color, the *African American and Latino (AALo) Male Empowerment Summit*. This was extremely rewarding because I could now teach social justice to young men of color, and they understood a lot of what I was talking about. My teaching of social justice was always through the lens of Critical Race Theory (CRT), a theoretical framework that posits first that racism is clear and apparent in American society, and we must accept and acknowledge this if we are to eradicate it.

After 4 years at UMKC, I accepted a position at CSUF, an HSI, but I would no longer be teaching educational foundations. I was hired to teach higher education courses and supervise master's and doctoral students. In my 3 years, I have primarily taught courses in research and academic writing. As expected, given the demographic of California and the central valley of the state, about half of my students are non-White. The majority of my students have been Latina/o, with a large number of Southeast Asians. Regardless of the different courses I have been asked to teach, I have never wavered in understanding the centrality of social justice in the curriculum I teach. I have found that teaching social justice to a predominately non-White population, and a White population that many have lived in diverse communities with mixed families, has been seamless. For example, in a research course that I teach, while some might think that this has nothing to do with social justice, I have been able to construct activities and examples related to research in communities of color. This has been so popular with students that many have taken my examples and developed them into their research topics for their culminating research projects and theses. Also, because of the focus on social justice in this research course, students have taken on projects that they tell me they never would have picked if I were not their professor, such as the influence of race/ethnicity on academic achievement, and the experiences of undocumented college students. Having a Latino professor helps my students have the freedom to do research in their communities, and my focus on social justice gives them the confidence to research controversial topics.


*Edwardo*


My experiences teaching at PWI have been different than those of Juan Carlos. Other than student's challenging my grading, I have not had many negative experiences in the classroom, which I believe is related to a department that focuses on issues of social justice and social change. That is, I am not the only professor in my department who teaches from a critical social justice perspective. Also, all of my courses are cross listed with the Women and Ethnic Studies Program and the faculty there also teach from a critical social justice perspective. As a result I am not isolated in the way in which Juan Carlos was and students know if they take a sociology course they will receive a critical social justice perspective. Further, I will make an announcement to students on the first day of class that I speak critically of the criminal justice system and if they do not welcome a critical approach, then this is the time to drop the course.

The students know or come to learn that if they are in my classes I respond timely to e-mail messages, and although I stand firm on deadlines, students know if they approach me in most cases I will work with them. In addition, I tell students they can submit papers ahead of due dates for me to look at. Also, I give students options for taking their exams and they seem to like this approach. Finally, I work with students outside of the classroom and hold frequent study groups with students prior to exam. This means I frequently meet with students in the library and this gives the students an opportunity to ask questions and to get to know the instructor at a different level because we will frequently have discussions on issues that may not be directly related to the syllabus. The one area I have struggled is in the online courses but this has been primarily because students do not like the boring lectures. In person, I am more dynamic, and there are more engaging discussions when students can learn from each other. Online there are discussions but they do not engage the students in the same way as in person.

Based on my teaching evaluations, when you are teaching from a critical perspective, and the discussions which help students understand different perspective, when this is missing, it affects how the materials are learned and my teaching evaluations. Unfortunately, I tried to make this argument when explaining my teaching evaluations when I went up for tenure. At the department level, they agree and gave me a rating of meritorious for teaching and this rating held up at the dean's review committee. However, at the chancellor's review committee I received an acceptable rating for teaching. It seems that although teaching online is valued and encouraged because of the additional revenue it brings the university, low teaching evaluations for faculty who teach from a critical perspective can diminish how colleagues outside the college and department view your teaching. Although I still received tenure, I was disappointed because I feel I am a wonderful instructor, and the review committees should consider how race, class, and gender shape teaching evaluations.

Another problem I experience teaching at a PWI is helping students to recognize how unconscious racism is promoted through everyday interactions, including through the use of media and language. I think it is challenging to help students understand how the social problems they identify are much more complex then they articulate and that sometimes the rhetoric they use to explain certain social problems perpetuates certain preconceptions about specific ethnic groups in the United States. A classic example comes from one of my online classes where I asked students to discuss a major contemporary issue facing our society. One student responded:

> Illegal immigration is a huge issue for our country, it cost our country and tax payers a lot of money. When I talk about illegal immigration I am not just talking about Mexico, as some people would think and not all illegal immigrants who enter the United States illegally but just happen to overstay their allotted time...

The student then went on to discuss how immigrants financially strain our criminal justice system when they are arrested, whereas citizens do not because they have paid taxes. The student also provided a link to a video demonstrating the impact of violent crimes committed by immigrants and provided statistics on the arrest of immigrants.

The problem was the video showed predominantly White victims and all the perpetrators depicted in the video were Latina/o. And, the statistics showed that Latinas/os were disproportionately incarcerated in prisons and jails. I gave the student full credit for her response since it was an opinion-based discussion but I warned the student to be careful with the examples she uses because they promoted a racialized image of Latina/o immigrants as violent, which countered her initial argument. The student responded:

> Although I respect your opinion I would have to disagree with everything but the video part. With the video it seems I did something that I was intentionally trying to avoid. Most people assume that all illegal immigrants are Mexican and that is not true at all. Thank you for pointing out the one thing I was trying to avoid.

However, we continued an exchange because she firmly believed arrests indicated the extant of the illegal immigration problem rather than racialized criminal justice policies that have targeted immigrants. Only occasionally do I have these interactions with students, and although I may not always help students understand a particular issue, I do manage to challenge them to reconsider a particular perspective they have on a social issue. I believed the student used her sense of White privilege to challenge my argument, but she was using a larger narrative of White privilege that promotes the idea that citizens, which through her examples are clearly White, are the racial group that has a legitimate presence in the United States. Therefore, the hardest aspect of teaching social justice issues is helping students to recognize various forms of privilege.

# RECOMMENDATIONS

As institutions diversify, it is important that they become more conscious of how historically marginalized groups view social justice and equity. Through our experiences in teaching social justice, we offer recommendations that institutions can implement.

(1) *Social justice in the college classroom needs to be more widespread* (Altman, Abraham, Bonebright, & Johnson-Licon, 2010; Skubikowski, 2010). While fields like ethnic studies might be more receptive to the teaching of social justice in the curriculum, a curriculum focused on social justice needs to be integrated throughout multiple fields, include STEM fields and the type of service oriented fields those students will serve a diverse public upon graduation (e.g., Brubaker, Puig, Reese, & Young, 2010; Garii & Rule, 2009). We believe that this could be done without major revisions to the curriculum, as social justice could be integrated with existing theoretical frameworks presently being taught in the service-orientated professions.

(2) *White students cannot be excluded in the teaching of social justice.* We believe that White students, being the majority of college students nationally, need to be included in the teaching of social justice. Often times White students are forgotten, particularly when the teaching of social justice goes from the classroom to the campus community, such as our example with the designing of the *African American and Latino Male Empowerment Conference* (AALo) to teach social justice to African American and Latino youth. We believe that new methods need to be created to teach social justice to White students in a way that they do not see themselves as the oppressors of non-Whites, but as important change agents in the transformation on American society. Higginbotham (1996) offers some suggestions for how to deal with resistance by White students and other students that are resistant to learning about social justice.

(3) *Social justice classroom pedagogy needs to focus on collaboration* (see Hays et al., 2010). We believe that often students come to class expecting to compete with other students, but the teaching of social justice requires a pedagogy that promotes collaboration among students. This can benefit not only students of color who come from pluralistic cultures, but also White students because it increases the chances that they interact with people who think different than them. We believe that the teaching and learning of social justice is not just an intellectual activity, but a social learning experience where students are affected emotionally as well as cognitively. We recommend in and out of class group activities between diverse groups. We also recommend the designing of grading systems that reward both the cognitive and social-emotions aspect of the learning of social justice.

(4) *The teaching of social justice can not only be related to racial/ethnic justice and equity* (Skubikowski, 2010). We believe that social justice needs to be oriented to justice and equity for all marginalized groups, which may include not only women but also men, and people of different physical abilities. We believe that professors need to not only focus social justice pedagogy to include marginalized communities in their communities (e.g., in the case of Fresno, California, this would include Latinas/os and Southeast Asians), but also go beyond it to give students the understanding that social justice is not a set of actions directed for the betterment of a particular group, but a philosophy rooted in justice and equity for all marginalized group, regardless of how marginalization is defined.

(5) *The teaching of social justice cannot be done exclusively in the college classroom.* Researchers have written about examples in where a social justice framework has been utilized across higher education institutions (see Altman et al., 2010; Nagda, Gurin, & Lopez, 2003; St.Clair & Groccia, 2010). We believe faculty who teach social justice have a responsibility to not limit this teaching to the classroom. The example that we presented earlier about the AALo conference showed the ideas of social justice had larger forums outside of the classroom, and faculty must find different venues to teach social justice. In another example, I, Juan Carlos, was recently informed that the university president had formed a commission on human rights and equity, and I knew this would be a way to influence the institutionalization of social justice. I immediately e-mailed the concerned administrators and asked if I could be a member on this commission, which spent the first year

developing a diversity strategic plan for the entire university, and I was able to influence the inclusion of social justice in the framework and writing of this plan. Also, faculty can serve as faculty advisor to student group on campus to help ensure a social justice perspective is being incorporated and that they are planning social justice events to expose other students to these issues.

(6) *Faculty need professional development to help them transform and ground their curriculum and pedagogy in social justice.* Faculty cannot merely be expected to teach social justice without some help in doing this. Universities, particularly their faculty teaching and learning centers, need to be involved in helping provide professional development. Skubikowski, Wright, and Graf (2010) offer examples of how to transform the curriculum in fields such as mathematics, the social sciences, and foreign languages. We do not believe professional development of this type needs to be made mandatory, but faculty need to be rewarded for participating and engaging in some type of curriculum redesign or for developing different pedagogical tools to use in the classroom for the teaching of social justice.

(7) *Chicana/o faculty need to be professionals in the teaching of social justice.* It is important that Chicana/o faculty understand that teaching social justice requires patience and understanding of students who come to the university with different frames of reference (see Solórzano & Delgado Bernal, 2001; Stanley, 2006). Many times White students have not had Chicana/o professors, and they are likely to generalize their first encounters to other potential encounters. This type of tokenizing is something Chicana/o faculty need to be aware of, and understand that teaching social justice does not have to be a struggle. Chicana/o faculty need to understand that pedagogical tools exist for teaching social justice in a way that students are less resistant.

(8) *Universities should allocate more funding for the teaching of social justice and use community experts to help teach social justice.* Students should be exposed to a variety of social justice perspectives and institutions should provide funding to bring in guest speakers. Also, faculty should be advocating for a public sociology as a way to help bring about social change. They should involve themselves in the community and even teach in the community if such opportunities exist. In addition, experts from the community who are working in social change should be brought in to present on local opportunities to bring about social change.

## CONCLUSION

As we reflect on our teaching of social justice, we understand that while social justice pedagogy differs based on race/ethnicity, gender, class, and ability of professors, being Chicanos focuses our pedagogy on our lived experiences. That is, the nature of our pedagogical practices are both rooted in social justice and rooted in our experiences as Chicano. This is our contribution in looking at how social justice works in the college classroom – looking at social justice pedagogy through a Latina/o lens. This means that the social justice that we practice always begins and ends with how Latinas/os are affected in society, and how Latinas/os are a part of a larger society focused on justice and equity. Also, from a Chicana/o perspective, social justice also means that Latinas/os and other marginalized groups are part of the discussion for justice and equity. Too often Latinas/os are left out of justice and equity conversations in PWIs, and usually only in HSIs are Latinas/os able to attain the necessary critical masses to demand a voice.

When it comes to the college classroom, Latina/o students are also ignored in favor of their White classmates. This is less likely to occur in HSIs, where Latinas/os may either be a majority in the classrooms, or have the critical masses to demand their voice. Especially when the faculty are Latina/o, Latina/o students are less likely to be marginalized, and many times the students go out of their way to develop intimate relationships with their professors. What is important for faculty of color teaching social justice to know is that it is okay to develop personal relationships with students from similar racial/ethnic backgrounds, but that a social justice framework calls for all faculty to give voice to all students, and develop inclusive pedagogies that make even their White students take ownership in the promotion of justice and equity for all in society.

This also means it is acceptable to focus topics around Latinas/os. As researchers we can see in the literature, especially in the study of crime and justice, historically the focus has been looking at a Black–White paradigm in crime. The Latina/o experience was ignored and although this is beginning to change today as more researchers are beginning to study the Latina/o experience, much of this research still does not address the complexities and regional differences found within the Latina/o category. For these reasons it is important to expose our students to a variety of theoretical and substantive topics that they may not receive in other classrooms. We believe that such an approach can help reshape popular perceptions of Latinas/os in the United States and help people to recognize the ways in which these groups have been unfairly perceived.

# NOTE

1. Persons mentioned in this chapter will purposely be left anonymous to protect their identity.

# REFERENCES

Altman, M., Abraham, N., Bonebright, T., & Johnson-Licon, J. (2010). A campuswide, ethics-based approach to social justice pedagogy. In K. Skubikowski, C. Wright & R. Graf (Eds.), *Social justice education: Inviting faculty to transform their institutions* (pp. 100–116). Sterling, VA: Stylus.

Bell, L. A. (2010a). Preparing teachers for social justice. In K. Skubikowski, C. Wright & R. Graf (Eds.), *Social justice education: Inviting faculty to transform their institutions* (pp. 26–41). Sterling, VA: Stylus.

Bell, L. A. (2010b). *Storytelling for social justice: Connecting narrative and the arts in antiracist teaching*. New York, NY: Taylor & Francis.

Brubaker, M. D., Puig, A., Reese, R. F., & Young, J. (2010). Integrating social justice into counseling theories pedagogy: A case example. *Counselor Education and Supervision, 50*(2), 88–102.

Cammarota, J. (2007). A social justice approach to achievement: Guiding Latina/o students toward educational attainment with a challenging, socially relevant curriculum. *Equity & Excellence in Education, 40*(1), 87–96.

Case, K. A. (2012). Discovering the privilege of whiteness: White women's reflections on anti–racist identity and ally behavior. *Journal of Social Issues, 68*(1), 78–96.

St. Clair, K. L., & Groccia, J. E. (2010). Higher education strategy. In K. Skubikowski, C. Wright & R. Graf (Eds.), *Social justice education: Inviting faculty to transform their institutions* (pp. 70–86). Sterling, VA: Stylus.

De Luca, S. M., & Escoto, E. R. (2012). The recruitment and support of Latino faculty for tenure and promotion. *Journal of Hispanic Higher Education, 11*(1), 29–40.

Dolby, N. (2012). *Rethinking multicultural education for the next generation: The new empathy and social justice*. New York, NY: Routledge, Taylor & Francis Group.

Duncan, K., & Stasio, M. (2001). Surveying feminist pedagogy: A measurement, an evaluation, and an affirmation. *Feminist Teacher, 13*, 22–39.

Fernández, L. (2002). Telling stories about school: Using critical race and Latino critical theories to document Latina/Latino education and resistance. *Qualitative Inquiry, 8*(1), 45–65.

Garii, B., & Rule, A. C. (2009). Integrating social justice with mathematics and science: An analysis of student teacher lessons. *Teaching and Teacher Education, 25*(3), 490–499.

Garrison-Wade, D. F., Diggs, G. A., Estrada, D., & Galindo, R. (2012). Lift every voice and sing: Faculty of color face the challenges of the tenure track. *The Urban Review, 44*, 90–112.

González, J. C. (2007). The ordinary-ness of institutional racism: The effect of history and law in the segregation and integration of Latinas/os in schools. *American Education History Journal, 34*(2), 331–345.

González, J. C. (2008). Damning historical visual archives: Deficit photographing of Mexicans and the "schooling" process. *American Education History Journal, 35*(2), 293–313.

González, J. C., & Portillos, E. (2007). The under-education and over-criminalization of U.S. Latinas/os: A post-Los Angeles riots LatCrit analysis. *Educational Studies, 42*(3), 247–266.

González, J. C., & Portillos, E. (2012). Teaching from a critical perspective/Enseñando de una perspectiva crítica: Conceptualization, reflection, and application of Chicana/o pedagogy. *The International Journal of Critical Pedagogy, 4*(1), 18–34. Retrieved from https://libjournal.uncg.edu/ojs/index.php/ijcp/%20article/viewFile/305/265

Hays, D. G., Arredondo, P., Gladding, S. T., & Toporek, R. L. (2010). Integrating social justice in group work: The next decade. *The Journal for Specialists in Group Work, 35*(2), 177–206.

Higginbotham, E. (1996). Getting all students to listen: Analyzing and coping with student resistance. *American Behavioral Scientist, 40*(2), 203–211.

Highberg, N. P. (2010). Beware! This is a man!. *Feminist Teacher, 20*(2), 157–170.

Holsinger, K. (2012). *Teaching justice: Solving social justice problems through university education.* Berlington, VT: Ashgate Publishing Company.

Johnson, K. R., & Martínez, G. A. (2000). *Crossover dreams: The roots of LatCrit theory in Chicana/o studies, activism, and scholarship* [Electronic Version]. Retrieved November 20, 2012, from http://ssrn.com/abstract=205210

Leonardo, Z. (2009). Reading whiteness: Antiracist pedagogy against white racial knowledge. In W. Ayers, T. Quinn & D. Stovall. (Eds.), *Handbook of social justice in education* (pp. 231–248). Now York, NY: Routledge.

Messner, M. A. (2011). The privilege of teaching about privilege. *Sociological Perspectives, 54*(1), 3–14.

Nagda, B. A., Gurin, P., & Lopez, G. E. (2003). Transformative pedagogy for democracy and social justice. *Race, Ethnicity and Education, 6*(2), 165–191.

National Center for Educational Statistics (2011). *Table 256: Employees in degree-granting institutions, by race/ethnicity, sex, employment status, control and type of institution, and primary occupation: Fall 2009.* Retrieved from http://nces.ed.gov/programs/digest/d10/tables/dt10_256.asp?referrer = report

Nichols, D. (2010). Teaching critical Whiteness theory: What college and university teachers need to know. *Understanding and Dismantling Privilege, 1*(1), 1–12. Retrieved from http://www.wpcjournal.com/article/view/5421

Portillos, E. L., González, J. C., & Peguero, A. A. (2011). Crime control strategies in school: Chicanas'/os' perceptions and criminalization. *The Urban Review, 44*(2), 171–188. doi: 10.1007/s11256-011-0192-z

Rakow, L. F. (1991). Gender and race in the classroom: Teaching way out of line. *Feminist Teacher, 6*(1), 10–13.

Rodriguez, D. (2010). Storytelling in the field: Race, method, and the empowerment of Latina college students. *Cultural Studies <=> Critical Methodologies, 10*(6), 491–507. doi: 10.1177/1532708610365481

Sartre, J. P. (1966). In W. Baskin (Ed.), *Essays in aesthetics.* New York, NY: Washington Square PressTrans.

Shaull, R. (1988). Introduction. In P. Freire (Ed.), *Pedagogy of the oppressed* (p. 15). New York, NY: Continuum.

Skubikowski, K. (2010). Social justice education across the curriculum. In K. Skubikowski, C. Wright & R. Graf (Eds.), *Social justice education: Inviting faculty to transform their institutions* (pp. 87–99). Sterling, VA: Stylus.

Skubikowski, K., Wright, C., & Graf, R. (2010). *Social justice education: Inviting faculty to transform their institutions.* Sterling, VA: Stylus.

Solinger, R., Fox, M., & Irani, K. (2008). *Telling stories to change the world: Global voices on the power of narrative to build community and make social justice claims.* New York, NY: Taylor & Francis.

Solórzano, D. G., & Delgado Bernal, D. (2001). Examining transformational resistance through a critical race and LatCrit theory framework: Chicana and Chicano students in an urban context. *Urban Education, 36*(3), 308–342.

Solórzano, D. G., & Yosso, T. (2002). Critical race methodology: Counter-storytelling as an analytical framework for education research. *Qualitative Inquiry, 8*(1), 23–44.

Stanley, C. A. (2006). Coloring the academic landscape: Faculty of color breaking the silence in predominantly White colleges and universities. *American Educational Research Journal, 43*(4), 701–736.

Stinson, D. W., Bidwell, C. R., & Powell, G. C. (2012). Critical pedagogy and teaching mathematics for social justice. *The International Journal of Critical Pedagogy, 4*(1), 76–94.

Stovall, D. (2006). Forging community in race and class: Critical race theory and the quest for social justice in education. *Race, Ethnicity & Education, 9*(3), 243–259.

Turner, C. S. V., González, J. C., & Wong (Lau), K. (2011). Faculty women of color: The critical nexus of race and gender. *Journal of Diversity in Higher Education, 4*(4), 199–211. doi: 10.1037/a0024630

Weiler, K. (1988). *Women teaching for change: Gender, class, & power.* New York, NY: Bergin & Garvey.

# CHAPTER 8

# REVOLUTIONARY REFORESTATION *AND* WHITE PRIVILEGE IN A CRITICAL RACE DOCTORAL PROGRAM

Amy A. Hunter and Matthew D. Davis

This chapter expresses the need for an increase or reforestation of Black scholarship and examines the complexity of race in a White privileged institution of higher education. It is written with an understanding of Critical Race Theory's counter-narrative benefits and models the power of voice in the classroom of a Black student and a White teacher and their roles in creating a "safe space for race talk" in the classroom.

Educational reform will need a new strategy and direction, particularly if students of color are to succeed where they too often do not. Despite what might be understood as a pedagogical hazard for "race talk" (Leonardo & Porter, 2010), White privilege has allowed, at times, for the "promot[ion] of a 'risk' discourse about race" in which the need for resistance and "reforestation" in the lives of Black students can be realized. (Reforestation alludes to the need for more Black scholars to rejuvenate the Ivory Tower ecology.) The lens of education that evokes liberation or "revolutionary" voice is essential for Black students in an educational system that continues to ask, "… how does it feel to be the problem?" (DuBois, 2008 [1903, 1989]). The necessary support of this revolutionary voice can and must be located in

**Social Justice Issues and Racism in the College Classroom: Perspectives from Different Voices**
**International Perspectives on Higher Education Research, Volume 8, 113–131**
Copyright © 2013 by Emerald Group Publishing Limited

ISSN: 1479-3628/doi:10.1108/S1479-3628(2013)0000008010

the classroom (Leonardo & Porter, 2010). A host of strategies will need to be created in order to encourage a revolution to reject and resist the White supremacy messages currently provided by professors, the curriculum, and even the institution of higher education. The term reforestation usually refers to foliage, land, and forestry. However, throughout this chapter we will explain what reforestation within the educational system would look like, mean, and benefit the field or research, study, academia, and higher education as a system. It will take intentional actions in favor of liberation in order for teachers and students to create a supportive growth or reforestation within the system of higher education.

Importantly, liberation is different from resistance; liberation evokes messages of freedom and personal power to educate, question, and liberate the mind, spirit, and soul of African American students. This strategy will include students of color being understood as citizens (Harris-Perry, 2011) in the sometimes sterile and majority White and male institution of higher education. The revolution will need multiple strategies, allies and supporting scholarship in order for the world to see, understand, and create change within the system of higher education. This will create a reforestation, a new planting of Black scholars within the field of education and within the research, publications, and articulations of race within the educational system. Additional education or ongoing education for the current scholars is also paramount to the success of this reforestation. This revolutionary reforestation will require a robust strategy. There is much written about the civil rights movement in the United States. There is endless scholarship written about the achievement gap – often by White scholars. However, without the intentional inclusion of authors and scholars of color being introduced, encouraged, and supported within the field of higher education, there will be little or no change.

This chapter is intended to express the need for White allies within system of higher education to be advocates for and encouragers to students of color, African American students in particular, to attend universities and pursue doctorate degrees, to include and accept their voices, and to encourage their counter-narratives (Yosso, 2005) and research about their culture, scholars, and children within classrooms. In order to create this far-reaching strategy, it is important to understand the historical context on "how did we get here" and the current perspective of "what is working." It offers an account of an "underground railroad of academia" while it is taking place. The difference here is that the White professor and the African American student in search of liberation are named. The risks are explained and the effect on the academic community that currently exists is explained in order to be mimicked and replicated within other universities.

As authors, we utilize the framework of "Critical Race Theory" (Bell, 1980; Ladson-Billings, 1998; Yosso, 2005). This CRT position is utilized in conjunction with that of "social justice in education" framework (Cochran-Smith et al. in DiAngelo & Sensoy, 2009). Further, we adopt the lens of Leonardo in his articulation of "White Privilege" – even White supremacy (Gillborn, 2005) – as it relates to that carried by the program leader. Our combined experiences will provide insight and voice to the challenges and triumphs of pursuing revolutionary reforestation in a White supremacy environment.

The doctorial process for an African American woman in a predominately White institution of higher education is complicated with the intersection of race and gender within the system of education (Crenshaw, 1993). The process of pursuing a doctoral degree is daunting enough; the entrance process, alone, is grueling and designed to only allow certain types of people into the programs. Being a Black woman in the system of higher education is politically and personally complicated (Harris-Perry, 2011). It is complicated for three dynamics in particular: (1) the intersection and micro inequities of politically navigating a majority White space with race and gender as a factor; (2) the pedagogical framework and scholars that are studied within the institution; and (3) the agency and alliances that are needed to resist and find liberation while completing and obtaining the doctorate degree.

I (the first author) was fortunate. I was introduced to a professor who would later be my advisor, Mathew Davis (the second author). Gil Scot-Heron said it best: "The revolution will not be televised" (1970). This replanting of Black scholars will also not be televised but is essential in creating strategies for liberation through education within the African American community. The loss of Black teachers within our communities (Delpit, 2012; Horsford, 2011) has also affected the way the Black students internalize education, the educational system, and their need or role in resisting the narratives that are being presented and creating strategies within and outside of the community toward liberation. Matthew was a new faculty member at the university. He was not from St. Louis (where the university is located), which offered him and me an opportunity to start a *fresh* relationship, absent historically local White/Black animosities. He has assisted me in navigating the institution, locating scholarship, and research from scholars of color, which provided me with the reality that I can and must become one of them and articulate the need for more Black scholars as an act of resistance toward their liberation and reforestation within scholarship and the "Black spatial imaginary" (Lipsitz, 2011).

Race and gender intersections in the academy also matter (Taylor, Gillborn, & Ladson-Billings, 2009). All women have been marginalized or objectified by men. Rarely is the argument of sexism as a significant factor and impact within systems and within societies around the world argued. However, what is rarely taken into consideration is the impact of race and gender within the academy of higher education or the system of education overall. These patterns of race and gender segregation in higher education have direct implications for gender and race gaps in occupational and income attainment (Mickelson & Smith Jacobs, 1996). In the quest for reforestation of Black scholars, it is paramount to support women of color within the institution of higher education. Their success within the institution will be a model and a path for the students of color, their monetary success as well as their academic success may encourage them to continually mentor, and support and provide insight to the double and sometimes triple consciousness needed to navigate the institution of higher education. My experience as an African American woman is a shared experience with other women of color. This is not to denote that the "Spicy Latina" or the "Suzy Wong" (Hill Collins, 1986) stereotypes are not also harmful and hurtful. I would like to offer that this shared experience on the intersection of race and gender intersectionality (Crenshaw, 1993) is a moment of sisterhood within the academic space, a "fictive kinship" (Harris-Perry, 2011) or understanding that as women of color our experiences are sometime similar, but that our strategy may sometimes be different. Our quest to find our voices in a White and male-dominated system, like higher education, not only is a time for us to reflect on the harm that has been done, to our souls, spirits, and minds but also is a moment to realize our own inherit goodness and intellectual ability.

Our chapter offers an opportunity to articulate that for African American women there are several stereotypes that may affect the way we see ourselves or the way that others see us and our need to navigate, to resist, and to search for liberation within the institution of education, as girls and as women. Therefore, my (Amy) story continues.

One complication is the stereotype threat of Black women as Sapphire, Jezebel, Mammy, or the Strong Black Woman (Harris-Perry, 2011; Hill Collins, 1986). This not only impacts Black female students but may also impact Black female professors. Many of the strategies it takes to combat and overcome the impact of the stereotype threats are shared but students and faculty. The morning of the interview to get accepted into the university's doctorate program I was concerned about my attire. I didn't want to look like the Jezebel and I had to be careful not to present myself as *the* Angry Black woman, the Sapphire. This is a worry that White women and men may not have to concern themselves within the process. I was not worried that they would see me as a Black woman trying to gain entrance to the doctoral program; I was worried about which stereotype they were going to pigeonhole me into during the interview. This is a concern I have managed daily throughout my experience within a variety of institutions. The weight of managing other people's perceptions of me has always been enormous. Liberation or freedom from feeling the need to manage or reject this is important in the reforestation of Black scholarship. Identifying with and claiming the need to resist the stereotypes is exhausting. The strategy to liberate myself within this particular institution required me to redefine my role, as a planted tree within the forest and find resources to support the planting of other African American students. This strategy took realizing the support to and for other students within the program and the support of my advisor.

Matthew, my advisor, noticed that there were few people of color in the doctoral program and decided to interrupt the sterile environment. Partly out of his desire to "fix the problem" of the lack of students of color in the program and the other part is to fulfill desire and role to be remembered as an inclusive educator. He came to the university with a clear understanding that "White Supremacy" (Leonardo & Porter, 2010) was present "in every institution in America" (Bell, 1989). His upbringing assisted in his general love for people and his ability to critically analyze systemic harm, White privilege, and his role within the system. His father, also a professor within the higher educational system, was instrumental in mentoring and supporting Latinos pursuing their advanced degrees in Texas. Matthew has a clear understanding that he would not be harmed or ostracized by his family or his Chair by assisting people of color in obtaining their degrees in higher education. He fully understands that the benefits, as an ally, outweigh the risks to his tenured career. He is able to bravely and boldly step forward to act as an agent, ally, and "safe house" in the Underground Railroad in higher education. The goal or hope is that his actions will assist in the liberation for students of color in the system of higher education. His strategy to assist is also complicated. He has acted as an informational guide to the African American students in politically navigating their way through the system. He has been instrumental in pointing out the career strategies, opportunities, and pitfalls within the system. This is important to the survival of the students. It is affirmation that they are standing in the "crooked room" (Harris-Perry, 2011) of higher education. He not only noticed that the system is in need of replanting, or reforestation of African Americans in higher education, teaching position, professor position, literary reviews, and on research panels, but it is his understanding of the impact their voices, their research could have on the system of education, and the African American community. His ushering of students through the political hurdles of education is not enough for their souls to become liberated nor for them to complete and graduate from the higher education institution. Liberation comes from within and from the external factors of the classroom. Safety in the classroom must be established in order for cross-racial conversations to occur, increase of Black voices, and counter-narratives to be shared, valued, and recognized. The understanding and appreciation of race talk within the classroom setting requires strategy and practice within the classroom.

Creating a safe space to discuss race in the classroom is essential to quality race talk. Many White professors and some professors of color would proudly pat themselves on the back and brag about creating a safe space for conversations regarding race. However, this self-auditing is hardly ever helpful or accurate in higher education. Instead, I (Dr. Davis or Matthew) entered the classroom with an understanding that "the violence is already there" (Leonardo, 2010). In order to establish a less hostile, not hostile in the sense of comfort, White students may never feel comforted by the conversation of race; they can, however, understand that often students of color enter the space harmed and with an understanding that if they participate, raise their hand, share an objective, thought, idea, or analysis, they may be ignored, dehumanized, or harmed by their professor or their peers. As a professor of Critical Race Theory, I had to not only unlearn the concept that my classroom was a safe space for all of the students, but also work to create the kind of space that may be perceived as "safe" where counter-narratives and the voices of the students of color were heard, recognized as valuable and brilliant and expected. It was helpful to have a Black student with a revolutionary view of education in my classroom to establish some safety for conversations of race. It is possible to establish a safe space but it takes longer without the counter-narrative and "other" voice and perspective. The strategy to creating this space is a top down, professor's role and bottom up, student's role approach. My role as the professor is only half the equation.

Creating the climate of safety was strategic, deliberate, and intentional. It went beyond my desire to be liked and my need to be "in charge" of the students. As a professor, I had to remember my Whiteness in the classroom at all times. I started my classes with a check in, with an understanding that students of color experience race or race-related issues and incidents daily, sometimes hourly. They came to class with the understanding that race matters and so does their voice at the onset of class. I was also assured that they were paying attention to the news and world events in a racialized manner. It was a practice for students feeling citizenship within my class. I wanted to encourage my White students to look forward to and to be able to articulate the intersectionality (Crenshaw) of race in the events, policies, and classrooms. Instead of scolding students for being a minute or two late I warmly welcomed them into the conversation, reminding them that I not only wanted them to attend my class, but also was looking forward to their feedback and perspectives on the assignments, their voice was often the counter-narrative to the material. I intentionally developed my syllabus including articles and books written by scholars of color. For many in the room, it was their first time reading an article or book by a person of color. It symbolized and affirmed their brilliance and revolutionary ideology that scholarship did not reside within Whiteness, it belongs to everyone. I wanted all of my students to become familiar with and practiced at looking for, expecting, and becoming scholars with clear and concise writing. The best way to model this for my students was to create it as a norm. The new norm became to read, understand, compare, question, challenge, critically critique, and form analysis around the assigned reading. It was also important to constantly remind them that people of color often have something to say; however, the system of racism invalidates, hides, or questions their voice. Critical Race Theory requires the framing by "others" becomes as valuable as the majority lens, in some cases more valuable. This counter-narrative culture was questioned and practiced in almost every class by my Black student. Her input in the class was often followed by students gazing at me to see if I would shut her down or make her stop talking or end allowing her voice to be heard. White and Black students watched to see what the punishment would be given to her for her clear unapologetic articulation of the materials presented, her ease to relate one article to the next or the article to current events helped to set the tone within the classroom for liberation across the color and gendered line.

As a teacher or professor, I worked closely with this student on articles and books not assigned in the classroom. I did this for other students who seemed extremely engaged and interested in the subject matter. She, however, assisted in modeling the scholarship what I wanted to see in all of my students. This was more than a "favorite student" moment, we were modeling CRT in the classroom. We were practicing the counter-narrative and "cultural capital" (Yasso, 2002) recognition in the classroom, it was becoming part of the cultural norm of the classes I taught. She came to class not only with the assignments read, but also prepared to learn, discuss, analyze, question, and draw parallels to the material. This skill and demonstration demanded that the other students come prepared to class, even if that preparation only included reading the material. Often students would look to her for insight on the assignment, and later they became more skillful at not just reading the material but analyzing the material. They had witnessed her being able to utilize her thoughts without verbal assaults from me, the professor. Instead she received a look or comment of appreciation from me and her peers for the thoughtful and thought – provoking analysis. This assisted in establishing a culture of appreciation for the counter-narrative and the Black scholar. It became clear from the students that this environment in my classroom was not the "norm" for their experience within higher education. They were excited to know that it could happen and that they could establish it within their own settings in the classroom. This excitement allows for the reforestation, replanting the seeds for Black scholars in education.

To address that strategy, teachers must introduce Black scholars to the curriculum, something missing from many classrooms. This became an important strategy after she, an African American student, questioned the lens of the White scholars presented to the class. It was the teacher's desire to affirm her as a student that prompted him into being an authority on Black scholars and Critical Race Theory. His understanding of the counter-narrative and the power and enlightenment of hearing the scholarship of the forgotten and oppressed promoted him to encourage "voice" and agency within his classrooms from and of the African American students. This permission to speak, boldly and confidently from the students of color, not only shocked the African American students, but also shocked the White students. However, the challenge to deliver effective preparation to teachers-in-training is to diversify and expand their knowledge and skill repertoires and enable them to "think like a teacher" about problems racialized and systemic issues of race in the institution of higher education and in the classrooms they occupy (Cochran-Smith & Lytle, 1999; Wilson & Berne, 1999). It not only helped the African Americans be better students and scholars, but also allowed all of the students to notice the "plantation model" schooling that had warmly accepted them and their roles within educational institutions (Jones, 2005).

The introduction of additional Black Scholars was a shared moment for me and my professor. I came into the program with an understanding that messages from the majority culture are usually jaded, misleading, and sometimes just false. The curriculum is slanted toward the Eurocentric views, the authors, scholars, and writers who are studied within the higher educational system often belong to the White majority. Unless a professor is deliberate about introducing Black and Latino scholars into the classroom it is possible for a college educated undergraduate and graduate student to only hear the majoritive view on education, which includes an "othering" of individuals and historical references with a White lens in their K-12 educational experience (Brown & Brown, 2010). This lack of information or education has a direct impact on the ability of teachers, teacher within the institution of higher education, to look for ways to link students to the subject matter at hand and to see students of color, not only as single agents but also as part of a larger movement toward repopulation or reforestation of scholarship within the community and within the institution. As a Black student I came into the institution well aware that there is more than a White perspective about most subjects, especially the subject of education. However at a majority White institution, students particularly Black students, questioning or challenging professors or assigned reading materials, authors is rarely if ever encouraged by White professors (Hill Collin, 1986). The impact of racism and sexism within the system of higher education has allowed the silencing of Black women's voices within the academy. The impact of the intersectionality of the two structurally oppressive systems requires that we encourage the voice and scholarship of women of color in higher education as students and as full faculty. It is not enough to tell students of color they belong within predominately White institutions, they too long for the "fictive kinship" of pride in professors who look like them (Harris-Perry, 2011). The reforestation of students is deeply related to living examples of possibilities and examples of inspiration. "Faculty of color" bring that inspiration to the institution when they "show up" to a classroom or serve on committees to implement change within the institution. Moreover, the need for faculty of color within the reforestation process is vital. Faculty of color, particularly African American faculty are the proof that obtaining a graduate degree and teaching in higher education is possible, their physical existence inspire students to obtain, and seek positions within the institution. Their role within the system of higher education is complex. The first role is as a counter-narrator. The practice of telling truths, or witnessing in the form of a narrative, is called a counter-narrative. Counter-narratives are an important part of under-standing the framework for Critical Race Theory. A Counter-narrative, the experience and reality of the "other" or the oppressed provide an opportunity for the majority to hear, understand, and utilize this body of knowledge to gain a rich and whole or complete picture to historical and current events. Counter-narratives are an important element in Critical Race Theory (Solórzano & Yasso, 2002).

The counter-narrative is not only researched, written, and spoken; it emerges as a shared, lived experience in historically all White male spaces. Thus the research by scholars of color presents claims for full citizenship for these writers within the system of higher education. Without their presence, research, lens, or guidance it is easy for all students, students of color as well as White students to believe the majority narrative that people of color are not as smart, brilliant, or capable as the majority scholars. The CRT practice of telling the other part, the counter position, the story from the oppressed view is possible when an institution values, supports, and encourages scholars of color. Professors of color are "witnesses" of the structural barriers within higher education and more importantly, they are survivors, heroes and even "sheroes" within the institution. The second role faculty of color play within the institution is as guides for the students of color through the tumultuous, often dangerous, terrain of higher education (Solórzano, Ceja, & Yosso, 2000). They have survived and triumphed within the institution and they are aware of the hidden agendas, strategies, and unwritten rules and hurdles that students of color will face within higher education. Professors of color may guide a student in a certain direction to protect them from the systemic and institutional pitfalls, they may direct them away from the most obviously racist professors or advisors, and they may prepare them for the academic rigor in a way that differs from a professor outside of their race or culture. They may be aware of the dirt, the landscape, or the structural racism within the institution and act as gardeners within the reforestation, tending to the seeds and supporting them throughout the process. The reforestation will require White allies to also work with students. The supremacist, structural system is designed for White men to succeed within the institution. They may often be privy to policy and strategies within the system that can also assist students of color through the process. They too may need some additional training, scholarship, and research in this area. Like the professors of color, caring about students and hoping they will endure the higher educational system are not enough to guarantee the success of students in the reforestation process. Moreover, it is a system and structure they may be accustomed to navigating and achieving positive results. I met a man like this in my quest for higher education in my first course.

My professor came into this work with a general knowledge of Critical Race Theory and a few Black scholars. Another challenge to reforestation of Black scholars in a White supremacy environment is closely tied to the historical nature of Critical Race Theory within education (Bell, 1989; Ladson-Billings, 1998). Racism according to Bell (1989) is a permanent fixture in American society (Delgado & Stefancic, 2001).

Critical Race Theory which is derived from Critical Legal Scholarships helps examine, explain, rationalize, and understand how the racial laws of American society affect the lives of Americans. It sets a basis for understanding the property rights of human ownership, land ownership, and the ownership of Whiteness as property in the United States.

Ladson-Billings (1998) article sets forth a framework for understanding the impact of CRT within the system of education, that the access to resources within the educational system is based upon the CRT premise of property rights. Property rights as defined in CRT scholarship include not only the physical property rights, like land or home ownership, but also the property rights of people and Whiteness. The impact of each of these rights is significant in understanding, why Whites have generated more generational wealth and how White skin affords even the poorest of White's citizenship and access to entitlement programs. Zoe Burkholder's (2011) *Race in the Classroom* offers a chronological history of how Whiteness – White skin privilege – was strategically aligned utilizing the system of education to create the White supremacy narrative we now understand as White privilege in America. It is to be understood that White privilege is a benefit that is received by all White people whether they want to receive it or not. White privilege may be compared to being on the riding and escalator, and believing that you are out pacing the person taking the stairs fairly (Leonard-Wright, 2004). The automatic, unearned privileges afforded to individuals based upon the racial identification or hue of their White skin is actualized in all institutions and systems.

There were several opportunities to practice "voice" within the classroom. For the first time for many of the students in the classroom there was a Black woman challenging the text, looking up the credentials, background, and other articles written by the authors presented in class and in front of the entire class "challenging" the materials as they were presented. What was unusual in this instance is that rarely are Black students "allowed" to challenge materials presented by White teachers, and rarely is it encouraged. The other Black students and White students looked on with amazement and were genuinely concerned that the student would receive a failing grade. This type of behavior was not welcomed by all the students in the class and at times some of the White students would verbally attack the Black students. With a clear understanding of White supremacy and White superiority and unsafe spaces in "race talk" (Leonardo & Porter, 2010), Mathew, the professor, took three key steps to create a different dynamic in his classroom. The first is to introduce the CRT to the entire classroom. It not only establishes that race and racism are real, but also affirms racism within the system of education. Critical Race Theory encourages the usage of the counter narrative, "stories [that]challenge the story of white supremacy and continue to give a voice to those that have been silenced by white supremacy" (Solórzano, 1998). The introduction of CRT and the counter-narrative encouraged multiple perspective and critical thinking on the part of the students. It also fostered an environment where all voices were heard and honored even if everyone did not agree. The second step was in selecting the students of color to speak on the topics at hand at the beginning of class. It set a precedent that their voices would be heard. And lastly, he supported the Black student's voices, sometimes with a nod and other times with additional scholarship when they were being attacked by their White peers. It wasn't unusual for a Black student to give their understanding or interpretation of the text or scholar and Matthew to support that understanding with other scholarship. For example, in understanding Critical Race Theory we not only studied Derrick Bell, but also looked at the intersection in education with Gloria Ladson-Billings and then the geospatial relationship with Gordon's Mapping Decline and the impact of land ownership, a tenant in CRT and educational attainment. He was not only brilliant at creating a space where scholarship and thought could be somewhat equally exchanged but also deliberate and intentional. The intentional aspect of this is a place for all professors to question if they have created this dynamic within their classroom and if they are providing cross-racial space for students to be validated, heard, and encouraged in their scholarship.

The oppression within the system and institution of education of people of color limits the agency, rights, and citizenship children of color are granted, if ever granted, within the system of education. The responses to this systemic and institutional oppression and stress are strategies toward resistance and liberation. The strategy is twofold, of resistance and liberation. To resist the racist ideology, scripting, teaching, and internalization of the oppressed narrative along with the struggle and fight for individual, collective, and community liberation is the key to the reforestation in the White supremacy space or the White spatial imaginary (Lipsitz, 2011). This will require a FULL education, an education that includes faculty of color and scholars within the system of higher education. In fact, as Turner (2002, p. 14) points out, "efforts to diversify the faculty continues to be amongst the least successful elements of campus commitments to diversity" So, why, despite the best intentions, are some of the programs designed to address the recruitment and retention issues; programs and policies failing to increase faculty/staff diversity? At the university the student and advisor attend and teach, a Dean's Committee on Social Justice was formed to address the strategies for diversity, including but not limited to recruitment, retention, and tenure within the university. While some faculty of color have been hired, few make tenure. The tenure track is a difficult and tedious track for professors of color. It is vital to the reforestation for students to "witness" professors of color within their institution. It would be ideal if tenure faculty of color became so normative that students assumed that the faculty of color were already tenured instead of adjunct or visiting professor status. If we want students to see themselves as capable of achieving great success within the system of education, it is helpful to model that practice within the system of higher education. With the "window of opportunity" for diverse hiring limited to the next five years or so of faculty retirements, many higher education administrators and bureaucrats are scrambling desperately to find an answer, especially since the growing gap between a multicultural student body and a monoculture faculty/staff has become an educational and political problem. This is not only important for the students of color, so that they can hear from scholars who look like them and at times represent their opposing view, but also important for White students to also understand that there are often more than one lens or perspective and that all voices are valued and deserve to be heard and recognized as scholarship.

This moment is the window for resistance, the practice of analysis and challenging of predominantly White scholars occurred in the classroom, strategically created by Matthew and actively acted on by his Black female student named Amy. This created a safe space on the Underground Railroad to be heard, listened to, and supported as smart. There were several students who worried and questioned that this space was real and safe. In order to replant, or create a space for personal and professional liberation, everyone will have to change, shift a little. It required Matthew to be brave and vulnerable at the same time as witnessing the infinite possibilities of supporting Black scholars on their way to the lives, and advocacy they were previously denied. The reforestation takes both parties to risk a little to gain a lot for the academic world and the community as a whole. When women of color are liberated within the system of education we will all benefit and be liberated (Giddings, 1996). But until their voices are recognized, heard, understood, admired, and accepted the institution or system of higher education is void of the knowledge and insight this body of humans can offer, bring, and contribute. It will take all of us to work toward liberation.

The collective work toward the resistance of White supremacy within the system of higher education along with noticing that other people who may be targeted by the system and the need to assist them in navigating the political nature of higher education was a role that Matthew assigned himself; in part for his own humanity and also in his recognition that liberation is something that his student Amy could only give to herself. He realized that Amy's goal was to live freely, heard, recognized, and appreciated that this is the goal for his other students. His sense of responsibility, and the ability to mourn for and at the same time recruit individuals who are missing from higher education is his acknowledgement that Whiteness and White privilege survives, thrives and is supported within higher education. This awareness offered him no other choice but to "do something" to change the historic reality that some people are allowed, encouraged and supported in higher education. Even though pursuing an advanced degree or even an undergraduate degree can be challenging for any person, the impact of race and racism is ever present.

Upon meeting Amy, a middle-aged African American woman, who believes that education is a form of liberation and an act of resistance in a racially biased educational system, Matthew decided to fully support her. The complexities of their strategy were not fully realized until he and she started this journey together. He decided to tell her and others in navigating the ins and outs of higher education, and also to learn from her and the other students. Together they decided to work to repopulate or begin the reforestation of African American scholars within the Ph.D. program at their university, where he is a tenured associate professor and she is an African American student. Reforestation is the restocking of existing forests and woodlands which have been depleted, an effect of deforestation. Reforestation can be used to improve the quality of human life by soaking up pollution and dust from the air, rebuild natural habitats and ecosystems, mitigate global warming since forests facilitate biosequestration of atmospheric carbon dioxide, and harvest for resources, particularly timber. Reforestation. (n.d.).

Together, we were inspired by the complexity and success of the Wangari Maathi's Green Belt. Wangari Maathi was the first African woman to win the Noble Peace Prize. She won this award after several years of fighting for a movement to assist women in economic stability. The movement grew and her safety was often threatened. The movement not only increased financial stability for women planting trees, selling wares, and providing their community with resources, water pumps, job creation and green spaces, but also created a reforestation, a movement of planting more trees to increase the air quality, to preserve the natural vegetation of Africa, and to maintain green spaces for African people.

This movement, as was our nascent reforestation of Black scholars, was met with resistance. Maintaining economic opportunities for people, financial independence, and environment gains within communities was more important to Wangari Maathi than her own personal safety. The courage and vision and determination she felt toward this movement is the same courage, vision, and determination we will need to create more Black scholars, to plant more African Americans within the system of higher education. The benefit, like the benefit of the Green Belt Movement, would include a generational wave of education as a form of resistance and liberation. As more Black scholars write more and interpret better the realities and strategies of Black people navigating the educational environment, the more Black people will be able to establish a movement, repopulating people, scholars within and outside of Black space and within and outside of White spaces. The benefit of trees is similar to the benefits of Black scholars, they are always needed, their infinite possibilities always exist, and their worth cannot be measured by their mere existence, the value is seen and unseen but necessary.

The Green Belt Movement and its application can be applied to schooling and education for Black students and scholars. Much of the language being used to describe the Green Belt Movement could also be utilized to describe the desolate reality of African American schooling, lack of resources, White superiority of curriculum, and desolate physical characteristics of the physical building of schools and the need then to replant, water, and provide sunlight to the endarkened community and educational system. But the system is far from the agricultural lens we see with reforestation. It is far from the lens of Wangari Maathi Green Belt Movement.

The goal in this movement has the potential to reach beyond the lives of our work; modeling, voice, and action have touched the lives, inspired, and produced graduates of the program. The model of support and reforestation of African American scholarship is important for future understanding, scholarship, publications, policy making, and leadership within academia and the community at large. The impact of this model can be replicated and may significantly impact: academia, research, future directions, strategies and actions within the community. It will call for a shift from a "plantation model" Jones educational model into an act of liberation or resistance on the part of Black and Brown students (Jones, 2005). The reforestation of African American scholars within the higher educational system is a complex strategy that will require the collaboration, organization, and support from the institution that oppresses students of color historically. The impact, like the Green Belt Movement implies a spiritual, economic, community building, and "sowing seeds," creating a community of scholars that can repopulate and replant the seeds. Reforestation will require deliberate and strategic movement towards liberation and education as a form of resistance and it will take a clear understanding of White supremacy and privilege within the system of education the thoughtful and strategic ally work that is needed and necessary to repopulate the higher education field.

The resistance of accepting, promoting, internalizing, and identifying with the negative narratives about Black people within the educational systems calls for a deep understanding of the ahistorical aspects of America and a strategic and deliberate strategy for people of color to utilize, create, demand, and resist the systemic White supremacy models in American institution of schools. This includes the understanding of CRT and the property rights of Whites and how landownership and "opportunity hoarding (Tilly, 1998)" take place and impact the system of education and higher education. The time is now for higher education to create strategies to repopulate their forests, or institutions with African American scholars. The resistances to the White supremacy within the higher education system will not lonely benefit students of color but White teachers in Black and Brown spaces will have more information to encourage Black students to become trees within and outside of their community. Wangari Maathi's example illustrates the endless possibilities that can arise from this movement and the impact it would have on communities, schools, and higher education would be significant. We encourage everyone to listen and learn from our experience, and work to populate higher education with African American scholars.

In conclusion, there is an enormous amount of strategy and implementation of the strategy within the system of higher education to begin a reforestation of Black scholars within the structural system of higher education. However, like the Green Belt Movement this is not an impossible task. As a matter of fact this task is possible on every campus. Like the Green Belt Movement the ripple affect on the community the Black community and the community at large will be significant. With more Black scholars and researchers and professors and educators in the community at large, it grants everyone the privilege of learning, growing, and critically collaborating on systemic and institutional issues within the community of education and society as a whole. The "cultural capital" (Yosso, 2005) of the counter-narratives provides a road map to creating strategies with people, individuals, and communities to acknowledge, address, and dismantle systems of structural inequality and repopulate the community with people who can assist in liberating communities and encouraging the resistance to stereotypes, racial scripting, and institutionalized messages of Black and Brown people. This movement can ignite agency and citizenship (Harris-Perry, 2011) within the system of higher education and provide the system of higher education with new "voice" and scholarship in multiple disciplines. Imagine a college where professors have information about Black people from Black people. Imagine a school or university where Black students are eager to learn and feel like their voices and opinions matter and are being recognized, respected, and heard. Imagine an increase of Black students graduating from universities and colleges and providing insight and collaboration on projects, utilizing their lens and experiences to add value and vision to research, and the articulation of the research. Imagine as many trees that were built as a part of the Green Belt Movement as students graduating from undergraduate and graduate schools. The impact within the Green Belt Movement also impacted the economic conditions of the people living in Kenya. Imagine the economic impact that increasing Black scholars would have on the Black community and the community at large. There would be more individuals making living wages and able to act as agents and living role models to children within the community. Their mere existence would articulate and provide an actual and living counter-narrative to the gangster, criminal, and negative images that are facing Americans and the world today. Instead of seeing Black women as angry we can see them as smart and passionate. This positive lens and narrative can also impact how Black women, men, and children see themselves within and outside of the community. Reforestation of Black scholarship in a White supremacy realm will take a model of resistance and liberation. It will take all of us, if not all of us then most of us each working toward restructuring the system of education and fighting for equality and liberation within the system.

# REFERENCES


Bell, D. (1980). Dialectics of school desegregation. *The Alabama Law Review, 32*, 281.

Bell, D. (1989). *And we are not saved: The elusive quest for racial justice.* New York, NY: Basic Books.

Brown, A. L., & Brown, K. D. (2010). Strange fruit indeed: Interrogating contemporary textbook representations of racial violence toward African Americans. *Teachers College Record, 112*(1), 31–67.

Burkholder, Z. (2011). *Color in the classroom: How American schools taught race, 1900–1954.* New York: Oxford University Press.

Cochran-Smith, M., Shakman, K., Jong, C., Terrell, D. G., Barnatt, J., & McQuillan, P. (2009). Good and just teaching: The case for social justice in teacher education. *American Journal of Education, 115*(3), 347–377.

Cochran-Smith, M., & Lytle, S. L. (1999). Relationships of knowledge and practice: Teacher learning in communities. *Review of Research in Education, 24,* 249–305.

Crenshaw, K. (1993). Mapping the margins: Intersectionality, identity politics and theviolence against women of color. *Stanford Law Review, 43,* 1241–1299.

Delgado, R., & Stefancic, J. (2001). *Critical race theory: An introduction.* New York, NY: New York University Press.

Delpit, L. D. (2012). *"Multiplication is for white people": Raising expectations for other people's children.* New York, NY: The New Press.

DiAngelo, R., & Sensoy, Ö. (2009). We don't want your opinion: Knowledge construction and the discourse of opinion in the equity classroom. *Equity & Excellence in Education, 42*(4), 443–455.

DuBois, W. E. B. (1903; 1989). *The soul of black folk.* New York, NY: Bantam.

Giddings, P. J. (1996). *When and where I enter: The impact of Black women on race and sex in America.* William Morrow Paperbacks. New York, NY: Harper Collins Publishers.

Harris-Perry, M. (2011). *Sister citizen: Shame, stereotypes and black women in America.* New Haven, CT: Yale University Press.

Hill Collins, P. (1986). Learning from the outsider within: The sociological significance of Black feminist thought. *Social Problems, 33,* S14–S32.

Horsford, S. D. (2011). *Learning in a burning house: Educational inequality, ideology, and (Dis) integration.* New York, NY: Teachers College Press.

Jones, B. A. (2005). Forces for failure and genocide: The plantation model of urban educational policy making in St. Louis. *Educational Studies, 37*(1), 2–24.

Ladson-Billings, G. (1998). Preparing teachers for diverse student populations: A critical race theory perspective. *Review of Research in Education, 24,* 211–247.

Leonardo, Z., & Porter, R. K. (2010). Pedagogy of fear: Toward a fanonian theory of 'safety' in race dialogue. *Race Ethnicity and Education, 13*(2), 139–157.

Lipstiz, G. (2011). *How racism takes place.* Philadelphia, PA: Temple University Press.

Reforestation. (n.d.). Dictionary.com Unabridged. Retrieved from http://dictionary.reference.com/browse/Reforestation. Accessed on June 29, 2012.

Scott-Heron, G. (1970). *The revolution will not be televised. On Small Talk at 125th & Lennox Ave. [Medium of recording: record].* New York, NY: Flying Dutchman.

Solórzano, D., Ceja, M., & Yosso, T. (2000). Critical race theory, racial microaggressions and campus racial climate: The experiences of African-American college students. *Journal of Negro Education, 69*(1/2), 60–73.

Solórzano, D., & Yasso, T. (2002). A critical race counter story of race, racism and affirmative action. *Equity and Excellence in Education, 35*(2), 155–168.

Taylor, E., Gillborn, D., & Ladson-Billings, G. (2009). *Foundations of critical race theory in education.* London: Routledge.

Tilly, C. (1998). How to hoard opportunities. In C. Tilly (Ed.), *Durable Inequality* (pp. 147–169). Berkeley, CA: University of California Press.

Turner, C. S. V. (2002). *Diversifying the faculty: A guidebook for search committees* (p. 14). Washington, DC: Association of American Colleges & Universities.

Wilson, S. M., & Berne, J. (1999). Teacher learning and the acquisition of professional knowledge: An examination of research on contemporary professional development. *Review of Research in Education, 24*, 173–209.

Yosso, T. J. (2005). Whose culture has capital? A critical race theory discussion of community cultural wealth. *Race Ethnicity and Education, 8*(1), 69–91.

# CHAPTER 9

# RESEARCH AS ACTIVISM

Linda Sue Warner

## ABSTRACT

*This chapter discusses the similarities and differences between native research methods and western social science research as it impacts American Indians in the academy. The chapter reflects on the requirements needed by young practitioners and their responsibilities to their tribal communities to produce research that is both informative and available. The chapter contextualizes the discussion in examples of indigenous activism.*

You taught me language; and my profit on't
Is, I know how to curse.[1]

A quote from Shakespeare as the prelude to a reflection on indigenous perspectives in research – I would guess you did not see this coming. Caliban, as the indigenous inhabitant of his land, uses the language of his oppressor to combat insult with insult. This quote from Caliban reminds me of the following poem, penned in the early years as an educator "wanting to make a difference." The reference to an ongoing war is perhaps, again, not what you expected in this chapter. But reflecting on both of these, in some odd combination of the intersection of colonization and activism and when we return to this at the end of the chapter, it should give you pause.

Social Justice Issues and Racism in the College Classroom: Perspectives from Different Voices
International Perspectives on Higher Education Research, Volume 8, 133–150

ISSN: 1479-3628/doi:10.1108/S1479-3628(2013)0000008011

# BATTLES[2]

I write about the yesterdays,
for it is in their freedom that we find ourselves.
Ours is an ageless time. Meant for
the strong and wise. Meant for us.
We begin the hunt with the same rites as before.
They sound metallic, but they still sound.
We begin the fight with the same strength of purpose
but we fight with our minds now; we win with gavels.
The faces and the weapons have changed, but the battle
to remain unconquered, the freedom remains.
It endures the rule changes;
it endures the seasons.
You and I choose the time for the final test,
faltering now, our grandchildren's sons will fight.
Even in the losing now, we win. It is still our
choice to wait. It is still our yesterdays that free us.
It is our tomorrow.

Most of the audience today will be researchers and native students who are contemplating a career in Indian Country; a career that links their works to home communities and is conceived and inspired by personal commitment and community need. This chapter, therefore, will not "preach to the choir"; I hope that most of you are familiar with the standards on indigenous research but if they are unfamiliar or you have not reflected in some time, please review Mihesuah (2003) or Smith (2005) or Wilson (2009). The tension between nonindigenous academy research, with its all familiar and sometimes personal stories of invasion, and the depth and sense of indigenous research is well established. To retell you the angst of colonization or to analyze it and denial of sovereignty in efforts to recover our own knowledge base would be redundant to exceptional work readily accessible. This chapter will reflect more specifically on what Smith describes as "an encounter" (p. 8). Then, hopefully, it will challenge you to begin your own "encounter." This chapter is intended to remind you that it is important to keep at this battle, the one described by Tahdooahnippah.

This encounter began with Caliban's cursed speech in a language foreign to him, but one that he successfully mastered. Caliban's motives are not perhaps our own, but these motives represent a necessary starting place. Caliban is ultimately physically beaten into submission by his oppressors; definitely not the conclusion expected in our efforts at activism through research. In the play, he draws attention to results of a society that does not respect individuals. If we expect a nonindigenous academy to "listen" to us, it is important to master the skills of their language.

The clearest memory of this type of experience is linked to The National Science Foundation's Systemic Initiatives. These began in the early 1990s and included three sets of initiatives: states, urban school districts, and rural school districts. One of the most successful of all three was the Alaska Rural System Initiative led up by Ray Barnhardt at the University of Alaska in partnership with the Alaska Federation of Natives (Kawagley, 1997). The project was so successful that it was funded for a decade and the research resulted in policy changes at the state level that were unprecedented in the other projects in the lower 48. Ray Barnhardt was successful in getting the academy (in this case The National Science Foundation) to listen to his story, but he was also successful in ensuring that the Alaskan natives in the communities they used as pilot sites heard what he was saying. Dr. Barnhardt and his team spoke two languages; not English and Yupik, but academic protocol and indigenous ways of knowing (Barnhardt & Kawagley, 1998).

But the key does not lie in just being able to translate fluently between these two languages. The real substance of Dr. Barnhardt's legacy is that the team documented the work they began. Research studies and evaluation instruments were initiated at the beginning of each activity and now form a sizeable corpus of documentation. Studies were produced and found their way into major academic venues across the United States and even internationally. These studies can be found in major academic journals because the research team used rigorous methods and sound practice; the researchers knew and understood western research methods. These studies met the requirements of academic rigor and peer-review and are readily available to others seeking to replicate this work.[3]

The work also made its way into native educators' workshops, tribal council meetings on educational policy, and the State Department of Education in Alaska. Each one of these venues required a translation of sorts because the utilitarian need for curriculum reform in the classroom required action research and an understanding of native ways of knowing but it also required funding. The changes essentially required that the same argument be made in three distinct venues, using language specific to that venue. The State of Alaska serves as the best case study of the implementation of native ways of knowing throughout the system. In fact, the initiative, The Alaska Rural Systemic Initiative, sought to change policy and practice. The systemic change of this State was accomplished by the following changes.

1. To change practice, the team developed curriculum and rubrics that were user-friendly to teachers, parents, and tribal council members in each of the six linguistic regions in Alaska. This included developing items in each of those dialects so that communities could reinforce the curriculum.
2. To change policy, the team developed the hypotheses and research that aligned rigorous rubrics to the state's content standards and then added the cultural component which was adopted by the State Department of Education for all teachers in all public schools.
3. Finally, the history of continued funding over this decade was predicated on Dr. Barnhardt's team's ability to convince the scientists and politicians on two points: First, that the native knowledge base used in this work was legitimate and could withstand the scrutiny of academic scientists, and second that the results would be institutionalized in policy and in practice.

This work took a decade and the impact can continue to be seen in the use of indigenous knowledge systems in the development of classroom activities. As a National Science Foundation program officer during this process, it is important to make a few objective observations. Dr. Barnhardt began this work with a highly respected career in place; he was an acknowledged expert within the State of Alaska and had built an academic career that provides a solid backdrop for this work. Further, he is not seen as an outsider in Alaska native communities, even though he is from North Dakota. His academic career and life's work in mathematics and science education in Alaska are testament to his commitment; the trust of native peoples across the State is a testament to his resolve. I suspect that Dr. Barnhardt would caution you not to read this as an endorsement of any single effort because he did not do this work alone. His body of work with Oscar Kawagley et al. can be reviewed on the Alaska Native Knowledge Network (www.ankn.uaf.edu) and continues to set a high standard in research and evaluation. In fact, that is one of the reasons it remains a standard; the work was done by a multitude of researchers and practitioners (native and non-native). The leadership, however, made absolutely sure that research accompanied practice and that this research was published and disseminated as widely as possible.

This last statement emphasizes that "research accompanied practice" and is perhaps the single, clearest parallel for indigenous and nonindigenous researchers. The separation comes when we do not widely disseminate our research findings from indigenous communities into mainstream academe so that we can refine the practices in the classroom. The majority of the work on native ways of knowing, as it affects curriculum, is in the K-12 classroom; it is important to complement this work with alignment in higher education. In the example I cited, the educators were careful to publish the results of their research in mainstream journals; they did not limit their dissemination of this work to the State of Alaska. The utility of the Internet facilitated the dissemination of information, but it is not the dissemination of information that makes this effort significant; it is the dissemination of well-crafted qualitative and quantitative research that uses both peer-review and subject matter expertise (community elders) and, therefore, incorporates local knowledge and culture into the effective practices used in high-performing classrooms. If we could reach down into the language preservation efforts of numerous tribes, we would find that significant findings are evidence in a range of practices. There are many examples of "reinventing the wheel" where projects are funded in native language literacy and then lost to the general academic consumer because it is not disseminated widely. For example, the U.S. Department of Education was known in the early 1970s for funding numerous Indian projects and shelving the results.

It seems we just forget to get them published in mainstream venues, or as my more practical colleagues will state, mainstream venues do not want to publish research on such narrow fields of study or these venues dismiss the rigor of our research methods. This begins the challenge of this chapter: Be sure your research reflects the highest quality in both methods and interpretation and that it is readily available in mainstream venues (Droogsma, 2007) (see Note 4). The opportunities are expanding in higher education through the work of classroom educators in colleges and universities designated as Native American Serving, Non-Tribal Institutions (NASNTIs). Using the research on native ways of knowing, these institutions are incorporating indigenous tribal values in courses across the curriculum.

The adage "publish or perish" respoke as "publish and perish" is appropriate here too. This reminds me of a second example of research in mainstream academy and how easily we can allow our own urgency to negate our purpose. As a facilitator at a national conference on Indian Education, I watched a young native scholar pile one overhead after another on a screen as the scholar attempted to discuss a major a "research" project. Without the benefit of senior scholars, like the ones in the first example in Alaska who would be able to translate the research findings to an audience of practitioners, this researcher explained findings after explaining the statistical test was a correlation coefficient which resulted in statistical significance.

I asked this young scholar to reposition the overhead listing the research questions used in the beginning of the presentation because I had remembered these questions as cause/effect, not relationship based. Clearly this young researcher did not understand the mathematical language being used and, therefore, was unable to present relevant findings. For this audience, the result was probably negligible because the audience was school board members and practitioners in reservation schools; unfortunately they would not have the expertise to question the results presented. These practitioners were not everyday consumers of research findings. The fundamental problem, however, is not their inability to ask the correct questions or to sort through the methods, but it is a problem if, as a scholar of original inquiry, you are unable to discuss your results and know when you have made such a fundamental error. The same presentation to an audience of researchers would limit this native individual's opportunities in mainstream academe and could result in dismissal of other native perspectives. The second lesson in our battle analogy then is to be prepared. The likelihood that indigenous scholarship will change mainstream academe is still remote, but not impossible; we need to be able to be prepared to speak both languages, that of the researcher and that of the practitioner, if we expect anyone to listen to our findings.

The second story I share is even more disturbing because it originated with a senior native scholar and produced work in a tribal school district. We had convened a set of papers at an international research forum and the lead investigator on this team invited local tribal officials to present the findings. The "study" was a set of demographic data and simple percentages. Some of the data contradicted other pieces of the presentation and each question had a different "$N$" which confounded the findings. The tribal officials were very proud to be working with the research university and the senior scholar. This work, they noted, produced findings which the tribal officials then used to make policy decisions for that school. The findings were presented to a group of mainstream researchers. The whole presentation was disturbing and embarrassing. The most significant "finding" for me as an observer was that even senior scholars lack a basic understanding of research. Knowing your colleague's intentions does not excuse sloppy methods; you have no control over their work, but you do have a personal commitment to your own, to your own tribe, and to tribal nations.

My final story is one of being a guest lecturer in a basic research class at Haskell, a tribal college. From the questions posed by the students, it was evident that there was a basic lack of understanding for even the most elementary vocabulary associated with research. For example, the students used the term "significance" with cavalier abandon and evidenced no understanding of the process for creating a research study. There was no evidence that the students had any understanding of theory or that any of the questionnaires been based in any logical framework. Students had already created sets of questions that they administered to as many willing classmates and peers as they could round up. The surveys were elementary and invasive. The instructor obviously lacked a general background in research and yet students would be awarded credit for a research project that lacked integrity or usefulness and ultimately three hours of credit for a class that actually taught them the wrong way to do research. Each of us is a mentor and while these incidents may have been a well-intentioned scenarios, it serves to remind us that we need to teach our students to be critical consumers and to continue to ask questions. We cannot do that if we are not competent researchers first.

For each of these somewhat disturbing stories, there are likely dozens of positive stories you can relate to quality research that was driven by a tribal community need and which ultimately added data to the decision-making process in that community. There are highly qualified indigenous scholars and researchers; you can likely name as many as I can. So these three stories are provided as examples of what we absolutely know not to do; these stories are provided to remind you that we need to be competent consumers of the research we produce or use for decision-making. Finally, these stories can remind us that we have colleagues who produce quality work and who are most willing to work with us. We live and work with native communities where sharing knowledge is valued (Sahota, n.d., 2007).

In a digital-tweeting-facebook age, this sharing would seem all too easy. You can post and posit any number of chapters and articles in a multitude of venues. You can create a forum, design your own website, post your own work, and pronounce yourself an indigenous activist-scholar. All of those efforts will not matter to the academy because the rules there are inviolate. It is important to remember Caliban's speech here. The colonizers need to hear us, no matter how softly your one voice sounds. The digital-tweeting-facebook audience is a different one than the policymakers we hope to educate, but that does not negate the effect that technology has on our ability to tell stories.

The sheer lack of numbers of trained indigenous researchers in mainstream institutions works to complement our research strategies; we do not work as individuals, we share the workload and the opportunity. Large-scale research projects need multiple perspectives and insights. Like

Barnhardt and Kawagley, it also provides the opportunity for senior researchers to mentor junior scholars and for both to work with practitioners. We begin this work with links to an indigenous community, but it does not hurt our cause to expand our distribution of findings to other communities. Just as we often look at theories across cultures to define our problem, other researchers may find our work adds a dimension to their inquiry – but they need access to it.

## TENSIONS

The tension between research based on native ways of knowing and western methods is that the academy has shown little regard for indigenous methodologies. It is ironic to think that western scientific communities devalue observation as a technique, when observation and replication form the core of mainstream research. Indigenous observation underlies the strategy found in oral histories and appears to have withstood the test of time (Bischop, 2005). The fact that a western-based academy does not embrace these methods or this delivery system does not negate the usefulness of the data collection. In an age of "data-based decision-making," native people understand that data held now in oral tradition is as valid today as it was when the original observations were made. Academics may require a doctorate in marine biology to substantiate oceanic research but that does not negate the observations of indigenous elders who have observed marine wildlife their entire lifetimes; it does not negate the observations of their ancestors who relied on such observations for their livelihood – and survived.

Habermas (as cited in Bernstein, 1978) and others posit that traditional science acts as tool of domination instead of a tool of enlightenment for native peoples and in multiple instances this statement appears to be true. This chapter was not designed to add rhetoric to that argument. Further, this chapter is not interested in the argument that the tenure process is so individually geared as to require a fundamental agreement that it serves the individual researcher more than it does the community being researched.

The argument here is not that one method (western science or native science) is better or more tested than another; the thesis is that we can learn from multiple perspectives. This thesis is true for research in the "hard sciences" as well as research in the social sciences. While western social sciences methods ignore practical implications until the end or conclusions section, it is incumbent upon indigenous researchers to "translate" these methodological restrictions to incorporate practice and the practitioner in the initial research process. Western social science research has long been actualized as a binary process that separates the researcher from the researched. The history of the dissemination of social science research and critical analyses highlight the privileged position of researchers and question the substantive link to change in indigenous societies, often noting that research benefits the individual researcher more than a community (Alfred, 2001; Denzin & Lincoln, 1998; Lafromboise, Coleman, & Gerton, 1993; Noah, 2003; Schiele & Hopps, 2009; Wax, 1991).

One of my earliest memories of social science research was a story told by my cousin about her grandmother's experiences with language researchers. Her grandmother's initial reluctance was framed as a lack of payment for her time, the hallmark of early non-Comanche researchers. After being assured that the researcher was a student and needed the translation of certain words for a paper, the elder agreed. But for me, as a researcher, the singular outstanding conclusion was the elder's response to her grand-daughter's question at the end of the interview. "Grandmother, did you tell her the truth?" to which the elder smiled and replied, "sometimes." This story substantiated the findings noted above; the individual researcher benefited more than the elder, or the community.

The ability to infuse cultural research methods into a substantive research agenda begins with our ability to ask ideologically informed questions about native communities. As indigenous researchers and scholars these questions will be derived from hundreds of languages and myriad experiences; it is our challenge to honor the tension between individual reward and community need. There is enough work to share.

## THE BATTLE

The chapter also began with a poem reflecting on modern battles. Some will be uncomfortable with the analogy of war or the oblique reference that it is "us and them" but those of us in the academy now have our own battle tales. The struggles for tenure, the demands of service to the profession, and the teaching – all these crowd out the time we have to devote to the one commonality that all native researchers share, regardless of discipline – a career that links our works to home communities and is conceived and inspired by personal commitment and community need.

The sheer intensity of the tenure process for minority scholars is documented and the culture of each specific institution determines the support network for untenured scholars (Aguirre, 1995; ASHE, 2012; Stanley, 2006; Ponjuan, Conley, & Trower, 2011). With 0.04% American Indian professors in higher education, the ability to impact classrooms and future American Indian students is minimal (American Federation of Teachers, 2010). Trower's study (2009) found the number of doctoral degrees earned by American Indians to have increased 40% from 1995 to 2005; a disproportionately high number based on the general populations, but she also reported an exceptionally low number of new faculty in research institutions (p. 40). Stanley's work (2006) categorizes all minority faculty the same and her work does not specifically provide evidence of American Indian faculty, most likely because the numbers are too small for any comparative analysis (p. 703). Finally, Taylor, Apprey, Hill, McGrann, and Wang (2010) article on Diversifying the Faculty (pp. 15–18) is written from multiple perspectives by minority authors, but does not include an American Indian voice. This is perhaps more telling about the lack of voice in higher education classrooms than the studies which mention the dearth of evidence. The extent to which research is valued in an institution may vary; so while the rules may change slightly, each individual who decides to work in a research institution with an expectation of an individual research agenda is prepared at the beginning of the first six years. The rules pretty much remain the same throughout the process, so it is unlikely that an individual scholar can attest that the criteria changed along the way. The indigenous scholar's colleagues do change, however, and each year a young scholar may find that the new addition to the faculty has no experience with indigenous perspectives; so the teaching begins again. As a young researcher in a mainstream institution, the challenge to gain a recognized "voice" is often diluted by the requirements of the university to get tenure, so that no matter how well intentioned your work, you find it complicated in all manner of ways you did not anticipate. Colleagues in these institutions appear to have an "unconscious privilege" about tenure as a meritocratic system (Trower, 2009). As an individual researcher, you are responsible for your own expertise and the first strategy to use in competing in this venue is to be sure that your "voice" is credible; that your research is well grounded, and that you are knowledgeable about both the methods for analysis and for the articulation of your results (p. 40).

The first component in this strategy for an activism agenda is to acknowledge that each of us will need to teach our nonindigenous colleagues about the usefulness of indigenous research methods so that they can be consumers of our research findings. We had to learn their language; now it is important for them to learn ours.

Alfred (1999) provided a governance framework in his indigenous manifesto for young scholars to move beyond colonization to self-determination that is particularly useful in a discussion on indigenous research. This work has been rethought and reconceptualized; it is particularly noteworthy that Alfred has moved beyond his discussion of sovereignty to one of freedom in his later works (2005). As loosely coupled as the entreaties by various indigenous scholars were in recent decades, each entreaty represented a similar, now familiar, line of thinking and each urged other scholars to continue to produce and publish. Our colleagues, other indigenous scholars, who have been most successful in this tenure process are scholars who, like Caliban, speak both the language of the academy/ oppressor and that of native peoples. These scholars are able to generate primary inquiry, test, and report the results, and they are also able to work in indigenous communities. They speak two languages.

The battle reference in the poem at the beginning of this chapter is a refrain similar to Alfred's call for an understanding of the nature of freedom for indigenous peoples. Alfred is characterized as a warrior-scholar in reviews of Wasáse. Both his writing and Tahdooahnippah's poem ask the reader to understand the past. Both call for action and, as indigenous scholars, our actions as researchers form an integral foundation for the movement of education, health care, and economics in our communities. To understand the battles as indigenous researchers that we face today, reflected in Tahdooahnippah's poem, we reflect on the grassroots activism of the past.

## ACTIVISM

Timelines for 20th-century Indian activism in the United States often start with the formation of the National Congress of American Indians in the 1940s. In the fifty odd years since that origination, there can be found executive orders, legislation, judicial decisions, as well as organizational formations, illustrating activism. The most recent timeline shows the latest activity as 2000, now ten years ago (20th-Century Indian ctivism; Humbolt University). Native scholars today may be too young to remember the tumultuous 1960s and 1970s, decades devoted to activism aimed at change not exclusive to American Indians. The strategy then was simple; it really was a battle. The activism for change included takeovers, occupations, and radical, even criminal acts (Johnson, Nagel, & Champagne, 1997). Even some thirty or forty years later, history has not decided if the changes were worth the price (Tinker, 2004).

Activism today is a different strategy and does not require we pick up a gun or set up a roadblock. Activism in the academy, the strategy proposed in this title, draws heavily on the first quote. We, as current indigenous educators, have the opportunity to use the tools of research taught to us in the established academy and the knowledge of our grandfathers to create data that can be used to make thoughtful, reflective decisions. Activism of this nature begins with an individual commitment to standards and quickly moves to a commitment to leadership.

The leadership and commitment that fueled the creation of many of the organizations was grounded in grassroots movements. In the academy, the grassroots are less dense and now are more scattered throughout the globe; the core of this commitment to indigenous research activism is not found in native studies curricula and is barely tolerated in mainstream research universities. As a community of indigenous social science scholars, we need to support each other's work; we need to ask for critical review, and we need to listen to each other and to ourselves (St. Germaine, 2000).

Indigenous scholars have plenty of mainstream scholars who will tell us that we do not know how "real" research is defined; typically, these mainstream scholars are quantitative researchers who do not see the value of qualitative research. They will argue that native ways of knowing are not a viable research lens. At the same time, we have plenty of relatives in tribal communities throughout the country who will tell us that we have lost our focus by hanging out with the establishment (the 1960s' term for the colonizer); they will argue that if we really wanted to help tribal people, we would work at tribal colleges and give up western ideas of research altogether. We will even have to cross some critical ground when it comes to knowing how much of our own tribal histories can and should be available, including the ethical questions of ownership of intellectual property. Through this career journey, we are ever mindful that failure is a singular event. If, as an indigenous scholar, you present ill-conceived questions, use the wrong treatment, or draw extraneous conclusions, then the body of work, as well as that of your indigenous peers, is denigrated. Because of our numbers, it is important that we do quality work that can be published in academic, peer-reviewed venues. Because of our numbers, your work will be looked at more closely than other scholars; it will be reviewed by your academic peers and your tribal relatives. Your work has to be able to withstand the scrutiny of both reviews; again, you have to be able to speak two languages.

The fields of education, health care, and economics remain critical throughout Indian Country; this set formed the genesis of the activism of the 1960s and 1970s and today forms the core of the indigenous social science research agenda, particularly as native peoples have incorporated technology as a cross-cutting variable in each of these. The use of indigenous social science research as a change agent strategy allows each of us to be an activist–scholar–educator. The ability of indigenous scholars to analyze the results of research through a lens of experience within a cultural community adds a depth to the analysis that outsiders will always struggle to understand. It is important, then, to continue to write and publish about our cultures and traditions from an insider perspective, exposing the nuances of language and role, and contributing to the knowledge base of indigenous pedagogy. Recognizing your own boundaries as an indigenous educator includes acknowledging that you do not speak for all native communities. Our contribution to activism also includes a commitment to the balance found throughout native epistemologies. As indigenous educators, our activist agenda includes creating a set of priorities; there are too few of us and much work to look forward to completing.

A review of the literature on indigenous research highlights a scattering of chapters intended to formalize a "research agenda." Typically the forum for this effort is federal or state policy papers, formed in collaboration with indigenous scholars in a think-tank atmosphere and presented at national meetings. These reports occasionally have federal input or sponsorship, but a deep analysis of the content of the summary findings would appear to yield similar suggestions over the past decades. For example, as Indian Nations At Risk, nearly twenty years old now, studied the current status and made recommendations for Indian students, the authors endeavored to incorporate priorities for research to augment the recommendations on developing tribal resources and partnerships (Charleston, 1991). The Final Report on the Roundtable Conference on American Indian Research Training Needs advocates close consultation with tribal groups and the use of a rigorously vetted, culturally appropriate Institutional Review Board (National Institutes of Health, 1999, August 23–24). The Research Agenda Working Group convened by The Department of Education identified five independent domains that affected school readiness as priorities. These domains incorporated educational curricula with physical well-being and motor development in efforts to identify effective practices (Strang, William; von Glatz, Adrienne; Research Agenda Working Group, 2001). In recent years, The National Congress of American Indians commissioned a set of research agenda papers which first described different ways to institutionalize research regulation in indigenous communities (Sahota, Research Regulation in American Indian/Alaska Native Communities: Policy and Practice

Considerations) and second, an interactive guide for indigenous communities in the review process (Sahota, Research Regulation in American Indian/Alaska Native Communities: A Guide to reviewing Research Studies).

Similarly, The World Indigenous Nations Higher Education Consortium highlighted six principles for Indigenous Research. These include:

- Respects local indigenous authority;
- Recognizes knowledge as part of a living and constantly adapting system that is grounded in the past, but continues to grow through the present and into the future and reinforces this in research approach;
- Uses the local language respectfully as a foundation for interpretation and meaning;
- Fosters a complementary relationship across knowledge derived from diverse knowledge systems;
- Acknowledges multi-ownership and levels of knowledge;
- Accesses community ownership of knowledge (WINHEC, 2009).

I am not advocating a new definition of an indigenous research agenda, nor would I find fault in the work we have come to rely on as the foundation of many of our studies. These reports highlight the needs for research and, again, we are back to education, health care, and economics. There is so much work to be done that it is unlikely we could replace these three with anything more meaningful in a newer version of a consensus research agenda or strategies.

## THE AMERICAN INDIAN LEADERSHIP PROGRAM

In the mid-1970s, I was a student at Penn State University; in the 1990s, I was fortunate enough to be the Director of the American Indian Leadership Program (AILP). The attention to standards and accountability, the expertise and experience of the professors, and the friendships formed with other alumni have had a profound effect on my academic scholarship and career. Currently, I and Holly Mackey are working on a research project that I started with Gerald E. Gipp. This project is a replication of a national study, but its basic question is: Who has influenced American Indian Education policy? I actually had to ask Dr. Gipp to resign from the project once the results started coming in. It is very clear that Gerald E. Gipp, the first Indian director of the American Indian Leadership program, has had a highly successful career and has influenced K-20 Indian education in policy and practice. The Alaska Rural Systemic Initiative that I discussed earlier as the most successful example of the fusion between indigenous theory and practice was Dr. Gipp's project at National Science Foundation.

When I began my Master's work at Penn State, the Director was Grayson Noley. Dr. Gipp, Dr. Noley, Dr. Tippeconnic (along with others) all colleagues in the 1970s formed the first American Indian/Alaska Native Special Interest Group (SIG) for The American Education Research Association (AERA). The AERA SIG is still around today, even though the name has changed, and you will find Penn State alumni more frequently than not as Chair of that group since its inception.

Mike Charleston, another former Director of this Program, was the lead writer on one of the most quoted national reports in recent history. Indian Nations at Risk (1999) has remained an important part of the research agenda for native people in this country. It addressed education, health care, and economics and called for an emphasis on research based practice.

Dr. John Tippeconnic, III, a former director of the AILP, has had a similar career. The findings in our study are showing that the American Indian Leadership Program has been one of the most influential forces in Indian education since its inception in 1970. A large body of the research, as opposed to expository essays, on American Indian Education has been produced by Penn State Graduates. Sure, there are a few outliers; but current students in the AILP inherit a legacy along with a degree. The expectations have not changed; the standard is not "adequate." It is important that we teach indigenous students so that they will move the research agenda forward.

How you define this research agenda when you intend to return to Indian Country and begin to practice in the schools that serve our children is an individual decision. This research can include action research projects on site that will help in providing useful data to make the changes so frequently called for in these schools (Warner, 2001; Crum, 2007). But even if you, as a practitioner, never begin a research project on your own, it is important to be a competent consumer of research. You do not want to make decisions based on sloppy research or unfounded conclusions; our children will live with the result of the day-to-day decisions you make.

While you are in Indian Country, you will live and practice in communities where the three strands of education, health care, and economics are intersected by our own personal community interests and local politics. I caution you that you still need to disseminate your findings. Economic researchers encounter practitioners, particularly in real estate, who tout the adage "location, location, location." Health care researchers can identify with replication studies and educational researchers acknowledge a sense of place in their studies. These groups know the importance of place, venue, or location. Our work needs to be visible if it is to be understood and replicated. The activist agenda requires that we publish. Where you publish is your own choice.

We need to understand mainstream research methods and we need our colleagues to recognize indigenous methodologies. Caliban-like we would have preferred that the invaders learn our languages first rather than our being required to learn theirs, but clearly they were not going to do this. Pedagogy treats this as a "learning moment." We can teach our colleagues how to think about indigenous research and methodologies; the goal is to represent our work in their language defining and clarifying our own tribal needs. Linking our work to the spirit of self and community is a goal all researchers should aspire to reach; perhaps while we teach our non-native colleagues the value of our research, they will learn to a little more about their own. Like Caliban, you are accomplished speakers of two languages and like Tahdooahnippppah's reflection, you will take the fight to a newer venue. The goal is not to replace current research methods; the goal is to be able to talk about our strategies in their language while teaching them ours. And, it is a battle.[4]

# NOTES

1. William Shakespeare, *The Tempest*, 1.2 (Caliban's outburst).
2. V. Jean Tahdooahnippah. (1985, June). "Battles" in Akwekon p. 104, #2/3. Akwesasne Press: Rooseveltown, NY.
3. See Alaska Native Network: www.ankn.uaf.edu
4. This Chapter was first presented at The Pennsylvania State University, Warner, L.S. (2010, March). Research as Activism. Symposium Series commemorating The Pennsylvania State University's forty years of Service to Indian Nations. Penn State University, State College, PA. The paper is a call to action to future AILP graduates.

# REFERENCES

Aguirre, A. (1995). The status of minority faculty in academe. *Equity & Excellence in Education*, *28*(1), 63–68.

Alfred, M. V. (2001). Reconceptualizing marginiality from the margins. *Western Journal of Black Studies*, *25*(1), 1–11.

Alfred, T. (1999). *Peace, power, righteousness: An Indigenous Manifesto*. Oxford, UK: Oxford University Press.

Alfred, T. (2005). *Wasáse: Indigenous pathways of action and freedom.* New York, NY: Oxford University Press.

American Federation of Teachers. (2010). Promoting diversity in the faculty: What higher education unions can do. AFT Higher Education Report, 36pp., Washington, DC.

American Indian Issues. (n.d.). Retrieved from http://www.humboldt.edu/~gol/kellogg/pdf/part3hndout.pdf

ASHE Higher Education Report. (2012). American Indian and Alaska Native Faculty. *ASHE Higher Education Report, 37*(5), 91–106.

Barnhardt, R., & Kawagley, A. O. (1998, Fall). Culture, chaos and complexity: Catlysts for change in Indigenous education. *Journal of School Leadership,* 1–18.

Bernstein, R. (1978). *The restructing of social and political theory.* Philadelphia, PA: University of Pennsylvania.

Bishop, R. (2005). Freeing ourselves from Neocolonial domination in research: A Kaupapa Maori approach to creating knowledge. In N. Denzin & Y. Lincoln (Eds.), *The sage handbook on qualitative research.* Thousand Oaks, CA: Sage.

Charleston, M. (1991). *Indian nations at risk: An educational strategy for action.* Washington, DC: Department of Education.

Crum, S. J. (2007). Indian activism, the great society, indian self-determination and the drive for an Indian college or university. *American Indian Culture and Research Journal, 31*(1), 1–20.

Denzin, N., & Lincoln, Y. (1998). *The landscape of qualitative research: Theories and issues.* Thousand Oaks, CA: Sage.

Droogsma, R. (2007). Infusing the critical research paradigm with activism: The case for activist research in intercultural communication. *92rd Annual NCA convention,* November 14, Chicago, IL.

Johnson, T., Nagel, J., & Champagne, D. (1997). *American Indian activism: Alcatraz to the longest walk.* Champaign, IL: University of Illinois Press.

Kawagley, A. O. (1997, January). Education Indigenous to place. In G. Smith & D. Williams (Eds.), *Ecological education in action* (pp. 1–20). Prospect Heights, IL: Waveland Press.

Lafromboise, T., Coleman, H., & Gerton, J. (1993). Psychological impact of Biculturalism: Evidence and theory. *Psychological Bulletin, 14*(3), 395–412.

Mihesuah, D. A. (2003). *Indigenous American women: Decolonization, empowerment, action.* Lincoln, NE: University of Nebraska Press.

National Institutes of Health. (1999, August 23–24). *American Indian research training needs.* Bethesda, MD: National Institues of Health and Indian Health Service.

Noah, B. A. (2003). The participation of underrepresented minorities in clinical research. *American Journal of Law and Medicine, 29,* 221–245.

Ponjuan, L., Conley, V. M., & Trower, C. (2011, May/June). Careet stage differences in pretenure teaching faculty perceptions of professional and personal relationships with colleagues. *Journal of Higher Education, 82*(3), 319–346.

Sahota, P. C. (n.d.). *NCAI PRC Publishes papers on research regulation in AI/AN Communities.* Retrieved from http://www.ncaiprc.org/research-regulation-papers

Sahota, P. C. (n.d.). *Research regulation in American Indian/Alaska native communities: A guide to reviewing research studies.* Retrieved from http://www.ncaiprc.org/research-regulation-papers

Sahota, P. C. (2007). *Research regulation in American Indian/Alaska Native Communities: Policy and practice considerations.* Washington, DC: National Cognress of American Indians.

Schiele, J., & Hopps, J. (2009). Racial minorities then and now: The continuing significance of race. *Social Work, 54*(1), 195–199.

Smith, L. T. (2005). *Decolonizing methodologies: Research and indigenous peoples.* New York, NY: Palgrave.

St. Germaine, R. D. (2000). *A chance to go full circle: Building on reforms to create effective learning.* Washington, DC: Department of Education.

Stanley, C. A. (Winter 2006). Coloring the academic landscape: Faculty of color breaking the silence in predominately white colleges and universities. *American Education Research Journal, 43*(4), 701–736.

Strang, W., von Glatz, A., & Research Agenda Working Group. (2001). *American Indian and Alaska native education research agenda.* Washington, DC: U.S. Department of Education.

Taylor, O., Apprey, C., Hill, G., McGrann, L., and Wang, J. (Summer 2010). *Diversifying the faculty* (pp 15–18). Peer Review. Washington, DC: Association of American Colleges and Universities.

Tinker, G. (2004). *Spirit and resistance: Political theory and American Indian liberation.* Philadelphia, PA: Fortress Press.

Trower, C. (2009, September/October). Toward a greater understanding of the tenure track for minorities. *Change,* 38–47.

Warner, L. S. (2001). *Urban Indian education research summit* (pp. 1–21). In S. Faircloth (Ed.), *Executive summary.* Milwaukee, WI: Indian Community School of Milwaukee, Inc.

Wax, M. L. (1991). The Ethics of research in American Indian communities. *American Indian Quarterly, 15,* 431–457.

Wilson, S. (2009). *Research as ceremony: Indigenous research methods.* Winnepeg (Canada), New South Wales: Fernwood Publishing.

WINHEC. (2009). *WINHEC research principals.* Palmerston North, NZ: World Indigenous Nations Higher Education Consortium.

# CHAPTER 10

# REFLECTIVE JOURNALING IN A COLLEGE MULTICULTURAL EDUCATION CLASSROOM: LOOKING PAST, PRESENT, AND FUTURE

Eunyoung Kim[1]

## ABSTRACT

*College classrooms are an important socializing site, preparing students to critically reflect upon their viewpoints and engage in democratic citizenship and civic leadership. Yet this very notion of educational environment can serve to produce racial inequality and ethnically and culturally blind pedagogical space. In this chapter, the author describes how students articulate their internalized social position and racism in a given college classroom and understands the process by which students' sense of self is internalized and (re)constructed through the practice of reflective journaling.*

Education either functions as an instrument which is used to facilitate integration of the younger generation into the logic of the present system and bring about conformity or it becomes the practice of freedom, the means by which men and women deal critically

**Social Justice Issues and Racism in the College Classroom: Perspectives from Different Voices**
**International Perspectives on Higher Education Research, Volume 8, 151–169**
Copyright © 2013 by Emerald Group Publishing Limited
**All rights of reproduction in any form reserved**
ISSN: 1479-3628/doi:10.1108/S1479-3628(2013)0000008012

and creatively with reality and discover how to participate in the transformation of
their world.

– Paulo Freire (2000, p. 34)

As a woman of color in the academe, I find it challenging to teach content
on diversity and to manage the tensions and interpersonal dynamics that
occur in the classroom, in part, because the work of racial minority faculty
members is often undervalued (Aguirre, 2005; Bradley, 2005; Turner,
González, & Wood, 2008). The literature reveals that faculty of color are
more likely than their white counterparts to advise students, take on
additional teaching loads, participate in community service, and "take
personal responsibility for applying their talents to the cause of social
change" (Antonio, 2000, p. 594). While teaching graduate-level courses, I
have observed that college classrooms are an important site of socialization,
preparing students to critically reflect upon their viewpoints and engage in
democratic citizenship and civic leadership. Yet this very notion of the
educational environment as a social institution can serve to (re)produce
racial inequality and ethnically and culturally blind the pedagogical space. I
have found it important to provide students with a classroom community
where individual voices can be validated, allowing a safe space for
disagreements. With this in mind, the aim of this chapter is to understand
how a group of graduate students from diverse racial/ethnic, class, gender,
and cultural backgrounds locate and negotiate identity within the context of
multicultural education (i.e., course content regarding issues of diversity in
higher education) by writing a reflective journal.

For the past four years, I have served as the faculty member in charge of
the master's degree program in student affairs at a private, independent
university in the northeastern region of the United States. This degree,
which is part of the university's Higher Education Program, is committed to
preparing students for various positions in student affairs administration. It
offers a balance of classroom-based academic learning and field-based
experiential learning opportunities. Students are introduced to theory,
research, policy, and practices related to the administration of higher
education, in particular that of student affairs administration. Graduates
from this program should be well equipped to pursue careers in student
affairs administration and management at any postsecondary institution
and/or to continue doctoral education in higher education administration,
policy, and research.

When I redesigned this program's curriculum, I developed a graduate-
level course to introduce students enrolled in both the student affairs

master's degree and the higher education doctoral program to issues of historical and contemporary-isms, politics of diversity, social justice, and campus climate in higher education settings, looking at the perspectives of various constituents including students, faculty, and administrators. During the semester, students in this class are asked to write reflective journal entries on a weekly basis, focusing on interpreting course content and class discussions in order to apply them in and outside the college classroom. This practice allows students to contemplate their own learning processes, looking at how they are affected by things like classroom dynamics, thinking critically about values, listening to others, and both challenging and being challenged by peers, particularly on issues related to diversity, oppression, white privilege, and racism.

In this chapter, I intend to describe how students articulate their internalized social positions and racism in a given college classroom through reflective narratives. I also attempt to understand the process by which students' sense of self is internalized and (re)constructed through the practice of reflective journaling. My discussion uses data collected from a cohort of students who enrolled in my graduate-level multicultural education course (the actual title of the course was "Diversity in Higher Education"). The class was one semester long (16-weeks) and consisted of roughly equal numbers of white and nonwhite students. Data sources include journals, notes on teaching, end-of-course evaluations, and other course-related projects. My experience with teaching students in this course and observing their reactions, both spoken and unspoken, points to the importance of creating a safe environment for discussing social justice and diversity issues and the student–teacher and student–student relationship.

## WHAT IS REFLECTIVE JOURNALING?

Reflective journaling is a form of reflection that documents our evolving thought process and an effective method that help us to make sense of our experience (Steven & Cooper, 2009). Reflective journaling is often used in social work, nursing, and both preservice and in-service teacher education, but is rarely part of graduate programs in the field of higher education. Reflective journaling is a powerful tool, allowing students and teachers to reflect on their learning processes and teaching practices, examine their experiences, (re)construct the meaning of the past and present, gain new perspectives, and thereby begin the process of transforming the self, or selves (Cooper, 1991). Through reflective journaling, students may discover an inner voice, exploring who they are, what they are learning, and how to act as functioning members of a multicultural society while facing the realities of social injustice, power inequalities, and privilege. Freire (2000) encourages students to act as active co-inquirers with their teachers, rather than passive listeners, and to be critically conscious of the world and themselves. He writes that:

> Authentic reflection considers neither abstract man nor the world without people, but people in their relations with the world. In these relations consciousness and world are simultaneous: consciousness neither precedes the world nor follows it. (p. 81)

Further, Freire (2000) also states, "As women and men, simultaneously reflecting on themselves and the world, increase the scope of their perceptions, they begin to direct their observations towards previously inconspicuous phenomena" (p. 82).

Communities in higher education, particularly college classrooms, ought to be places where cultural, ethnic, and racial diversity are promoted (Hurtado, Milem, Clayton-Pedersen, & Allen, 1998). College students must be cognizant of ways in which they can promote diversity while eliminating racialized institutional policies (Rendón, 1994; Rendón, Jalomo, & Nora, 2000). As I developed a curriculum for multicultural education, I emphasized the importance of reflecting on the process of learning and the social (re)production of race and racism in educational environments. During self-reflection, students begin to think authentically on past and present experiences of race, oppression, intolerance, and injustice that are inconspicuously embedded within the college classroom as well as outside of higher education. Students reflect upon their own development and practices as well as the issues they face in daily life by paying close attention to the process they are going through as part of the course – how they react, what they think, feel, wish they had or hadn't said, or wish they were able to say. Students are required to devote some time to writing on the issues discussed in class and how they understand themselves in relation to these issues.

Reflective journal writing seemed unusual to the students who entered my class. Though all held undergraduate degrees in disciplines from business to humanities and some even had another master's degree, few had written reflectively on their learning during their academic careers. In her first journal entry, one white female student wrote that she recognized her life experience differed from that of other students:

> So, we're supposed to be keeping a journal. I have never kept a journal. Not as a young child, not as a teenager, not as an adult. I was given journals, but I used them to doodle and write down proverbs, or book quotes that I found compelling. I am excited about

the idea of writing journal to discuss my thoughts on everything I learn in this class to help discover myself. What do I know about being diverse? I am a 23-year old white female who grew up in upper-middle class suburban Maryland. I have never experienced racism or genocide, and have never really experienced different cultures…I hope to learn about the history of diversity in this class…Perhaps I can contribute slightly since I am a woman in what I still believe is a male dominated world, but my insight is lackluster to those born in different countries and of minorities. I am very excited to see where this class is going to take me in both my understanding of diversity as a functioning part of higher education and in my growth as a person.

Another white female student reflected on the first day of class and her expectations in the following entry:

After attending class one, I'm much more excited to be a part of this class. I think it is full of a great variety and diverse group of students who will make the class and discussions that much more interesting. I'm actually excited to be keeping a journal for class. I'm often more comfortable expressing myself through writing than I am verbalizing my thoughts to others. Especially in a class such as this, I know that we are all supposed to be grown, mature adults who can hold an intellectual conversation, but I feel as though I might be a bit reluctant to speak, in particular when it comes to issues of race. I grew up in a very diverse town, and was the minority in high school by my senior year. It is unfortunate, but based on the way other groups spoke to and treated "white" students, it instilled a bit of both anger and fear in me. So I will be quite honest in saying that I walk into class with a bit of a chip on my shoulder. I truly hope this class will open not only my eyes, but the thoughts and actions of other in the class as well. I hope the classroom can be a place of understanding, learning, and developmental growth for everyone. I am taking this class with an open mind, and am excited to see how this can play out not only in my personal life, but in the workplace as well. We encounter issues dealing with diversity often.

Another white female student noted similar concerns. She was worried that being white and having white privileges would make her somewhat uneasy in this diversity course. She wrote:

I am looking forward to this class, I am very open-minded and I hope to learn a lot from the readings and from my classmates about diversity and its effects. We are also a diverse class, which I hope brings a fresh look into diversity. I am also very intimated to speak, since I am white. Many of these issues are things I have never personally dealt with or have been exposed too[sic]. I hope to gain the courage to share my stories and life experiences with the class.

In their journals, students expressed they were ready to grapple with the guilt and many "isms" in which oppression is manifested, such as racism, white privilege, classism, and sexism. They wanted to openly take up issues of inequity, race, class, and gender.

# CRITICAL PEDAGOGY AND GRADUATE STUDENTS IN HIGHER EDUCATION

Critical pedagogy is a form of instruction that "rejects oppression, combats injustice, gives voice to marginalized people, fights the maintaining of the status quo; [it] is achieved through a reflective search for wholeness" (Milner, 2003, p. 199). Rooted in Marxist and neo-Marxist critical theory, critical pedagogy represents a transformational educational response to "inequalities of power...the false myths of opportunity and merits for many students, and...the way belief systems becomes internalized to the point where individuals and groups abandon the very aspiration to question or change their lot in life" (Burbules & Berk, 1999, p. 50). As an educator, my role is to help students become critical thinkers empowered to seek justice and emancipation. Students should be able to not only recognize injustice but, for the purposes of critical pedagogy, be able to take action to transform and change it. Among leading critical pedagogical thinkers (Freire, McLaren, and Giroux), Freire (1985) is particularly concerned with the development of critical consciousness (*conscienticizao*); the task of critical pedagogy is to bring the oppressed to a critical consciousness of their situations as a beginning point for their liberatory *praxis*: "reflection and action upon the reality in order to transform it" (Freire, 2000, p. 51). Students can critically reflect upon their learning and interpret the world that surrounds them as well as act to change the world. As Freire (1970) puts it, "critical consciousness is brought about not through intellectual effort alone but through praxis – through the authentic union and reflection" (p. 48).

Working as a faculty member in a program that studies higher education, I have found that issues of race and social justice have often been pushed to the periphery in students' thinking on presuppositions, choices, experiences, values, and positions of privilege in the hierarchies and power structures associated with the learning environment. College classrooms prepare students to critically reflect upon their standpoints and engage in a healthy discussion of democracy and diversity-related issues. Yet this space also serves to promote the privileged and advantageous social position of a certain group rather than "creating psychologically beneficial pedagogical space for all students" (Macedo & Bartolome, 1999, p. 20).

The premise of critical pedagogical theory is that systems of formal education maintain and reproduce an exploitative capitalist system and stratify the socioeconomic class (Apple, 1990; Mayo, 1999; McLaren, 2003). Some scholars have identified disciplinary practices for classrooms that contribute to the reproduction of these values. One example makes use of the classroom's hidden curriculum: the unspoken and unwritten norms, rules, and values manifested in the behaviors and interactions among students and faculty (Apple, 1990). Teachers may encourage students to engage in civil, open debate when controversial statements are made. Although there is no clear consensus on how to practice critical pedagogy, three central components must be facilitated in the college classroom: *dialogue, critique*, and *praxis. Dialogue*, the active participation in discussion by both teacher and students, combats a culture of silence (Freire, 2000). College classrooms are social institutions where students' psychological, social, and intellectual development is promoted, so teachers must be cognizant of the power dynamics between students and teachers, becoming aware that this relationship can often silence and invalidate students' social and cultural voices in the classroom (Delpit, 1988). Silence should never go unnoticed. While teaching a course on diversity in higher education, I have consciously attempted to understand my students' perspectives, frames of references, and their positionality, and have been prepared to address and discuss controversial issues posed by the course materials. For example, after an in-class group activity on defining "diversity," one student wrote:

> We were asked to formulate a diversity statement for an urban university. Not an easy task. Someone in the group kept speaking of "blending" as the goal. That word bothered me. Blending is too close in meaning, at least in my opinion, the word that I find as offensive as the word "tolerance." I don't want to blend; I don't want to be tolerated. I want to be respected as a person.

Through active participation in the classroom and in reflective journal writing, students may gain a sense of emancipation and develop a critical consciousness of societal issues and problems (Braa & Callero, 2006).

*Critique* refers to the systematic examination of one's self and society, paying special attention to issues germane to inequality, oppression, exploitation, domination, and social injustice of class, gender, race, and ethnicity (Darder, Baltodano, & Torres, 2003). *Praxis* means the actual application of knowledge in life beyond the classroom. Students may connect their critical reflections to action to promote social transformation (Braa & Callero, 2006). With these core components of critical pedagogy in mind, I used classroom discussion and reflective journaling as a basis for ongoing critique and dialogue. I constantly reminded students that they should not be solely concerned with their individual learning objectives but should also set individual goals to change their communities. The excerpt below from a student's journal illustrates a developing critical consciousness of issues of race and ethnicity:

> The readings have been extremely interesting, but definitely a lot of information to shift through, digest, and consider how they affect me personally. Several thoughts run through my mind. Can things truly change? Issues of race, gender, ethnicity, sexual orientation, religious beliefs, and culture is ingrain into a person's psyche. Can individuals who have not been directly affected by bigotry or prejudices truly understand with those who have dealt with bigotry, prejudices, and ignorance? Even those with the best of intentions have, unbeknownst to them, engaged in behavior that can be offensive. Sometimes I prefer the outright bigotry than the "pretend" I believe in equality/diversity that one finds in all levels of society – I'd rather know what I am up against. Thought and questions that come to mind are: Do whites fear that they may be overstepping if they say certain things? Does this take away from the discussion of equality and diversity (which I see as two different issues, but many with whom I have spoken in the past see it as the same thing)? Do people of color who have lived in a protected world understand how bigoted, racist, and sexist policies, attitudes, beliefs, stereotypes affect people of color? One word seems to come up in many of the reading: Assimilating. A word I dislike for a variety of reasons. What exactly does it mean? One writer indicated that it was speaking English and forgetting the "foreign culture" that one comes from. I say "hog wash" assimilation = White. It doesn't matter how well one speaks English, forgets one's culture (or how many generations since one's ancestry arrived in the US), one can't change skin color.

## CREATING SPACE FOR DISCUSSING RACISM AND SOCIAL JUSTICE IN A COLLEGE CLASSROOM

If I want to cause my graduate students to become critical thinkers and develop a social consciousness, I truly believe that they need to feel encouraged, not judged, in the college classroom. I have learned that it is important to look at the influence I may have on student interactions and behaviors. Students should not just accept things I value or opine, but should critically evaluate them. At the outset of the class, I made it clear to my students that it was extremely important for them to become comfortable expressing their views, beliefs, and opinions openly. Acknowledging the power dynamic and political and social relations embedded in student–teacher and student–student interactions is the first step toward creating a space for students to discuss their personal experiences with social injustice, inequity, and privilege; it may also help them confront the bias and guilt they have experienced in daily life as well as in association with the curriculum. A black male student wrote that everyone should be treated equally and with respect in a classroom, also asserting that what students shared should move beyond the classroom setting:

> The professor was conscious enough talk about the sensitivity of the topics that we are going to cover in class. She talked about confidentiality and the respect for each other's opinions and perspectives about the issues that we will be discussing in class. It was amusing that the students shared the view of confidentiality whilst respecting personal views and differences. I agreed with the decision of the rest of the class; however I found it necessary that the class should share the discussion with their peers so that they too can understand what other students think about issues surrounding diversity and what they have experienced. This may ease dialogue and understanding among the students. During the class, Dr. Kim asked us to share our experiences with the rest of the class. The question was 'whether any of us has experienced prejudice?' It was fascinating to hear my classmates narrate their stories. I came to understand that the term prejudice means a negative attitude toward an entire category of people such as a racial or ethnic minority group. The stories of my classmates help me understand that prejudice may vary from racial slurs, subordination of women to the extent to discrimination. One of the students talked about the tension between Ibos and Hausa in Nigeria, for mere fact that one group is Christian and the other Muslim. The in-class practice on "sharing our experience" really helped me. It helps me understand my classmates; and it can also relate to them in some circumstances even though our experiences are different. I hope one day we can put these practices into practicality so that we can open the door of understanding among all people regardless of their gender, religion, ethnicity, and national origin.

On the other hand, a Latina student wrote that her classmates were not open enough:

> I was a bit frustrated that discussions didn't move forward. Could it be because it's our first class? Can we openly discuss issues from various view points? Are we concerned that we might be seen as radical or on the opposite end of the spectrum? It will be interesting to see how things develop. I'd truly like to see how others view and understand the multiple issues that diversity and/or multiculturalism touch our lives.

In the fourth week of the semester, the class participated in an activity called "The Game of Oppression." This "game" is designed to challenge individuals from different backgrounds and experiences to engage in authentic dialogue with people who they don't normally interact with in a safe space. The objective of this classroom session was to allow students to confront their understanding of issues surrounding oppression, providing opportunities for them to interact with class members through dialogues and connect to their personal and professional lives. A white female student recalled the session in her journal entry:

> Today's class was very interesting and a lot of fun with the game of oppression. I had a really good time listening to everyone's experiences and especially when we had the

jury cards. A couple of the stories were pretty clear cut but a couple of them actually stirred discussion which was very interesting. I lucked out with the spots I was landing on because I kept racking my brain throughout the whole game of times when I felt oppressed and I really wasn't thinking of anything. I like when other people are telling their personal stories because most of their experiences are so different from mine. I feel very thankful that I haven't had some of these negative experiences that classmates talk about but at the same time I feel bad about the things that other people go through. It makes me feel like I should be more aware of how I deal with other people because I don't ever want to make someone have experiences that they will remember like some of these people did today…After last week's game of oppression we talked more about the actual definitions of oppression and the different types that are normally seen and experienced. It was really interesting to hear more personal stories from everyone about different times that they felt oppressed, and it had a different perspective than last week's class. Anthony's (a white male) story was pretty interesting when he talked about his teacher being specifically against male students and that's why his grade was lower. It was very different story than the one that a lot of other people were telling because it wasn't based on race or ethnicity. As shallow as it sounds I felt like I could relate more to his story because gender oppression is something I identify more with. Last week I was struggling to think of situations where I was oppressed and it was hard for me because I think I kept my mind in the racial and ethnic lines of oppression. When I thought of gender though[sic] I started to think about times where being female was a point that made someone oppress me. Hearing other people's personal experiences helped me to see some of the situations that people go through every day that I have ever had to experience. It gives me a different perspective on how much oppression really does go on in American society.

Similarly, a white male student expressed in his journal how uneasy he felt with the word "oppression" on the day of game and attributed the lack of educational success for students of color to characteristics often rooted in their abilities and cultures:

Playing the game of oppression made me realize that I do not experience what many others do. I guess there are indeed advantages to being a white male. I found it difficult to come up with personal instances where I felt oppressed or even discriminated against. I actually felt a bit embarrassed with the examples I provided due to the fact that they paled in comparison to the experiences of others. I initially viewed Peggy McIntosh's article on White Privilege: Unpacking the Invisible Knapsack as a bit shallow. However, after reading it and reflecting on it, I wonder how many things I take for granted. For example, I do not have an issue finding an appropriate colored band aid or birthday card. While this may seem trivial, there must be a cumulative effect if you are constantly faced with these small issues on a daily basis. One thing that did bother me is the over use of the word oppression. There were many examples cited in class that people were calling oppression that were a real reach. Perhaps some of the issues or lack of success were due to individual performance and not some grand conspiracy of oppression. I hope we are careful to not make those types of generalization.

On the other hand, a black female student observed that not knowing one another prevented students from more openly revealing their stories:

> The questions asked of The Game of Oppression are as provocative as its name. I am hoping that in playing, I will gain a deeper understanding of each of my classmates and an appreciation of their life experiences. The challenges in revealing personal information is creating an environment where each person feels valued and invested in the experience. I am not that certain that we are all at that point yet. After observing the game and how we interacted with each other, we were probably as forthcoming as I thought we would be. There were some real opportunities for self-reflection; particularly in the "Moment of Privilege Space," and the "Reality Check Space." We were cautiously guarded and in this regard, I felt that there weren't any surprises. I wonder how our answers would change if we knew each other better. As an observer, I was able to focus on the discussion of the playing participants. For me, this was the most enjoyable aspect as I was less encumbered by keeping up with the pace and rules of the game. It was very difficult to rationalize a hurtful experience for someone else. Overall, I gained an appreciation for the opportunity to do some self-reflecting. I think that in the end, the true value of this course will come from the new insights I will gain about myself.

This student went on to note that it took time to establish a safe and supportive environment in which students could challenge their understanding of issues related to social justice and racism:

> Over the semester, I have enjoyed the readings and topics of our coursework. I have also felt that our class (students) was too guarded to really delve into any type of critical examination of racial relations on an institutional and societal level. Today, however, we seemed to turn a corner. When the professor asked about our pre-college experiences, we experienced a breakthrough. It seemed as if finally, we felt comfortable enough to share our personal histories and opinions about integration, assimilation, and racism in this country. I feel like I learned more about my classmates today than I have throughout the entire semester. Confronting issues about oppression, racism, and diversity is really more difficult than I imagined it would be. The subject matter feels like a sensitive one that never quite heals.

Several students came to similar conclusions, observing that the class finally became willing to openly share personal experiences: "[T]he class today seems as if we were all willing to contribute to the conversation about our personal experiences as it related to race and the classroom environment."

## RACIAL/ETHNIC COGNIZANCE IN A MULTICULTURAL EDUCATION CLASSROOM

I was keenly interested in observing students' social (i.e., racial/ethnic) identity (re)construction and the role race plays in the learning process throughout the semester. Racial identity is an evolving concept, originally categorized biologically in terms of physical and character traits, and more recently established as a social construct based upon personal identification with a group (Chavez & Guido-DiBrito, 1999). In other words, a contemporary understanding of racial identity "refers to a sense of group or collective identity based on one's perception that he or she shares a common heritage with a particular racial group" (Helms, 1993, p. 3). Existing research on ethnic and racial identity provides a theoretical structure for understanding how individuals negotiate culture and examines the interactions between self and group (Chavez & Guido-DiBrito). Racial identity development theories attempt to present the psychological stages associated with identity changes as experienced by oppressed people as they try to understand what it is to live as a minority in a society ruled by a dominant group's norm.

Among the earliest minority identity models is the concept of psychosocial *Nigrescence*, a black racial identity model developed by Cross (1971, 1991). *Nigrescence* refers to a "re-socializing experience" by which an individual's identity transforms, moving from non-African American, to African American, and then to multiculturalism. This model consists of five-stage sequential processes: pre-encounter, encounter, immersion-emersion, internalization, and internalization-commitment (Cross, 1991). Such a psychological identity model for blacks provides a conceptual framework for how African Americans move from being unaware of their own identities to internalizing identity in a multicultural context. Following Cross, subsequent racial identity models were established to help to describe how other racially oppressed individuals understand and negotiate identity development. Atkinson, Morten, and Sue (1979) proposed a five-stage Minority Identity Development (MID) model based on earlier studies of oppressed groups (e.g., Cross). Atkinson et al. proposed that black identity development can be generalized to other minority groups because they too are oppressed. The MID model outlines five stages of development that "oppressed people may experience as they struggle to understand themselves in terms of their own minority culture, the dominant culture, and the oppressive relationship between the two cultures" (Atkinson et al., 1979, p. 194).

For Helms (1995), racial identity theory emerges from "the tradition of treating race as a sociopolitical and, to a lesser extent cultural construction" (p. 181). Helms (1990) proposed a model of white racial identity development on the basis of progression toward a nonracist white identity. Her underlying assumption about race in the United States is that racial groups experience either supremacy or repression. Helm's white racial identity model has two primary phases: abandonment of racism and the definition of a nonracist white identity. The search for this identity is a process that involves a complex interaction of attitudes, emotions, and behaviors (Helms, 1993).

Returning to the college classroom, would my students also indicate identification with a segment of a larger society whose members are thought of by themselves or by others to have a common origin, a shared cultural experience, and to have participated in communal activities? A Latina student wrote in her journal:

> I was speaking to some friends today about the growing number of Latinos who are trying to discover their roots. A good friend talked about how she believed that by distancing herself from her ethnicity and her culture and by accepting the culture of White America, that she would fully accepted as "American." She believed in the melting pot theory. She believed that as a fair-skinned, green-eyed woman her acceptance into mainstream society would not be questioned. She refused to learn Spanish and had no interest in her ethnic history. Years after she started her transformation into White America she discovered that she would never be fully accepted as "White." She yearned for the feeling of belonging to a group of people that understood her struggles, her needs, and wants. She now finds herself in no-man's land where she is neither "American" nor "Latina."

This student critiqued the racial position of a friend who believed she could become "white" and therefore more effectively navigate the racial power structure embedded in society at large. She also went on to say:

> When I was once asked whether I see myself as an American or as a Puerto Rican, I answered without hesitation, Puerto Rican. Not that I am anti-American. I don't consider myself superior to or less than any other racial group, but I stand proud of my ethnic roots.

Course materials with a consciousness of racial and ethnic issues provided a real eye-opening experience for students. Sharing personal experiences with peers revealed for many a new reality with respect to identity. Students began to realize how little they knew about racism and social injustice and become increasingly aware that race matters, and may impact people profoundly. A white female student noted that because she is white, it was difficult to comprehend even the existence of racism, as well as to understand the racism encountered by racial/ethnic minority students:

> This was certainly eye opening for me. Many of my classmates surprised me when questions were read with, "Have you ever felt you were pulled over by a police officer solely on your race? Or something similar. I guess ignorance is bliss, and having never felt this way, I was shocked that anyone did. It's incredibly naïve of me to believe that

someday there won't be racism or oppression based on absolutely anything, but in the 'bubble' that I live in. Race shouldn't be a privilege, and it is hard to accept it when you are on the 'receiving' end of that privilege. What is my reaction supposed to be something like that? How can I help people to feel that way no matter what race?

Another white female student acknowledged how little interaction she has had with racially diverse groups and her lack of understanding of racial equality issues:

> Overall, I have no experience anything like along the line of racial diversity. I grew up in a white community and attended all white college. I joined an all white women's sorority and have many white friends only one African American friend. I am still very close friends with my high school. So, diversity is not something I have been exposed to. This is something I am trying to change. I want to try and immerse myself into topics and ideas that make have me readdress my current ideals.

Whiteness as a multidimensional position refers to a set of locations that are politically, historically, culturally, and socially produced, and are linked to the hierarchical differentials in power and the dynamic structure of domination (Dyer, 1997; Frankenberg, 1993; Roediger, 1998). Even though whiteness may be understood as a mechanism for the oppression of racial/ ethnic minorities (Roediger, 1994), racial identity theorists argue that a white person can transform whiteness, becoming comfortable with the self as well as others of color (Helms, 1990). Helms contends, "in order to develop a healthy white identity, defined in part as a nonracist identity, virtually every white person in the United States must overcome one or more aspects of racism" (p. 49). Several white students in my class began to work through whiteness to develop a healthier white sense of self, and were able to identify racial advantages and white privilege. For instance, a white male student wrote:

> We have focused on racial and ethnic diversity in class and I believe that this will continue. Being a white male allows me to empathize but I do not have the wealth of personal experience that other do. I realize that race and ethnicity are important.

Interestingly, a black male student noted his own biases with respect to whites and highlighted the development of his sense of self throughout the semester:

> The class allowed me to get to know myself better. As a minority one tends to believe that one does not hold biases, but we do. It may not be overt, but the biases exist. I was surprised to hear words like "cracker" in an urban northeastern setting and that whites brought up in a bigoted home were rejecting their parents' view. I realized that despite my belief that many whites did not understand or refused to understand diversity, many were actually open to hearing about the experiences of nonwhites.

These students' narratives reveal that interaction with diverse groups of students and exposure to multicultural education is precedent to the development of racial cognizance. For white students, interaction with students of color in a sustained and direct way is critical to recognizing the ways in which students racialize themselves and others, allowing them to identify, and begin to change, their own racialized practices.

## STUDENT EVALUATIONS

As a scholar and educator, I seek to foster an inclusive and safe classroom environment whereby students are able to examine their own values, listen attentively to others, and intellectually challenge or be challenged in a respectful way (Chan & Treacy, 1996; Garcia & Van Soest, 1997). However, a successful increase in students' critical consciousness of social justice and diversity is not easy to measure using standard course evaluations. I hoped students would go beyond a change in attitude and move toward becoming active social agents. One black student wrote in his final journal entry:

> The last day of class was very wonderful and enjoyable. I did my presentation on affirmative action in South Africa. Furthermore, it was "food day" for the class. The students brought different dishes or food from their culture or preferences. All the different kinds of food were delicious. It was good to interact in such as an atmosphere of family and acceptance of another at that moment given. I think that the world should have such harmony so that we continue to accept diversity. I was also fascinated by the story of our visitor from Georgia, Kelly. It helped us understand that race is socially constructed. In Russia, she is "black" while in the USA is "white." It further tells us that discrimination can lead others to label other people whom they think are different them[sic]. Kelly's testimony can be an eye opener to people who think in racial lines to revisit themselves. Finally, the diversity course taught by Dr. Kim was really a good experience. The Higher Education program should maintain such relevant courses like diversity to help the students understand the reality of issues surrounding racial discrimination in universities; more importantly, the students will also understand the plight of the disadvantaged and discriminated people in the world. The course, Diversity in High Education, was successful; and I will recommend it to any student, faculty and administration. In conclusion, I thank Dr. Kim and my classmates for helping me learn a lot in the class and develop myself as a person. Million thanks to all.

A white female student reflected on her own learning and began to look at herself, others, and society differently:

> As I reflected back on this class the past semester, I believe I have come a long way personally in my views on diversity. This class certainly opened my mind to all the various issues that exist within the topic. But I have also grown a lot as a person. I do not

judge people so quickly anymore. I owe a lot of this not only to the material that was presented and discussed in class, but also especially to hearing the stories of my fellow classmates. They really opened my eyes. I thoroughly enjoyed hearing about their thoughts and experiences, even though at times they were intense. I think a lot of the success of this class had to do with the diverse makeup of the students who were in it. If it had been a more homogenous class I do not know that students would have gotten as much out of it. I hope this class does continue to be offered in the future. It presents information on a whole other side of higher education that is normally not discussed in our other courses. This topic seems especially relevant to the current population of students in higher education, and is also quite applicable to the current work scene. The United States is only going to continue to become more diversified in its people, thoughts, and cultures. It only seems appropriate that such a course would be included in the curriculum to address the current and future trends of our society.

The following quote comes from a student who wrote an end-of-semester course evaluation that pointed out the positive outcomes of taking the course:

After review of the syllabus, I believe that we can state that we have accomplished most of the stated objectives of this course. It is true that we are able to recognize issues involving diversity in higher education from both micro and macro levels. We were exposed to and now have a better understanding of theory, research, and scholarship on diversity topics in higher education. We have also considered the historical and contemporary perspectives of diversity issues in higher education including the politics of equity and access. Stated objectives provide measureable data for which to assess learning outcomes. In the broadest sense, this awareness helps to advance the goal of diversity in higher education. The real work, however, comes after the course is over. As future faculty administrators at educational institutions, we each must now become change agents in order to realize the goals of creating a true diverse environment. We can affect campus climate by welcoming all student constituencies and challenging our institutions to become more proactive in its effort. We can create better outreach programs, suggest and recommend the inclusion of more diverse literature in the classroom, and individually extend ourselves beyond our comfort levels to get to know others unlike ourselves. There is a popular saying, "Be the change you wish to see." For me, that slogan should be the last stated objective of this course. If we can accomplish that, maybe we will realize a truly diversified environment here, one student at a time.

A Latina student summed up the value of taking a diversity class in her course evaluation:

I decided to take a couple of minutes to think about the class as whole. It was new experience since I had never taken a "diversity" class per se, or at least not like this one. I had always questioned that fact that my ethnicity or nationality was never discussed in my history books other than many a line or two. The course provided me with interesting readings which have either enhanced my understanding of the topic discussed or opened new areas of diversity to think about.

College education, whether undergraduate or graduate, must facilitate students' consciousness of issues related to diversity, multiculturalism, and social and racial inequality; class activities and assignments should be systematically structured so that "all students, regardless of their gender and social class and their ethnic, racial, or cultural characteristics, should have an equal opportunity to learn" (Banks, 2003, p. 3), rather than relying on the ability of individual professors to engage students in the curriculum and the content.

## CONCLUSION

Reflective journal writing enables students to articulate their internalized social positions and racism in the college classroom. Understanding internalized racial relations among students from varied backgrounds, including both students of color and white students in the classroom, is critical for college educators to reduce the (re)production of the inequities of race/ethnicity, social class, and gender in the classroom environment. Reflective journaling as a means of critical pedagogy helps students to engage in the critical examination and documentation of their own thoughts, views, and emotions when they are introduced to content that challenges the fundamental beliefs they may hold about themselves and society. Even though reflective journaling has not been commonly used in the traditional higher education classroom, the use of this activity should be advocated, as it allows movement away from a hierarchical authoritarian model that serves to reproduce social injustice and inequality. I have found it effective and enlightening as a tool to understand what students have actually learned and how they internalize their own knowledge, beliefs, and values, as well as those of others. A set of questions posed by Steven and Cooper (2009) helps me to bring to mind the key benefits of using reflective journaling in college classrooms: Do my students critically examine their underlying assumptions and biases when they interact with and respond to other students' world-views, beliefs, and values? Do my students reflect about their experiences and learning in terms of social justice? Do my students connect course concepts and content to their real-life experiences? Do I create a nurturing and comfortable environment where my students are encouraged to think out of their "comfort zone"? With these questions in mind, it is important to promote college classrooms as places where students may take certain risks without being judged, think critically for themselves and others, voice their positions and views, and ask questions more openly. What is equally important is to promote the college classroom as a place where students can connect with the world outside of college by transforming reflection to action in an accurate and authentic sense of social realities.

## NOTE

1. Eunyoung Kim, Ph.D., is an assistant professor of Education Leadership, Management and Policy at Seton Hall University.

## REFERENCES

Aguirre, A. (2005). The personal narrative as academic storytelling: A Chicano's search for presence and voice in academe. *International Journal of Qualitative Studies in Education, 18*, 147–163.

Antonio, A. L. (2000). Faculty of color and scholarship transformed: New arguments for diversifying faculty. *Diverse Digest, 3*(2), 6–7.

Apple, M. (1990). *Ideology and curriculum.* New York, NY: Routledge.

Atkinson, D. R., Morten, G., & Sue, D. W. (1979). *Counseling American minorities: A cross-cultural perspective.* Dubuque, IA: W.C. Brown.

Banks, J. A. (2003). Multicultural education: Characteristics and goals. In J. A. Banks & C. A. Banks (Eds.), *Multicultural education: Issues and perspectives* (pp. 3–30). New York, NY: Wiley.

Braa, D., & Callero, P. (2006). Critical pedagogy and classroom praxis. *Teaching Sociology, 34*(4), 357–369.

Bradley, C. (2005). The career experiences of African American women faculty: Implications for counselor education programs. *College Student Journal, 39*, 518–527.

Burbules, N., & Berk, R. (1999). Critical thinking and critical pedagogy: Relations, differences, and limits. In T. Popkewitz & L. Fendler (Eds.), *Critical theories in education* (pp. 45–65). New York, NY: Routledge.

Chan, C. S., & Treacy, M. J. (1996). Resistance in multicultural courses: Student, faculty, and classroom dynamics. *American Behavioral Scientist, 40*(2), 212–221.

Chávez, A., & Guido-DiBrito, F. (1999). Racial and ethnic identity and development. In M. C. Clark & R. S. Caffarella (Eds.), *An update on adult development theory: New ways of thinking about the life course* (New Directions for Adult and Continuing Education No. 84, pp. 39–47). San Francisco, CA: Jossey-Bass.

Cooper, G. (1991). Telling our own stories: The reading and writing of journals or diaries. In C. Witherell & N. Noddings (Eds.), *Stories lives tell: Narrative and dialogue in education* (pp. 96–112). New York, NY: Teachers College Press.

Cross, W. E., Jr. (1971). The negro-to-black conversion experience: Toward a psychology of black liberation. *Black World, 20*, 13–27.

Cross, W. E. (1991). *Shades of black: Diversity in African-American identity.* Philadelphia, PA: Temple University Press.

Darder, A., Baltodano, M., & Torres, R. D. (2003). *The critical pedagogy reader.* New York, NY: Routledge.

Delpit, L. D. (1988). The silenced dialogue: Power and pedagogy in educating other people's children. *Harvard Educational Review, 58*(3), 280–298.

Dyer, R. (1997). *White.* New York, NY: Routledge.

Frankenberg, R. (1993). *White women, race matters: The social construction of whiteness.* Minneapolis, MN: University of Minnesota Press.

Freire, P. (1970). *Pedagogy of the oppressed.* New York, NY: The Seabury Press.

Freire, P. (1985). *The politics of education: Culture, power, and liberation.* South Hadley, MA: Bergin Garvey.

Freire, P. (2000). *Pedagogy of the oppressed.* New York, NY: The Seabury Press.

Garcia, B., & Van Soest, D. (1997). Changing perceptions of diversity and oppression: MSW students discuss the effects of a required course. *Journal of Social Work Education, 33,* 119–129.

Helms, J. E. (1990). Toward a model of white racial identity development. In J. E. Helms (Ed.), *Black and white racial identity: Theory, research, and practice* (pp. 49–66). New York, NY: Greenwood Press.

Helms, J. E. (1993). Introduction: Review of racial identity terminology. In J. E. Helms (Ed.), *Black and white racial identity: Theory, research and practice* (pp. 1–3). Westport, CT: Praeger.

Helms, J. E. (1995). An update of Hemls' white and people of color racial identity models. In J. G. Ponterott, J. M. Casas, L. A. Suzuki & C. M. Alexander (Eds.), *Handbook of multicultural counseling* (pp. 181–198). Thousand Oaks, CA: Sage.

Hurtado, S., Milem, J. F., Clayton-Pedersen, A. R., & Allen, W. R. (1998). Enhancing campus climates for racial/ethnic diversity: Educational policy and practice. *The Review of Higher Education, 21*(3), 279–302.

Macedo, D., & Bartolome, L. I. (1999). *Dancing with bigotry: Beyond the politics of tolerance.* New York, NY: Palgrave.

Mayo, R. (1999). *Gramsci, freire & adult education: Possibilities for transformative action.* London: Zed Books.

McLaren, P. (2003). *Life in schools: An introduction to critical pedagogy.* New York, NY: Pearson.

Milner, H. R. (2003). Reflection, racial competence, and critical pedagogy: How do we prepare pre-service teachers to pose tough questions? *Race, Ethnicity and Education, 6*(2), 193–208.

Rendón, L. I. (1994). Validating culturally diverse students: Toward a new model of learning and student development. *Innovative Higher Education, 19*(1), 33–51.

Rendón, L. I., Jalomo, R. E., & Nora, A. (2000). Theoretical considerations in the study of minority student retention. In J. Braxton (Ed.), *Rethinking the departure puzzle: New theory and research on college student retention* (pp. 127–156). Nashville, TN: Vanderbilt University Press.

Roediger, D. R. (1994). *Towards the abolition of whiteness: Essays on race, politics and working class history.* New York: Verso.

Roediger, D. R. (1998). *Black on white: Black writers it means to be white.* New York, NY: Schocken Books.

Stevens, D. D., & Cooper, J. E. (2009). *Journal keeping: How to use reflective writing for effective learning, teaching professional insight, and positive change.* Sterling, VA: Stylus.

Turner, C. S. V., Gonzalez, J. C., & Wood, J. L. (2008). Faculty of color in academe: What 20 years of literature tell us. *Journal of Diversity in Higher Education, 1,* 139–168.

# CHAPTER 11

# CLASSROOM EXPERIENCES THROUGH THE LENS OF SOCIAL JUSTICE: THE POSTSECONDARY EXPERIENCES OF THREE BLACK FEMALE STUDENTS

Katrina M. Hubbard, Annette M. Burris and Ashley L. Gray

## ABSTRACT

*This chapter examines the educational perspective of three black, female graduate students within the context of a social justice framework. The US educational system has a long history of racial discrimination, which has created an environment that is in many ways hostile to those who are different. For many students of color, negotiating this culturally hostile environment can lead to feelings of invisibility and isolation. This chapter explores these dynamics and their impact upon an individual's educational, social, and personal development from the perspective of non-dominants in a dominant culture. Through the exploration of our own experiences, we highlight the various coping mechanisms employed by three minority students to deal with the socially constructed hierarchies*

Social Justice Issues and Racism in the College Classroom: Perspectives from Different Voices
International Perspectives on Higher Education Research, Volume 8, 171–194
Copyright © 2013 by Emerald Group Publishing Limited

ISSN: 1479-3628/doi:10.1108/S1479-3628(2013)0000008013

*that exist in the classroom environment as a result of differences across racial and gender lines. It is our hope that this chapter will provide insight to educators who desire to develop a well-balanced classroom experience for all students.*

## WHO ARE WE?

We begin our narrative by offering insight into our backgrounds. By doing so, we hope the lens through which we experience life and our educational experiences might be more clear.

### *Black Female #1*

I grew up in a middle-class family in the suburbs of a Midwestern metropolitan city. My father, a factory worker, and my mother, a university professor, came from a generation of black Americans that viewed education as a crucial foundation for a better quality of life. My parents own educational histories were full of roadblocks and hurdles imposed by the racial climate of their time, the socioeconomic standing of their families, and the prevailing attitudes of their environment.

The year my father was to start high school, the district in his small rural town desegregated. In his freshman year, he was one of two black students in a high school with a total enrollment of 500. Athletically gifted, he earned a spot on the varsity football team in his freshman year and was a starter through his senior year. While he desired to go to college, a concert of events, beliefs, and circumstances proved to be too large of a hurdle for him to overcome. His mother believed that "boys don't need an education because they can get a factory job, but girls need an education for security." His high school football coach was the sole person who encouraged him to go on to college. However, due to the lack of finances, encouragement, and adequate preparation, he only stayed a week before returning home. Unable to find work, he enlisted in the military and at the end of his term began the first in a long career of factory jobs.

My mother was from a small farming community in the Deep South where desegregation was slow to flourish. Her parents were sharecroppers and made a modest living that was not enough to afford higher education for their three children. As a child, she always wanted to go to college and become a registered nurse (RN). When she shared her aspirations with an uncle, also a farmer, his response was, "yeah, you'll be an RN all right, a regular nigger!" At that time, blacks were not admitted to white nursing schools or bachelor of science in nursing (BSN) programs in the south, and admission for black students to any BSN program was extremely rare. The National League of Nursing had affiliate programs with black four-year colleges that would award a bachelor's degree after two years at the college and three years in a nursing diploma program. A high school counselor took an interest in my mother and arranged for her to take an entrance exam at a black college that was part of the affiliate program. With a scholarship from the United Negro College Fund, she enrolled in college. Upon completion of her second year, she traveled north to the Midwest to begin the nursing part of her education. The year she entered the nursing diploma program, the National League of Nursing discontinued its affiliate programs. After her five years of education, she was left with the equivalent of two years of college and no degree. Determined to become an RN she sought fellowships and scholarships and enrolled in a local university in what would become her new hometown to repeat the last three years of college and earn her BSN.

These experiences, among others, inspired my parents to expose my sister and me to the best quality education they could afford. My childhood was peppered with the expectation that I would go to college. In my younger years, my mother frequently worked after hours and on weekends; she would take my sister and I along with her to the office. I grew to have a certain level of comfort on a college campus and saw it as a part of my future. While I fully expected to go to college, I was unprepared for the sheer cost of a college education. My top choice school awarded me less than $8,000 in financial aid to cover an annual tuition of over $20,000. As the dependent of a university employee where my mother taught, I was able to afford the cost of tuition with student loans and scholarships, which also allowed me to live on campus. I completed my undergraduate education at a private Jesuit institution in the Midwest where I double-majored in French and Spanish. Upon graduation I entered the workforce and unintentionally made my way into a career in international education. After an 11-year hiatus, I returned to college to earn my master's degree in adult and higher education.

*Black Female #2*

I am an African-American woman and I am 25 years old. I was born and raised in St. Louis, MO. I am the youngest of three daughters from my mother, a single parent. After a 20-year tenure, my mother was laid off from her position as an insurance agent. This abruptly and drastically changed our socioeconomic status. We were not wealthy prior to the dismissal, but we became working poor soon after. Throughout this time I attended school at a suburban, St. Louis County public high school. I was a part of the Voluntary Interdistrict Choice Corporation (VICC) program, affectionately referred to as "deseg" by the participating students. This required me to wake up at 5 am every morning to catch the bus. I was very involved in school and that drastically affected my schedule. There were only two school bus options available after school for students involved in a sport or club. I arrived home each night after the sun had set, just to get enough rest to wake up before it rose the next day. The school I attended was predominantly white. Out of my graduation class of 635 students, only 20 were African-American.

I completed my undergraduate degree in African-American studies, with a certificate in women's studies at a Midwestern, Jesuit, research institution. This was a predominantly white institution (PWI) as well. African-Americans accounted for 7% of the total population. While there, I became very interested in race relations and social justice. I was a first-generation college graduate.

I graduated in August 4, 2012 with a master's degree from a Midwestern, public research institution in adult and higher education administration. I plan to obtain a doctorate in the near future. I currently work in student affairs, where I feel most connected to the students I'm serving.


*Black Female #3*

I am African-American and I am a first-generation college graduate. I received a bachelor of science degree in business administration in 1995 from a doctoral granting research institution in the Midwest, although I began my collegiate experience at a southern Historically Black College and University (HBCU). I spent two years at the HBCU and two and a half years at a predominantly white research institution in the Midwest. After 10 years in corporate America, I pursued a master's of science in finance at a Midwestern master's level university, graduating in 2008. In 2009, after adjunct teaching for two years, I decided to go back to school, yet again, to obtain a doctorate in educational leadership and policy studies with an emphasis on higher education. I will complete my degree with the successful defense of my dissertation by summer of 2013. I also graduated with a master's of education in adult and higher education administration on May 13, 2012, a bonus accomplishment that was not originally planned. As a result of the 15 years I have spent in corporate America, I have climbed the corporate ladder and my income is within the top 25% of all US households. I was not privileged nor born into a life of privilege or surplus. My mother raised my sister and me on a nondegreed nurse's salary, putting us in parochial schools our entire K-12 education. Money was tight and often lacking. My mother is a licensed practical nurse (she did not pursue a college degree) and my father has a college degree from a Midwestern divinity school. I stated that I was a first-generation college graduate because I was not raised in the same household as my father and did not actually become aware that he held a degree until I was an adult. None of my mother's siblings graduated from college, although two of her brothers did attend for a certain length of time. Of my generation, I was the fourth person to attend a four-year university and graduate. I was the second person to obtain a master's degree and I will be the first person to obtain a doctorate.

## FACTORS CONTRIBUTING TO CLASSROOM EXPERIENCES

Important background elements must be introduced in order to make sense of the authors' journey as African-American female college students. The examination of how minority students may experience interactions at PWIs necessitates a review of how African-Americans make sense of their racial selves, and their racial identity; how individuals and institutions in the dominant culture communicate racial attitudes and perpetrate discrimination; and, how people of color experience those interactions. In particular, it is critical to understand racial identity development, racial microaggressions, and the sense of invisibility that microaggressions produce.

### *Racial Identity*

The Nigresence model by William Cross provides stages of African-American racial identity (Tatum, 1999). This model asserts that individuals can progress and regress at any given time within their racial identity due to social factors. The term nigresence translates from French to English as becoming black. This model was one of the first to shed light on racial identity of African-Americans and has served as the foundation for many other identity theories. The basis for Helm's Theory of White Identity was founded upon Cross' findings within the Nigresence model (Tatum, 1999).

Cross (as cited by Tatum, 1999) asserts that there are five identity stages through which African-Americans traverse. Stage one of the Nigresence model is pre-encounter phase. This stage involves a pro-dominant culture belief where individuals turn away from all things "black" while valuing Western aesthetics (1999).

Stage two of the identity model is the encounter stage. During this phase the individual endures a traumatic or multiple, small events that cause them to question their identity. The individual internalizes the event, which leads to the identity conflict.

Stage three of the identity model is the immersion/emersion phase. This stage promotes a change in dress and vernacular to express an affirmation of African-American culture. During this phase most individuals feel a lack of control over their identity. Internalization is the fourth stage of the Cross model. During this phase the individual is able to achieve balance concerning anti-white sentiments and expresses positive affirmations of African-American culture.

Internalization commitment is the fifth and final stage of Cross' model. This phase highlights a long-term commitment to positive racial identity and to the community.

## Racial Microagressions

Racism in the United States has evolved from the blatant and overt displays of racial hatred and bigotry that marked the civil rights era into more modern and subtle forms (Sue et al., 2007). Within this context, bias and discrimination have taken on an invisible quality that makes racism difficult to identify. Everyday occurrences of subtle racism can be characterized as racial microaggressions, which Sue et al. (2007) define as "brief and commonplace daily verbal, behavioral, and environmental indignities, whether intentional or unintentional, that communicate hostile, derogatory, or negative racial slights and insults to the target person or group and are expressed in three forms: microassaults, microinsults and microinvalidations (p. 72)" (as cited in Sue et al., 2008, p. 330). Sue et al. (2008) describe microassaults as being akin to "old-fashioned racism" in the sense that they are overt actions that are unmistakably racist in their orientation, while microinsults are verbal or nonverbal actions that demean one's racial identity, and microinvalidations are ambiguous actions that negate one's experiences.

Racism expressed through microaggressions can have a detrimental impact on the psychological well-being of persons of color; due to its nebulous nature the aggression is often inflicted without the awareness of the perpetrating parties, covertly communicating racial inequality throughout multiple contexts of interracial interactions in society (Sue et al., 2007). Regarding the black American experience "[m]icroaggressions reflect an unconscious worldview of white supremacy that directly assails the racial reality of black Americans" (Sue et al., 2008, p. 331). People of color primarily depend on their past experiences to provide the context for making sense of present interactions (Sue et al., 2007). Because microaggressions are often invisible to the perpetrator, the recipient is often left questioning whether the racialized incident in fact occurred. Sue et al. (2007) have noted that researchers have found when examining the microaggression experiences of black Americans that the cumulative impact of these interactions generated "emotions of self-doubt, frustration and isolation" (p. 279). Victims of microaggressions are often left wondering how to appropriately respond when these incidents occur; weighing the benefits and risks of making no response or pretending that it did not happen against addressing the behavior or striking back at the perpetrator (Sue et al., 2007).

Within the context of the classroom environment, students of color who encounter racial microaggressions from peers or from their professors may often find themselves in this situation. What are the risks of challenging an overt or subtle racist statement made by the professor or a classmate in a group project? Will addressing it directly place the individual in a stereotypical box of the "angry black woman" or "angry black man"? Will the response be easily dismissed under the social assumption that "black people make everything racial"? Will responding negatively impact one's grade, or jeopardize one's chances of being invited to collaborate on future projects? From the perspective of a risks-to-benefits analysis, the possible negative outcomes can prove to be too high of a risk for many minority students to accept.

> Deciding to do nothing by sitting on one's anger is one response that occurs frequently in people of color. This response occurs because persons of color may be (a) unable to determine whether a microaggression has occurred, (b) at a loss for how to respond, (c) fearful of the consequences, (d) rationalizing that "it won't do any good anyway," or (e) engaging in self-deception through denial ("It didn't happen"). (Sue et al., 2007, p. 279)

Sue et al. (2008) assert that researchers have also noted that micro-aggressions attack a person's sense of integrity and can communicate an invalidation of one's cultural self. Black Americans in particular have noted a myriad of negative emotional feelings (racial rage, frustration, low self-esteem, depression, etc.) in reaction to incidents of microaggression (p. 331). The damage inflicted by these subtle racist interactions is not contained to the immediate interaction or even the moments following the interaction. The emotional after effects of microaggressions can produce a lasting harmful psychological impact that can remain for years (Sue et al., 2008). When we apply this knowledge to the context of the black student experience, it is conceivable then that the stress of mentally and emotionally making sense of covert racialized experiences and dealing with the psychological fallout of those experiences adds an additional layer of stress to the academic and personal demands native to the college experience (Banks, 2010). The additional stress can increase the likelihood of negative outcomes for black students (Banks, 2010).

*Invisibility*

Many black Americans develop adaptive behaviors in an attempt to deal with the effects and stress produced by repeated racial slights, and in an effort to avoid the interactions altogether whenever possible (Franklin & Boyd-Franklin, 2000; Sue et al., 2008). Franklin and Boyd-Franklin (2000) assert that experiencing repeated racial slights can produce feelings of invisibility in black Americans; the sense that others do not see or value their feelings, talents, beliefs and abilities (p. 33).

> ... [A]ccumulated experiences of racial slights reinforce the perception that perpetrators of these acts are truly blind to the "personhood" of the individual they have encountered. The recipient feels disregarded and disrespected as – and because of being – a person of African descent ... It becomes increasingly likely for individuals in this "racialized context" to believe that their true personality and unique abilities are hidden by a cloak of psychological invisibility woven by attitudes of prejudice and discrimination on the part of others. (Franklin & Boyd-Franklin, 2000, p. 34)

In addition to creating this sense of invisibility, racial microaggressions also function as "status reminders" by the inherent message of unworthiness that microaggressions communicate; they indirectly convey the message to "stay in one's place" (Franklin & Boyd-Franklin, 2000). The continuous effort to manage racial slights and their impact upon the psyche can destabilize one's resilience and diminish an individual's ability to cope on both a momentary and long-term basis (Franklin & Boyd-Franklin, 2000). The struggle for visibility and personal identity provokes the emergence of adaptive behavior to promote a sense of personal efficacy and psychological well-being. Franklin and Boyd-Franklin (2000) also state that efforts to achieve visibility while simultaneously preserving one's integrity and dignity is a stressful psychological process for many black Americans that often involves coping with significant emotional pain and disillusionment brought on by racial slights.

# A REVIEW OF WHAT WAS: OUR INDIVIDUAL EXPERIENCES

*Speak Now or Forever Hold Your Peace ... Black Female #3*

*A Unique Journey to Academia*
I went to Catholic schools all of my life, but they were schools that had a majority African-American student body population. My mother forced me to attend a southern Historically Black University (HBCU) for college because my sister was already attending. Don't get me wrong; it was one of the best moves I ever made. I went there for two years and left only because I could not afford to continue after my sister graduated. The school cut my financial aid. So, I transferred to the predominantly white doctorate granting institution back home and was shocked by the difference between the two schools. The campus was a student commuter campus with minimal, if any, student activities and opportunities for socialization.

As a student at the HBCU, being social and active in campus activities was the norm. I felt the sense of family and support that had carried me through the first 12 years of schooling. I was an honor student in the School of Business (number four in my class). While attending the HBCU, I experienced two types of tensions. My friends and I, even today, have numerous discussions about the classism that was prevalent at the school. The more affluent students looked down upon students like me, who did not come from wealthy families. I remember feeling alienated by my first dorm roommate because she made me feel like I was beneath her (although I was ten times smarter than her). Another form of classism in which I was probably a participant was the social tension between the college students who attended the university and the local residents of the small town where the school was located. "Locals" didn't like us, the students, because they felt we looked down on them. And there were probably many instances where students were arrogant in their dealings with local town residents. On the other hand, were we supposed to want to fraternize with persons who were uneducated and immature, regardless of their place of birth!! I can remember feeling uncomfortable going to the local grocery store because of encounters with local guys in the town, which was an inevitable experience.

The other tension I experienced was racial tension. The racial tension experienced at my HBCU was internal, black on black racism. In the early 1990s, it was still a common occurrence for black people to care about the hue of your skin. On campus, light skinned, long-haired girls received more attention and were viewed more favorably by the guys on campus. I was 120 lbs, chocolate complexioned, 5'8 tall with very little shape to my body so no one paid attention to me. I had been the same in high school so nothing had really changed. I suffered from low self-esteem because I felt unattractive for most of my life compared to others. This didn't change while I was at this Southern HBCU. I was depressed the entire first semester of my college experience and felt completely isolated and alone. Those feelings changed as I matriculated and just when I was starting to love being a student there, I had to leave.

At the PWI, I went to class and went home or to work. My classroom size at the HBCU, at its largest, was approximately 30–35 students. At the PWI, I experienced auditorium size class with over 150 students. Most of the time, I felt like a number and felt equally invisible which was completely new to me. In my past, I would attempt to make a favorable and lasting impression on my teachers/professors because of how smart and outgoing I was. At the PWI, I felt that my intelligence was immaterial and irrelevant.

*And So It Begins …*
I decided to pursue my PhD later in my life. I applied to a local Midwestern doctoral granting institution and was accepted. I started my degree program in August of 2009. What was most interesting about the program, in my opinion, was the fact that the two professors responsible for my discipline were also African-American females. They were tenured professors at a predominantly white doctoral granting research institution.

One point of contention for me, during my experience, was the overwhelming sense of mandated excellence because I am also a black female pursuing academia. From the beginning of the program, I felt that I must not only participate and do well in class, but I also had to be better than most other students, especially the Caucasian students. My professors never expressed this type of mandate to me directly. My fixation on the mandate stems from years of self-imposed requirements on myself. I was immediately comfortable taking classes with my professors because I identified with them. I definitely had to exceed expectations, while striving to be the best. See, as a child, attending predominantly black elementary and secondary schools, I was always taught that as a black child, I had to be better than white people in everything that I do because I had to protect myself from the negative effects of prejudice and racism that have long plagued the African-American race. If I were just average, I would never have the benefits that white people were able to experience simply because of their race at birth. So I did, I studied and played harder in order to rise above the rest ... rise above everyone.

In addition to my self-imposed bar that I set, I also felt the need to speak intelligently on all topics, but specifically as a voice for the black race. The pressure that I placed on myself was always greater than any pressure I may have felt in the classroom. Because I was an education major, a number of the discussions during my courses would venture to topics of racial discourse, racial identity, and how race relations in America affected the educational system. Not only would I speak up, I also felt compelled to educate those who may not understand what race issues have done to African-Americans as a group of people. I remember having discussions in class where we debated on the inherit disadvantages faced by African-Americans due to generational class differences that are the ramifications of the forced servitude experienced by our ancestors. Think about it, black people helped build this country but have nothing collectively to show for it. We are not major land or business owners. White Americans own most wealth in the United States. White students in class voiced the opinion that every opportunity they are afforded is available to students of color. I attempted to explain that could not be further from the truth because higher education is not free. As it is not free, it is not accessible to all and everyone cannot afford it. If whites own the majority of the wealth in the United States, then whites will have greater access to advancement and opportunities by the mere fact of being able to afford further education. In addition, public school funding is disproportionately skewed in that most inner city schools, which educate primarily students of color, are under-funded compared to public schools in the suburbs and rural communities. I felt it was important for everyone to gain an understanding of our perspective as African-Americans because we are forced to live within the perspective of others.

Had my experience in graduate school been what I expected it to be? Not at all ... throughout the program, I wondered if I really had the ability to be successful. I know part of my self-doubt is because of years of unconscious self-hatred that black people are forced to come to terms with, but it is a constant battle. Centuries of slavery engrained in us that we, black people, are less than others and we are less intelligent than others. I, internally, affirmed and reconfirmed my skills and talents on a regular basis. I went back and forth between confidence and doubt. In the end, though, I will reach my goal.

### *Fight, Flee, or Teach? ... Perspective of Black Female #2*

"Racism doesn't exist. I don't see color. I'm not a racist ... my friend is black. It doesn't matter what race you are." Comments like these are often a part of the everyday conversations that happen in the classroom environment. Having gone to PWIs all my life, I can set my watch by the frequency that I am told comments like these. I guess you can say my curriculum is trifold. I find myself having to make a difficult choice: Do I fight, flee, or teach? Do I completely fly off the handle and vent my frustration at these comments? Am I supposed to just avoid the comments and conversations about race relations? Or, is this a teachable moment? I think this is a unique component of the classroom that is often learned by trial and error. If I react, will I perpetuate stereotypes of my people? This has been a personal struggle of mine. How do I react if I'm asked a racially offensive question? What are the ramifications of my chosen response? In the classroom setting when presented with these questions or comments, I have found that teaching is more effective than fleeing or fighting. Teaching requires patience and tolerance that comes with experience; thus, my ability to teach has developed with time.

### *Fight*

I will admit that sometimes I'm so offended by the questions that a teachable moment is the last thing on my mind. When asked offensive questions I sometimes want to retaliate. There have been times in the classroom setting when I have responded and received punishment or social isolation. I have had teachers pull me to the side and explain to me that I had no reason to be angry, because it wasn't my peers' intention to be offensive. In other cases, if I respond, I face social isolation such as finding a partner for group work. This task is difficult enough, but after a peer has seen me respond negatively I am labeled as an angry, black student.

As an African-American woman, hair is a major part of my identity and culture. During my sophomore year as an undergraduate, a white, male student petted my hair, saying, "Wow, I didn't know nappy hair could be so soft." I had the option here to explain to him that his comment was offensive and to explain why my hair feels different (teachable moment), walk away to avoid this conversation (flee), or bluntly let him know he has offended me and insulted my culture. I chose to respond brashly. He didn't understand why I would be angry at that statement, he thought of it as a compliment. He was thoroughly surprised that a black woman could have soft hair. He had no idea that throughout my entire academic career at PWIs people had commented on my hair and I had been petted like an animal. He had no idea that as I child, I lost my best friend over my hair. She insisted that we could never use the same brush because my hair was different. I internalized that to mean because I was black and my hair could not be washed daily that using her brush was out of the question. In the split second before my reaction I didn't feel like it was my responsibility to explain this to him. I knew social consequences would soon follow. After telling him off I immediately felt the backlash. It was a 200 level Biology class with 200 + students yet finding a partner was like finding a needle in a haystack. No one wanted to work with the "angry black woman" in class. I began to feel like it was easier to cope with being offended than to be socially outcast. In my mind I was just defending my body, my identity, and my culture. I had reverted back to Cross' Nigresence model Stage 3. I've immersed myself in all things black, which included dropping a major where I was one of a few African-American Students. For once, I wanted to be around people that looked like me and faced similar challenges as me. I changed my major to African-American Studies. Dr. Beverly Tatum explains this phenomenon of wanting to be near other African-American students in her book, *Why Are All the Black Kids Sitting Together in the Cafeteria*? "The developmental need to explore the meaning of one's identity with others who are engaged in a similar process manifests itself informally in school corridors and cafeterias across the country" (Tatum, 1999, p. 71).

*Flee*
As a means of coping with the racial climate at this Midwestern Jesuit institution, I began to be less vocal in response to offensive comments. I began to avoid race relation talks and even walked away when conversations about race got too heated. I felt horrible walking away from these conversations because it felt like a cop out. I was tired of not being able to

find a partner in class, or just tired of the same circular talks that led to nothing. I became silent. The burden of trying to get others to acknowledge and deny their privilege became too heavy. I recognize this as fleeing the situation. While in undergrad the historical case in Jena, Louisiana was taking over media outlets. Having followed the case closely I decided to plan a rally for justice. All students were invited to participate. The participants were overwhelmingly African-American. I felt a sense of pride and accomplishment that I, much like my predecessors, had fought for equality. After the rally I went to class. A few students had seen me in the quad passing out flyers and holding up signs. They wanted to know what the case was about. I was amazed that they were unfamiliar because every major network had run stories on the case. I thought to myself that privilege created provision for oblivion. But I explained it anyway. After the explanation, students became offended that I implied race as a factor in the case. It had seemed blatant to me. Instead of continuing the dialogue I changed the subject. First, I was the only black student in the class. Second, it seemed like common sense to me and third, I needed that class to graduate. There were large amounts of group work and peer evaluation; therefore I felt the need to just avoid race relations in class all together. "Talking about racism is an essential part of facing racism and changing it. But it is not the only part. I am painfully aware that people of color have been talking about racism for a long time. Many people of color are tired of talking, frustrated that talk has not led to enough constructive action or meaningful social change" (Tatum, 1999, p. xix). In hindsight, I'm not sure that this was the best way to handle this situation, but it felt right.

*Teach*
As cited in Tatum (1999), James Baldwin was noted as saying, "Not everything that is faced can be changed. But nothing can be changed until it is faced" (Tatum, 1999, p. xix).

Teaching has been one of the most difficult, yet rewarding responses to offensive questions. It has challenged me to think beyond my personal feelings and to share some knowledge with someone else. Teachable moments are humbling. They require a great deal of patience and care. I can recall sitting in a graduate level class and listening to a peer say that he did not see race. He insisted that the reason we have racial issues was because people chose to identify themselves by their race. He just wanted us to be a part of the human race. He insisted that he was not racist because he had a black friend. As previously stated, comments like these happen at all academic levels. The notion of being color-blind to avoid the truth of privilege and domination has always been a source of frustration for me. He went on to insist that he had been discriminated against because of his race. I had several options: I could respond harshly, walk away, or teach. I chose to teach. It was clear to me that race-related conversations brought him great discomfort. I shared some of my personal experiences and explained to him that being discriminated against for an African-American person was a daily struggle. I can't assert that all teachable moments have resulted or will result in instant change; however, I truly believe that a seed of understanding was planted. That is the power behind teachable moments. They have the ability to be life-changing moments.

*Where I Stand*

When I was first exposed to the Cross Nigresence model it was an enlightening moment. It gave me perspective about where I stood, but also where my African-American peers stand. Currently, I am in stage four (Internalization). I am able to build some relationships with peers outside of my race. Because of my experiences and my scholarly research about social justice I am able to discuss race relations openly. More importantly, I have made a commitment to the betterment of African-Americans and society at large. The one thing that I struggle with currently is, I have no close friends of a different race. I recently had a conversation with a classmate about how I have not had a close friend of another race since I lost my childhood friend. I never knew that a hairbrush has so much meaning and power to destroy relationships. I decided at the age of 9 that all my friends would be the same race as me because then at least we would have things in common. The encounter experience as described by Tatum has the ability to be world shattering. Freshman year of college I realized I had only built close bonds with African-Americans. Currently, I have plenty of colleagues, peers, and co-workers that are not the same race as me; however, I can't say that I am particularly close to any of them. Having talked to my classmate (Caucasian female), I decided to be open to building close bonds with people of other races. I don't want to trivialize my desire to have a white friend, but instead I want a true bond not based on our pigment. I truly believe that friendship has no color.

*Welcome to the Hallowed Halls: Be Sure to Read the Fine*
*Print … Black Female #1*

I entered higher education full of hope and the expectation that all of the promise and potential the college experience had to offer would be mine. As a teenager I was a devoted fan of *The Cosby Show* and *A Different World* and I couldn't wait until I had the chance to engage in the kind of classroom discourse, camaraderie, and mentor relationships that I saw depicted in the television episodes. My actual experience was a far cry from my expectation. I chose to attend a Jesuit PWI in the Midwest and quickly discovered that it was in fact a different world.

While I had attended predominately white schools for the majority of my elementary and secondary education, the overall population was small, which fostered a tight knit community atmosphere and the black student enrollment was enough to create a sense of acceptance and belonging. There were 98 total students in my high school graduating class. I went from an environment of approximately 400 students, to a college campus of thousands. When I arrived for move-in, I did not encounter a single other person of color, of any color, in the three-wing, 12-floor building where I was assigned to live. I consoled myself with the assurance that I would meet other black students at freshman orientation; however, I instead found myself as the single person of color in a room full of hundreds of white students. I began to question if there were any people other than white students at the institution. Determined to be optimistic, I set my sights on the first week of classes, convinced that circumstances would improve.

The first week of classes came and went and the reality of my situation began to sink in. I was one of two black students on my floor in the residence hall, and I was either the only black student or one of two, in each of my classes. I was alone, in an environment where most of the people around me did not acknowledge my presence or respond favorably to my attempts to initiate friendship. It was an incredibly isolating experience that provided a regular supply of negative encounters that assaulted my confidence and my sense of self. While I was able to put on a brave front to face the day, inwardly I struggled to combat the self-doubt and lack of confidence that was flourishing as a result of my campus experiences. In this section of the chapter I will explore some of the classroom experiences I encountered during my undergraduate and graduate programs as a minority student at PWIs that have framed my identity development.


*You Don't Belong Here*
Being a person with introverted tendencies I was used to spending time alone, but what I experienced at college was a new phenomenon; I was frequently alone in the midst of other people. While it felt foreign at first, I became used to walking into a room full of other students and not

interacting with anyone. I expected to be ignored by my fellow classmates but I did not quite expect to be met with hostilities from the professors.

My first attempt at freshman composition ended in defeat. I had always been a strong student and enjoyed a positive relationship with my instructors. The professor in this course took an almost immediate dislike to me. A quarter into the semester I had yet to receive a grade higher than a D on any assignment. The professor would return my manuscripts overflowing with cryptic remarks in pencil. I was thankful he had used pencil instead of red ink so that I wouldn't be embarrassed during class. I knew how to write, didn't I? I had attended a college preparatory high school and earned top grades in writing courses that were eligible for college credit; why couldn't I earn higher than a D in this class? After each paper I would visit his office hours in an attempt to find out what I was doing wrong only to be told that if I didn't know what his comments meant, there was nothing he could do to help me. I was determined to succeed in the course but despite my focused efforts, I continued to receive the same results. The culminating event that finally convinced me to drop the course occurred during class. There were two other black students in the course with me; after discovering each other in the first session we sat together whenever possible. One day while the professor was writing instructions for an exercise on the board, one of the other black students made a comment. After he finished, he took his seat at the front of the room and called me up to the desk. He proceeded to tell me in full voice in front of the entire class that he didn't give a damn if I didn't care about my education but he was not going to allow me to disrupt learning for all of the other students. I was too shocked to defend myself, and my classmate made no moves to speak up and tell him that she was the person who had spoken out. This was the first time any adult had used profanity with me. The silence in the room was deafening. I knew that all of the other students in the class had heard every word of the humiliating exchange. I returned to my seat and thankfully, I managed to retain my composure through the end of the class. Finally convinced that I could not turn the situation around, I made the decision to drop the class. I knew that no matter what I did, I would never earn a decent grade in this man's class.

In my senior year I was taking upper level literature courses that were cross-listed with graduate sections. I had become used to being the only person of color in my Spanish and French courses once I passed beyond the 12 credit hours necessary to meet language proficiency requirements. I thought I was used to the isolation but I encountered a new level of invisibility in the graduate courses. In one particular class we had assigned seating in a semi-circle to facilitate discussion. When the professor would pass around the handouts the student on my left would get up from his seat and walk around me to give the handouts to the person next to me, which required me to wait until the papers had made their way back to the professor before I could retrieve a set of the handouts from the front of the room. No one, including the professor, saw fit to intervene or disrupt the practice and by this point in my educational experience at this institution I was well conditioned not to challenge the behavior but to adapt. Being invisible was normal to me. I expected to be ignored and I thought it strange when my presence was acknowledged. This sense of isolation and invisibility put an incredible strain on my psyche. I had no allies; I knew that I could not expect help from my fellow classmates in the form of getting notes from a class I had missed, or getting into a study group. I was on my own. Where other students benefited from the sense of community and the collegial labor sharing and support that occurs within a student community, I was on the outside. There were no other black students in my major at this level and I could not gain entry to the inner circle of the dominant group.

Experiences such as these sent the repeated message that I was somehow less than and an outsider who did not belong. While I didn't realize it at the time, I internalized the message of being the perpetual interloper who had to justify her presence by extraordinary performance. Yet despite my GPA and semesters on the dean's list, I still believed myself to be in an omega position when compared to my peers. This created an enormous internal pressure to be perfect and to perform above what is required as well as a fear of falling short of expectations that I still manage to this day.

*Don't Rock the Boat*
One of the dynamics I became very adept at discerning was when I could safely contribute observations about race-related issues, or speak about personal experiences where race was a salient factor. At times I felt brave enough to forge ahead even though I knew I would meet a stiff challenge from others in the class, yet there were other times where I dared not take the risk. A primary factor in making the decision to speak or remain silent was the tone and atmosphere established by the professor. A secondary factor was the personality dynamics present in the room. During my graduate program there were white students in my cohort who were extremely expressive, some to the point of being aggressive and belligerent, when it came to discussions of race and privilege. When I found myself in a class with any of these individuals I censored myself and mentally over-analyzed my comments before saying anything. One of the most valuable

aspects of the educational experience is the opportunity to be impacted by other perspectives and knowledge outside of one's immediate sphere. This knowledge does not only come from the curriculum, the lecture, or the professor, but also from the collective experiences and viewpoints present in the room. However, as someone outside of the dominant culture I felt acutely aware of the unspoken message that my perspective was not necessarily welcome and that viewpoints on race and privilege were generally considered as controversial threads that would take time and focus away from the course material. From my perspective I saw them as overlapping threads that provided context to what we were learning, threads that had the potential to impact someone's understanding and change how a person approaches an issue or a people group.

In a research methods course, I had the opportunity to do a topic paper. Our assignment was to write an academic paper that examined our chosen topic from multiple perspectives; we were to review the existing literature and come to some basic conclusions based upon that review. The professor gave us complete freedom in choosing the focus of our paper. I admired his approach to learning and I felt safe in choosing to examine white privilege and its implications for student affairs work. Students who chose to do a topic paper were required to do a presentation to the class explaining the topic and their approach to examining it. The purpose of the presentation was to broaden your investigative approach by getting input from the professor and the other students. When I learned that this was a requirement of the topic paper assignment, I almost decided not to pursue it. There were several white male students in the class who were very vocal and very free with their opinions, one of which was a student that had unleashed a tirade upon me in a previous class together; in his opinion I was racializing things that had nothing to do with race. I sat one row in front of them and over the course of the semester I regularly overheard their before-class conversations. These exchanges convinced me that I would face an aggressive challenge from these men when I discussed my topic. My anxiety over the presentation continued to increase as the date drew nearer. I finally decided to communicate with the professor about my worries. I expressed concern over the nature of my topic given the composition of the class (out of 30 students there were only 6 people of color in the class). I communicated that it had the potential to be a very polarizing and inflammatory topic and I was uncertain about my bravery to handle the reactions from various students in the course. His response while overall positive and supportive included a sentence that served to remind me of the tacit contract for discussing race and privilege in dominant culture spaces. He told me that we were master's students in a graduate research methodology course and as such we should all understand the concepts of critical research. He continued to say that if it became evident that we did not understand those concepts he would use my presentation as an opportunity to re-present them. Up to this point, I was feeling confident; then came the last part of his response. He continued on to say that all of the students in the course should be beyond basic emotional bigotry and he expected thoughtful rigorous analysis from everyone, including me. Did he think that I was going to purposefully use incendiary language, or use the presentation as an opportunity to accuse white people of their collective wrongs against minorities? Why would he need to include that reminder to me? Wasn't this an academic assignment based on the body of work produced by the academic community? Hadn't he been clear on the parameters of the assignment? Why was it necessary to caution me against emotional bigotry and to remind me to keep my comments to "thoughtful rigorous analysis" of the topic? I didn't challenge his comment, or ask for clarification. I thanked him for his input and moved on. However, the seed had been planted that while on the surface he was supportive, if the conversation moved to choppy waters I may find myself on the receiving end of his censure, and I had no real way of determining what would trigger that reaction.

When the day of the presentation came, I was careful to discuss white privilege as an idea, as something that perhaps was not yet proven to exist. I framed my investigation as an exploratory effort to find out if white privilege exists and if it does, how would it impact the minority college student experience. Despite the fact that there is a solid body of academic work on this topic from which I could speak, I was more concerned with managing the white students' reactions and avoiding the anger that often comes after asserting that a system exists in this nation that provides advantages to those in the dominant culture and perpetuates disadvantages on those outside of that culture group; primarily because I was uncertain about the level of support I could expect from the professor.

While the academic sphere purports to be a place of learning and a free space for investigation and inquiry, in my experience it is only such for members of the dominant culture. As a minority student I was constantly made aware of the expectation to stay in my place. I was allowed to be in this space and contribute but only within the acceptable boundaries. I was not really free to be myself and speak my mind and to develop intellectually and personally in the same way as my white counterparts. I had to maintain an awareness of "the Dominant" at all times to ensure that others would perceive me favorably. I knew that I needed their favor in order to gain access. I was acutely aware of the fact that if I was labeled as "controversial" or "combative" that those labels would follow me throughout my time at the institution and certain "perks" (such as letters of recommendation, invitations to collaborate on projects, scholarship opportunities, etc.) would not be made available to me. I survived the PWI and I learned to play the game, but at what personal cost? Almost two decades after my undergraduate experience, I am still unraveling some of the internalized messages that have been harmful to me, and working to over-write them with positive affirmations. It is my hope that my transparency in sharing my experiences will impact educators and students in the educational sphere so that someday our educational spaces can be equally accessible and edifying for all regardless of race, color, creed, gender, or difference.

## WHAT DOES IT ALL MEAN

*Higher Education's Contribution to Social Justice on Campus*

*Perceptions*
In his article titled Redefining the Issue of Racial Preference: Minority Access to Higher Education, Renner (1998) expounded on the misconception shared by most white people that affirmative action has provided undue access to higher education for blacks and other minorities. While affirmative action has been an accepted practice by higher education institutions in admissions practices, Renner confirms that access to higher education has not increased for minorities, in general, and blacks, in particular, as a result (1998). Attendance growth for white students has far outpaced the attendance growth of black students and other minorities. Renner also points out that the population growth of blacks and minorities has outpaced their growth in attendance at postsecondary institutions.

Why has matriculation through postsecondary schools not increased at the same or similar rate of population growth? Several scholars have noted that black students perceive a sense of social alienation on college campuses in the United States (Gildersleeve, Croom, & Vasquez, 2011; James, 1998). And the further a minority student matriculates through the ranks of higher education, the more alienated they feel (Gildersleeve et al., 2011).

As cited in the article by James (1998), The Kerner Report, which was issued in 1972, stated the nation was moving toward two separate societies, one white and one black. The report further stated that most white people find it difficult to accept the idea that, for the most part, America remains a racist society. Even today, this dual, racist society permeates and manifests itself on college campuses across the country. Black students have been documented as feeling both social estrangement and social alienation, which are defined as a feeling of loneliness and the lack of perception of fit within an environment, respectively. In James' study, results revealed that 25% of the black student population's self-image worsened as a result of attending a predominantly white university and 61% of the population felt they were not properly prepared socially or academically for their college experiences by high school teachers. Black students tend to feel powerless, meaningless, and disenfranchised on college campuses, especially predominantly white campuses (James, 1998). The findings of James' study and other research provide reasons that there has not been a significant increase in the number of black students choosing to pursue higher education.

*Solutions*

How can faculty help alleviate the alienation and isolation that black students feel on college campuses? How can a more just and equitable society be established on college campuses to help African-American students? Several researchers have posed this question and provided potential solutions for faculty to consider. Radloff (2010) discussed the use of social justice course requirements for graduation. He found that requiring more than one course that focuses on issues of race and diversity increased the likelihood that students would support race-based policies such as affirmative action and diminished modern racism and its practices. We suggest that faculty should attempt to incorporate a discussion on social justice issues in every course they teach. The discussions that occur will enlighten not only the students that participate, but faculty as well.

In addition, the presence of black faculty in the classroom and on campus provides unexpected benefits to black students, such as providing the students the ability to feel included, minimizing that sense of alienation. Black faculty, more frequently, include black students in conversations, which encourage black students to participate and feel valued. Black students expect that faculty of color will provide curriculum and course content that is diverse and will further validate the research interests of black students (Tuitt, 2011). The availability of black faculty will also provide students of color access to mentors that we so desperately need in order to succeed in a world that feels foreign to us.

Gildersleeve et al. (2011) suggested that persistence is a struggle in the everyday life of students of color. If faculty would recognize this struggle, they could begin to develop more equitable environments, relations, and culture in graduate education. Students would feel encouraged and motivated to stay the course and complete their programs of study. Increased opportunities for socialization into the collegial society are also afforded when faculty of color embrace their important role in the graduate student experience, thereby reducing feelings of alienation.

We also feel that African-American students would benefit from faculty who take the time to engage in self-evaluation and identify their own areas of bias toward others who are different in some way. Ideally, engaging in this type of self-evaluation would make it easier to identify one's own behaviors and reactions that introduce elements of discrimination to the classroom environment. Because of the power differential in the classroom, faculty members have the potential to both initiate and disrupt the negative dynamics that develop in student-to-student and professor-to-student interactions. It is the responsibility of faculty members who claim to be committed to social justice to take it beyond dialogue and into action.

In addition to examining themselves, we encourage faculty to engage in diversity initiatives outside of the ones mandated by the university. If diversity is not a personal commitment, it will translate into the classroom setting. In our experiences though, racial dialogue is best facilitated by faculty who have genuinely embraced diversity and acceptance. Faculty who are committed to diversity, must be practitioners. If the only time, as a faculty member, you are focused on diversity initiatives, is during a mandated professional setting, you have missed the mark. Make the investment in becoming a social justice practitioner for the sake of your students of all races. Remember, professors are in a power position and they intervene with, advocate for, and educate their students.

From a personal point of view, a spiritual grounding or a belief in one true God who is watching, guiding, and caring was essential for persisting through our higher education experience. When times were difficult and stressful, prayer was definitely part of our solution. Also, having an outlet to discuss and vent frustrations was vital. It could be a relative, a close friend, or a professional's couch. The outlet could take many forms, but an outlet was imperative for maintaining sanity in a sometimes, insane situation.

Successfully navigating the racial division that exists in higher education requires much endurance, patience, and a strong support network. Endurance is built over time as an end result of every struggle, conflict, and challenge, regardless of the outcome; and patience is a choice. As minority students we must not give up in the face of hostile environments, but we must keep pressing forward so that we can make a difference for all who come behind us. Our experiences have instilled qualities in each of us, which have helped us in our student careers as well as our personal and professional lives. The process of writing this narrative has connected us through the thread of our shared stories and has established a sisterhood and friendship that will forever be cherished.

# REFERENCES


Banks, K. H. (2010). African American college students' experience of racial discrimination and the role of college hassles. *Journal of College Student Development, 51*(1), 23–34. doi: 10.1353/csd.0.0115.

Franklin, A. J., & Boyd-Franklin, N. (2000). Invisibility syndrome: A clinical model of the effects of racism on African-American males. *American Journal of Orthopsychiatry, 70*(1), 33–41.

Gildersleeve, R. E., Croom, N. N., & Vasquez, P. L. (2011). "Am I going crazy?!": A critical race analysis of doctoral education. *Equity & Excellence in Education, 44*(1), 93–114. doi: 10.1080/10665684.2011.539472

James, R. (1998). The perceived effects of social alienation on black college students enrolled at a Caucasian southern university. *College Student Journal, 32*(2), 228–239.

Radloff, T. (2010). College students' perceptions of equal opportunity for African-Americans and race-based policy: Do diversity course requirements make a difference? *College Student Journal, 44*(2), 558–564.

Renner, K. (1998). Redefining the issue of racial preference: Minority access to higher education. *Change, 30*(2), 26–33.

Sue, D. W., Capodilupo, C. M., Torino, G. C., Bucceri, J. M., Holder, A. M., Nadal, K. L., et al. (2007). Racial microaggressions in everyday life: Implications forclinical practice. *American Psychologist, 62*(4), 271–286.

Sue, D. W., Nadal, K. L., Capodilupo, C. M., Lin, A. I., Torino, G. C., & Rivera, D. P. (2008). Racial microaggressions against black Americans: Implications for counseling. *Journal of Counseling & Development, 86*(Summer), 330–337.

Tatum, B. D. (1999). *Why are all the black kids sitting together in the Cafeteria.* New York, NY: Basic Books.

Tuitt, F. (2011). Black like me: Graduate students' perceptions of their pedagogical experiences in classes taught by black faculty in a predominantly white institution. *Journal of Black Studies, 43*, 186–206. doi: 10.1177/0021934711413271

# CHAPTER 12

# THE EXPERIENCE OF CONDUCTING A STUDY OF RACIAL OR ETHNIC DYNAMICS: VOICES OF DOCTORAL STUDENTS IN COLLEGES OF EDUCATION

Aimee Howley, Renée A. Middleton, Marged Howley, Natalie F. Williams and Laura Jeanette Pressley

## ABSTRACT

*A large body of literature focuses on ways that learning experiences in colleges of education can combat racist stereotypes while promoting cultural competence. However, because limited research investigates how student research projects (e.g., master's theses and doctoral dissertations) can accomplish these same purposes, additional studies are needed. For this reason, the current exploratory mixed methods study addressed the following research question: "How does the racial identity development of doctoral students from colleges of education align with their experiences of conducting dissertation studies focusing on racial and/or ethnic dynamics in schools, universities, or human service agencies?" The research team used well-established scales to measure the racial identity*

Social Justice Issues and Racism in the College Classroom: Perspectives from Different Voices
International Perspectives on Higher Education Research, Volume 8, 195–227
Copyright © 2013 by Emerald Group Publishing Limited
All rights of reproduction in any form reserved
ISSN: 1479-3628/doi:10.1108/S1479-3628(2013)0000008014

*development of Black and White participants. The team also conducted a series of three interviews with each participant to learn about how racial identity statuses contributed to and responded to the experience of conducting dissertation research with a focus on racial and/or ethnic dynamics. Analysis of interview data pointed to the salience of "advocacy" in the experiences of participants. Advocacy connected to doctoral research by affording opportunities for personal advancement and by affording opportunities to promote social change. Further interpretation revealed differences in the importance of the two types of advocacy for White and Black participants, especially in consideration of their racial identity statuses. Despite such nuances, the experience of conducting dissertation research reinforced all participants' previous commitments to social justice and advocacy, but it did not help them develop more wide-ranging and systematic strategies for working as advocates of social justice.*

A large body of research literature focuses on ways that didactic programs and field experiences in colleges of education can combat racist stereotypes and practices as well as promoting cultural competence (e.g., Cochran-Smith, 1995; Katz, 2003; McIntyre, 1997). Limited research, however, investigates how student research projects (e.g., master's theses and doctoral dissertations) can accomplish these same purposes (cf. Herman, 2009; Johnson-Bailey, 2001). Nevertheless, studies of the impact of dissertation research on graduate students show that the dissertation experience contributes in a formative way to intellectual development by cultivating critical and independent thinking and helping candidates assimilate the role of scholar into their personal identities (Andrews, 2007; Gardner, 2008). Findings from these studies suggest that dissertation research focusing explicitly on racial and ethnic dynamics might offer a powerful basis for lifelong scholarship and advocacy.

Despite potential benefits to emerging scholars, the process of conducting research that challenges prevailing racist and ethnocentric paradigms can be particularly frustrating, especially for students of color (e.g., Davis & Sutherland, 2008; Gonzales, 2007). Dissertation work often cleaves to conventional assumptions about research – a circumstance that tends to keep new scholars from using inventive methods, offering groundbreaking insights, engaging in critique, or influencing practice in their fields (e.g., Adams & White, 1994; Horton & Hawkins, 2010; Ponticell & Olivarez, 1997). Dissertation research focusing on dynamics of race and ethnicity often does challenge such conventions (e.g., Davis & Sutherland, 2008; Gonzales, 2007), and the experiences of graduate students who undertake it can contribute to a wider understanding of the intellectual commitments, self-discipline, and mentoring support that make it possible.

To provide a beginning point for research of this sort, the current study examines the dissertation experiences of seven recent doctoral graduates from colleges of education. As an exploratory mixed methods study, it addresses a broad research question: How does the racial identity development (RID) of doctoral students from colleges of education align with their experiences of conducting dissertation studies focusing on racial and/or ethnic dynamics in schools, universities, or human service agencies?

## RELATED LITERATURE

Although little prior research has explicitly investigated the ways dissertation research in education contributes to increased cultural competence, three bodies of literature offer relevant insights. First is literature about approaches faculties in colleges of education use to expand the cultural competence of their students. Second is literature about how dissertation research, at least in some fields, supports students' emerging competence as scholars. A third body of relevant literature concerns the transformations that some students experience through the process of conducting doctoral research. Following discussion of these three bodies of literature, our discussion of related literature turns to the theoretical framework undergirding the study, namely the theory of RID as conceptualized by Cross (1971) and Helms (1990).

### *Increasing Cultural Competence of Students in Colleges of Education*

Both normative and descriptive literature describes strategies that faculty members in colleges of education use to improve the cultural competence of their students. This literature identifies the aims of such strategies as (1) developing cultural awareness; (2) providing knowledge about cultures, races, and ethnicities that differ from the mainstream; and (3) cultivating skills for interacting with individuals from different cultures in educational and other environments (Canen, 2007; Watt, Robinson, & Lupton-Smith, 2002). Because the scope of cultural competence is so broad, colleges can adopt any number of different strategies to accomplish these aims (Chao, Wei, Good, & Flores, 2011; Dickson, Jepsen, & Barbee, 2008).

One widely used approach for improving cultural competence has been to offer (and often to require students to enroll in) a single course that focuses on multicultural issues (Chao et al., 2011; Malott, 2010). Not only is this approach used in many undergraduate teacher preparation programs, it is also used in some master's and doctoral programs in colleges of education (Johnson-Bailey, 2001). According to Watt and associates (2002), such courses incorporate activities calling for introspection and dialogue with peers in order to help each student achieve a more accepting attitude toward diversity and perhaps also a more sophisticated racial identity. Through such activities, students expand their appreciation of their own cultural group as a basis for gaining greater appreciation of other cultural, racial, and ethnic groups (Canen, 2007; Dickson et al., 2008; Watt et al., 2002).

Despite the popularity of using a single self-contained course as a way to expand students' cultural competence, some commentators claim that multicultural learning must become part of many or even all experiences in colleges of education (e.g., Chae, Foley, & Chae, 2006; Foldy & Buckley, 2010). Moreover, according to several writers on multiculturalism (e.g., Dickson et al., 2008), experiential activities such as internships and practica often work better than formal didactic courses to increase cultural competence. Such activities allow candidates to work with diverse populations and to reflect on these experiences as the basis for examining, and perhaps changing, their personal values (Dickson et al., 2008). For graduate students, this broader approach encourages engagement with diverse perspectives, expanding these students' horizons while minimizing the Eurocentric norms of the typical university experience (Foldy & Buckley, 2010).

In addition to internships and practica, some teacher educators have described the use of projects involving action research as a way to increase candidates' cultural competence (Carillo, 1990; Martin, 2005). Martin (2005) described a project in which students first immersed themselves in a community to identify important research questions relating to cultural diversity and then conducted action research by selecting a question to investigate, developing an action plan, implementing the plan, collecting and analyzing data, and reflecting on the findings. Although thesis and dissertation work sometimes entails action research of this sort, we could find no articles that described how such research – or any other type of dissertation research – has been used systematically to contribute to graduate students' cultural competence.

### Students' Need for Support as They Encounter Challenges of Doctoral Work

Whatever their specific features, efforts to cultivate students' cultural competence require faculty to take responsibility for structuring the experience, providing guidance and critique, and offering ongoing support (e.g., Martin, 2005). Although all teaching implicates these requirements, learning experiences that challenge students' long-held assumptions about the world or ask them to develop complex new skill sets may depend even more heavily on faculty's ability and willingness to perform these roles. Teaching to expand cultural competence represents one example of instruction that places such demands; dissertation advising is another.

Arguably the demands are intensified when faculty members advise dissertations with the potential to encourage deep reflection about candidates' own racial identities or about racial dynamics in schools and universities, human service agencies, or society at large. Students who take on such projects are likely to need even more support than dissertation writers typically need. Some studies do speak to the support structures that assist dissertation writers, but these studies relate to fields other than education, such as library and information sciences (Sugimoto, 2012), history and chemistry (Gardner, 2008), visual arts (Kantawala, Hochtritt, Rolling Jr, Serig, & Staikidis, 2009), and nursing (Kirton, Straker, Brown, Jack, & Jinks, 2011).

### Students' Transformation Through Doctoral Research

According to some research, doctoral students frequently see the experience of conducting a dissertation study as transformative (Johnson-Leslie, 2009; Kantawala et al., 2009). Often their transformation involves the process of becoming a scholar – a process with implications for self-efficacy and identity formation (e.g., Gardner, 2008; Kantawala et al., 2009; Martin, 2005). A few studies also explore the transformation in terms of growth in perspectives about identity – including race and/or ethnicity, gender, and sexual orientation. These studies tend to use autoethnographic methods, thereby enabling new researchers to reflect on their own experiences of dissertation work and the impact of those experiences.

Nixon-Cobb (2005), for example, described her experience of the dissertation process to show how it fostered a shift in her conceptualization of issues of oppression and racism. At the start of the process, Nixon-Cobb felt enraged and immobilized by her sense of powerlessness as a woman of color who was required to navigate a doctoral program dominated by patriarchal politics. She encountered prejudice during the comprehensive exam and felt that her only option for completing the dissertation would be to subordinate her culture and experiences to the prerogatives of the dissertation committee. Nevertheless, the dissertation process did not turn out to be as restrictive as she had imagined. Even though her dissertation chair was not a person of color, she and her chair were able to find common language for exploring their experiences with oppression. Their common language then supported open, reflective dialogue about race relations and oppression. According to Nixon-Cobb, her willingness to confront her own assumptions and to see the value in the stories of others helped foster a dialogue with her dissertation chair that added to the meaningfulness of the dissertation process.

Also focusing on the importance of shared perspectives and experiences, Davis and Sutherland (2008) described the mentoring they received in a "boot camp" for African American doctoral students and junior scholars. The aim of the week-long experience was to help these emerging scholars increase their productivity as writers. The boot camp, in fact, assisted the women in making a transformation from feeling restrained by obstacles (such as disabling stereotypes) to seeing themselves as competent writers. According to the authors, one of the major reasons why the experience was so successful was that it provided a support system for emerging scholars. The women of color who served as mentors helped the junior scholars decrease their stress levels, cope with feelings of isolation and marginalization, and gain greater confidence in their abilities to conduct research and write research reports, including dissertations in many cases.

Jackson's (2007) article about her own dissertation work provided another reflection of how the dissertation process affected an individual whose identity category – in this case, her sexual orientation – at first seemed like an impediment to dissertation work but later made that work transformative. For her, the ability to use participatory qualitative research methods to study educators who also were gay or lesbian provided a way to make meaning in league with sympathetic compatriots. A supportive committee also made the process sufficiently safe to provide an important learning experience for Jackson herself and an opportunity for her participants to tell their stories.

# RACIAL IDENTITY DEVELOPMENT:
# A THEORETICAL FRAMEWORK

Whereas previous research has described the transformation many doctoral students undergo as a result of the dissertation process, the current study will explore the role of RID among doctoral students in education and related fields who conduct studies on topics related to race and ethnicity. The construct of racial identity is described here to illuminate the theoretical framework that served as the basis for the current inquiry.

Racial identity refers to a person's psychological response to his or her race. It entails not only a person's beliefs about and attitudes toward his or her own racial or cultural group but also that person's psychological reactions to the ways his or her group functions in relation to other groups, especially with regard to the group's status and power in the wider social setting (Carter, 1995; Phinney & Rotheram, 1987; Rosenthal, 1987).

As a psychological construct, RID reflects the extent to which identification with one's own racial group influences thinking, perceptions, emotions, and behaviors toward persons from other groups (Carter, 1995). The concept of RID has gained prominence over the last 40 years with the pioneering work of several racial identity theorists (Cross, 1971; Hardiman, 1979; Helms, 1984; Jackson, 1975), providing a major impetus to empirical research and further theorizing. Although several authors have created models and instruments to conceptualize and operationalize the constructs associated with racial identity, psychologist and researcher Janet Helms is among the most widely cited. Her work provided theories describing the developmental stages (later referred to as "statuses") of both White and Black racial identity (Helms,1990, 1995).

*White Racial Identity Development*

The five statuses of White RID in Helms' theory include: Contact, Disintegration, Reintegration, Pseudo-Independence, and Autonomy. The Contact status describes a position in which an individual who identifies as White has yet to encounter circumstances that involve close contact with racially different others. According to Helms (1990), Whites in the Contact status benefit from certain privileges and advantages as a result of their race, but are ultimately unaware of these advantages. The Disintegration status is described as a period of "dissonance" (Festinger, 1957) in which Whites begin to challenge previously learned negative assumptions about and attitudes towards Blacks (Helms, 1990). In the Reintegration status, cognitive dissonance begins to subside as feelings of White superiority become more salient; behaviors in this status may be active or passive, but often include negative actions and attitudes toward Blacks (Helms, 1990). The Pseudo-Independence status is characterized by intellectual acceptance of Blacks, accompanied by reduced feelings of White superiority (Helms, 1990). Attitudes in the Autonomy status include antiracist sentiments and commitments, supportive of actions to demonstrate the value of diversity and to promote inclusion (Helms, 1990).

### Black Racial Identity Development

Helms' (1990) theory of Black RID also contains five statuses: Pre-Encounter, Encounter, Immersion, Emersion, and Internalization. The Pre-Encounter status is characterized by denigration of traits associated with Blackness, accompanied by the tendency to idealize traits associated with Whiteness (Helms, 1990). Attitudes characteristic of the Encounter status are often shaped by a specific event that causes an individual to challenge or reject previously held negative beliefs about being Black. The Immersion status builds on the Encounter status and includes physical and psychological rejection of the dominant culture and in-depth immersion into the individual's own interpretation of Black culture (Helms, 1990). Individuals with racial identity attitudes described by the Emersion status are often more stable in their development than those in the previous statuses, tending to hold positive views of Blackness as a result of their increased knowledge, awareness, and appreciation for Black culture (Helms, 1990). The Internalization status is typified by attitudes similar to those characterizing Emersion, with an added propensity toward activism and advocacy; individuals in this final status function as change agents, working to combat racism and oppression (Helms, 1990).

As noted above, our broad research question is: How does the RID of doctoral students from colleges of education align with their experiences of conducting dissertation studies focusing on racial and/or ethnic dynamics in schools, universities, or human service agencies? Providing a context for this question is an extremely limited body of empirical work that sheds light on ways in which dissertation studies focusing on racial and ethnic dynamics might shape the identities of new scholars. Moreover, the extant studies most closely aligned with the research question all rely on autoethnographic methods. With such a limited set of relevant studies, many subsidiary questions associated with our overarching research questions still remain unanswered, specifically, (1) What personal attributes and commitments lead some doctoral students in education and related fields to choose dissertation studies that focus on racial or ethnic dynamics? (2) How do doctoral students whose studies focus on racial or ethnic dynamics interpret their experiences of the process of conducting dissertation research? (3) How do doctoral graduates who studied racial and/or ethnic dynamics for their dissertations apply what they learned to their personal and professional lives?

# METHODS

Discussion in this section focuses on the methods used to collect and analyze data pertinent to the experiences of dissertation writers whose research focused on racial and/or ethnic dynamics. It considers study design, instrumentation, selection of participants, collection of data, and data analysis.

## *Study Design*

The research used a mixed methods design because this approach, which combines quantitative and qualitative methods of data collection and analysis, provided useful tools for answering the overarching research question (and the related subsidiary questions) posed in the study. In particular, we used a sequential, balanced, mixed methods design (Creswell, 2009) whereby we collected quantitative survey data first, followed by the collection of qualitative data through semi-structured interviews. For this study, the design enabled us initially to gather descriptive statistical data on participants' RID, as assessed by the White Racial Identity Attitude Scale (WRIAS) and the Black Racial Identity Attitude Scale (BRIAS), and then to use in-depth, individual interviews to collect data about participants' experiences. The interview schedule included questions that elicited information about the relationship between participants' RID and their experiences conducting dissertation research on a topic relating to race and/or ethnicity. The study was balanced equally between the two methodologies; both the interview data and participants' scores on the WRIAS and the BRIAS were of equal importance during data collection, analysis and interpretation.


## Instrumentation

As noted above, we collected quantitative data using instruments designed to assess the RID of African American and White participants. To collect qualitative data, we relied on three researcher-developed interview schedules.

### Racial Identity Development Instruments

With White participants we used the WRIAS, a 50-item instrument, with 10 items representing each of the five subscales. The instrument is scored on a five-point Likert scale, with response options ranging from 1 to 5 (strongly disagree to strongly agree). The internal consistency reliabilities for each subscale are as follows: Contact $=.57$, Disintegration $=.77$, Reintegration $=.78$, Pseudo-independence $=.60$, Autonomy $=.53$ (Carter, Helms, & Juby, 2004). Despite these relatively low internal consistency reliabilities, some researchers have reported more robust test-retest reliabilities, with coefficients ranging from .64 to .86 over a one-month interval (Lemon & Waehler, 1996).

For African American participants, we used the BRIAS Long Form, which also includes 50 items scored on a five-point Likert scale, similar to the design of the WRIAS; however, unlike the WRIAS, the BRIAS Long Form has a different number of items in each subscale. Helms and Parham (1996) reported internal consistency reliabilities for the 50-item version of the BRIAS Long Form; Pre-Encounter (18 items) $=.60$, Encounter (6 items) $=.54$, Immersion/Emersion (12 items) $=.83$, and Internalization (14 items) $=.76$. The test-retest reliabilities for the BRIAS Long Form subscales over a one-month interval ranged from .52 to .66 (Lemon & Waehler, 1996).

As the relatively low reliability estimates on some subscale suggest, scores from both the WRIAS and the BRIAS need to be treated circumspectly. Furthermore, some research has found that these instruments are susceptible to social desirability bias (e.g., Abrams & Trusty, 2004).


### Interview Schedules

We developed three interview schedules that allowed participants to reflect and comment on (1) their RID, (2) the focus and findings of their dissertation

***Table 1.*** Interview Schedules.

| Interview | Questions |
| --- | --- |
| First interview | In what ways did the results of the WRAIS or RAIS-B represent what you see as your racial identity status? |
| | In what ways did the results disagree with how the WRAIS or RAIS-B results characterize your racial identity status? |
| | What else do you want to say about your racial identity? |
| | How does your racial identity reflect the way you were raised as a child and adolescent? |
| | How does your racial identity influence how you interact with colleagues and clients in the workplace? |
| | How does your racial identity influence your moral commitments? |
| Second interview | What did your dissertation study concern? |
| | Why did you choose to study this topic or issue? |
| | What were your findings? |
| | What was surprising in your findings? |
| | How did your findings influence your construction or interpretation of the social world? |
| Third interview | How did the dissertation process affect your life? |
| | How did the particular focus of your study influence your interactions with your committee members or the construction of your committee? |
| | How did the particular focus of your study influence your interactions with other candidates in your program and/or college? |
| | How did the IRB work to enable you to conduct (or restrain you from conducting) the study you wanted to conduct? |
| | In what ways did the focus of your study influence the character of your interactions with study participants? |

studies, and (3) the connection between their dissertations studies and their lives. The questions structuring each interview are presented in Table 1.

## *Participants*

To select participants, we reviewed dissertations completed in three Ohio colleges of education between 2005 and 2011 and identified all such dissertations that related to racial and/or ethnic dynamics in the United States. Once we had assembled this list, we contacted the doctoral graduates who had written these dissertations to ask if they would be willing to participate in the study.

Our study focused on seven participants, all of whom had recently completed dissertations relating to racial and/or ethnic dynamics. Four of the participants were White, and three were African American. Five were women, and two were men. Their programs of study included Higher Education (two participants), Educational Administration (two participants), and Curriculum and Instruction (three participants).

## Data Collection

We mailed consent forms to each of the individuals who indicated willingness to participate along with a copy of the Black Racial Identity Attitude Scale (BRIAS; Helms, 1990, 1995; Helms & Parham, 1996) and the White Racial Identity Attitude Scale (WRIAS; Helms, 1990, 1995; Helms & Parham, 1996) so that the participant could complete the correct form. We included an ID number on each of these forms and asked participants not to include their names. We also included two self-addressed stamped envelopes for participants to use in returning (1) the WRIAS or BRIAS in one envelope and (2) the consent form in the other envelope. This process assured that no one other than the researchers would able to identify the individual who completed the WRIAS or BRIAS.

Following the receipt of a participant's consent, one of the researchers conducted an introductory semi-structured interview with the participant. Following this interview, a member of the research team arranged a second and then a third interview with each of the participants. All interviews were audio recorded and transcribed verbatim. The transcripts of the interviews formed the data set that the researchers analyzed for the qualitative portion of the study.

## Data Analysis

Qualitative data analysis proceeded in three steps. First, one of the researchers read a participant's three interviews and coded relevant passages. Second, that researcher used a structured protocol for characterizing in an individual profile the participant's dissertation experiences and responses to those experiences. A second researcher also coded the data for each individual and verified the accuracy of the profile created by the first researcher. The profiles became the basis for cross-case analysis. This third step in the process involved all researchers in a discussion of the codes and categories used to construct the separate profiles. This discussion led to the identification of (1) important similarities across participants, (2) important differences among participants, and (3) patterns that might help explain the relevant similarities and differences. The researchers used matrices to characterize similarities and differences and to verify the existence of relevant patterns.

Quantitative data analysis entailed scoring the racial identity instruments completed by all of the participants. For each participant, we produced a graph showing the pattern of scores. We also created graphs of all scores for participants from each racial group. We used the individual and combined profiles to help explain patterns that emerged from the analysis of qualitative data.


# FINDINGS


In order to contextualize the thematic findings, we first present aggregated information about the participants. Then we turn attention to one of the most salient themes revealed in our cross-case analysis.

Scores on the BRIAS and WRIAS showed that all participants tended to score higher on the subscales measuring the final two statuses, while scoring lower on the subscales measuring the first three statuses. The fact that participants primarily operated in the higher statuses of RID may have played a role in their selection of dissertation topics related to race and/or ethnic dynamics. Although all participants, African American and White, scored higher in the latter statuses of RID, the White participants' scores on the Contact subscale were higher than their scores on the Disintegration or Reintegration subscales (see Fig. 1). This finding indicates that attitudes and behaviors associated with the Contact status (such as limited interaction with racially different others) may be more readily available to and easily accessed by these participants than attitudes described by the Disintegration or Reintegration statuses. For this group of participants, scores were highest in the Pseudo-independence and Autonomy statuses, indicating positive attitudes and expressions of White identity, with an intellectual awareness of and stated commitment to eliminating racism (Helms, 1990).

For the three Black participants, the latter statuses of Emersion and Internalization scores were the highest subscale scores, while the earlier statuses of Pre-Encounter, Encounter, and Immersion scores were lower, suggesting that attitudes and behaviors described by the latter two statuses

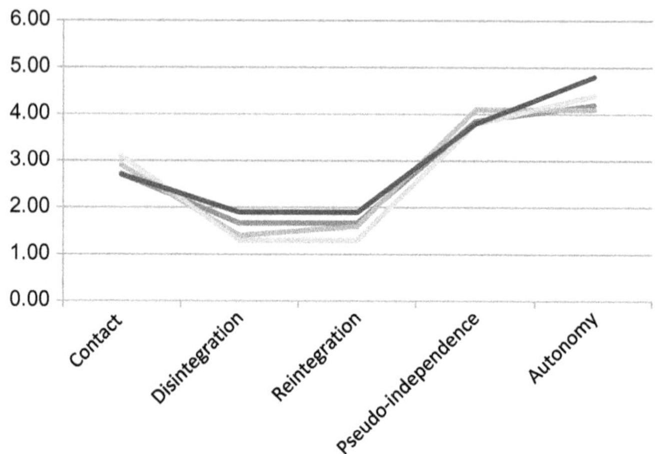


*Fig. 1.*   Combined WRIAS Profiles.

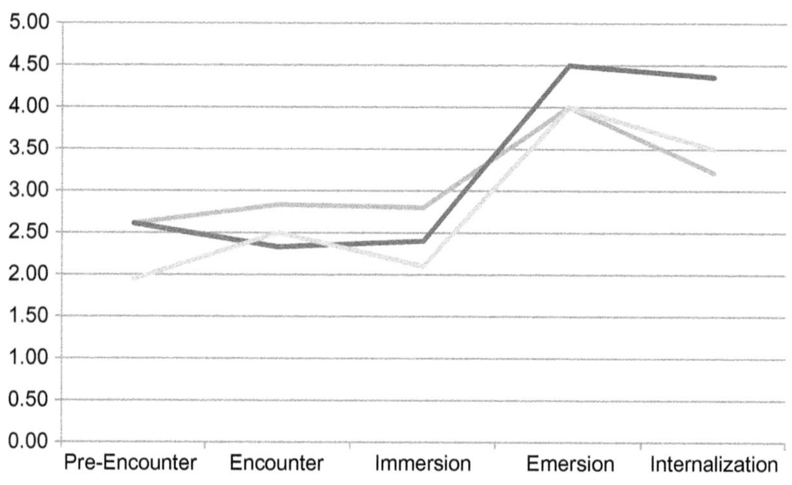


*Fig. 2.*   Combined BRIAS Profiles.

were more salient for these participants (see Fig. 2). Participants in this group likely possess positive attitudes toward Black identity and culture, exhibited by highest scores on the Emersion scale for all three participants. The second highest scores for this group were on the Internalization scale.

While the Emersion status is highlighted by an increased level of comfort with racially-similar peers, individuals who operate in the Internalization status may be described as stable in their own racial identity while also able to engage effectively with racially different others (Helms, 1990).

Comparing between-group differences among the responses of the two participant groups, a few findings are worth noting. As mentioned previously, the White participants scored higher in the first status, Contact, when compared to their scores on Disintegration and Reintegration. While the average Contact subscale score was 2.85, the subscale scores for Disintegration and Reintegration were 1.57 and 1.62, respectively. The average scores for the African American participants on the second and third statuses of Black RID (Encounter and Emersion) were about one point higher at 2.55 and 2.43.

Although the WRIAS and BRIAS are separate instruments, measuring distinct constructs, the underlying theories share certain parallels; both models are progressively developmental, and the authors of each model note that more than one status may be accessed at any given time (Helms, 1990; Helms & Parham, 1996). While participants in both groups were more likely to access attitudes in the latter statuses of RID, as indicated by higher subscale scores, the African American participants might have been more likely than the White participants to revert to the attitudes and behaviors of the previous two statuses of development (i.e., Encounter and Immersion on the BRIAS and Disintegration and Reintegration on the WRIAS).

### Interpretation of Participants' RID Scores

For participants in this study, in-depth exposure to concepts related to race and racial identity theory during the dissertation process could have played a role in RID, leading to identification with higher statuses, within both participant groups. Although all participants in the current study scored highest in the final two statuses of RID (Pseudo-Independence and Autonomy for Whites and Emersion and Internalization for Blacks), we acknowledge social desirability might have played a role in both sets of responses. Abrams and Trusty (2004) found evidence that the BRIAS was not immune to social desirability, especially in response to items on the Internalization scale. In contrast, dissertation research by Jome (2000) and Kurtzweil (1996) showed that WRIAS scores were not particularly responsive to social desirability. Nevertheless, we remain open to the possibility that either our African American or our White participants may have chosen response choices that portrayed them as further along the developmental continuum than they actually are.

In addition to the potential for social desirability, fluctuations between scores for both groups could also be explained by technical limitations of the WRIAS and BRIAS, including relatively low subscale reliabilities. Notably, the lower test-retest reliabilities of the measures provide limited evidence to suggest the WRIAS and the BRIAS may identify "state" as opposed to "trait" personality characteristics; whereas state characteristics of personality vary in response to recent circumstances or events, trait characteristics are more stable (Lemon &Waehler, 1996).

In their interviews, the African American participants described ongoing challenges they perceived to be related to their race, such as barriers to promotion and fear of unemployment. Such challenges were significant in the lives of these participants and may have contributed to moderate elevations in scores in the earlier statuses of development (Pre-Encounter, Emersion, Immersion). For White participants in this study, higher Contact scores, paired with lower Disintegration and Reintegration scores may also be reflective of current environmental characteristics as opposed to more enduring personality traits. For example, several White participants discussed limited interaction, currently, with people who are racially or ethnically diverse. Additionally, this pattern may also speak to the fact that there is a mental acknowledgement and desire to eliminate racism. However, the interviews with White participants contained limited references to active antiracist advocacy – a set of commitments and practices that higher scores on the Pseudo-Independence and Autonomy subscales implicate.

Further examination of scores on the middle two statuses for both groups of participants (Disintegration and Reintegration on the WRIAS and Encounter and Immersion on the BRIAS) also yielded unanticipated findings. As mentioned previously, the Black participants scored, on average, about one point higher on these two middle statuses, when compared to the White participants in the study. Again, we acknowledge the WRIAS and BRIAS are separate instruments, measuring distinct constructs; however, the developmental parallels are worth noting. For the Black participants, Encounter and Emersion scores near mid-range of the scale (around 2.5 on a 5 point scale) could be indicative of conflict and turmoil as a result of ongoing struggles related to race and ethnicity, on the one hand or of social desirability bias (i.e., a tendency to "blame the Man" for one's problems), on the other. For the White participants, lower scores on Disintegration and Integration (between 1 and 2 on a 5 point scale) could potentially indicate a genuine rejection of attitudes of denigration toward Blacks or the desire to appear less racist by providing socially desirable responses. An alternate explanation could be a combination of both factors, or simply limited interaction with Blacks, reducing the likelihood of critical incidents related to race.

In addition to fluctuations between scores associated with earlier developmental statuses, the findings also revealed unexpected results on scores in the latter statuses of RID. For all three Black participants, subscale scores on the Emersion status were higher than scores on Internalization. One explanation could be the presence of daily micro- aggressions related to race, a circumstance described clearly by Black participants in their interviews. Reactions to environmental factors, such as institutionalized racism in workplace settings, as mentioned by one participant, can potentially lead to an ever-present and heightened sense of awareness. For these participants the status of Emersion might reflect the need for a refuge where they can feel free to be themselves while being supported by Black friends and colleagues without judgment, evaluation, or the need for explanation. These individuals might, therefore, maintain a high sense of self-worth and a positive view of the world yet may not fully actualize the "common people-hood" attitudes described by the Internalization status (Helms, 1990, p. 31).

## Thematic Interpretation of Data

Analysis of interview data revealed two categories explaining commonalities across participants and constituting a theme best described with the phrase, "the centrality of advocacy to the professional mission of participants." This theme and the two categories comprising it enabled us to make sense of the role that doctoral study played in the lives of the seven doctoral graduates we interviewed. We named the two analytic categories "research as an opportunity for advancement (advocacy on behalf of self)" and "research as an opportunity for promoting social justice (advocacy on behalf of others)." As denoted by their subtitles, both categories represented forms of advocacy – the details of which we discuss below. Before we consider each category separately, however, we provide a brief explication of what advocacy meant for the participants in general and how it connected to their research efforts.

First, despite their use of different terms – "advocacy," "being an ally," "hearing their voice," "mediating," and "mentoring" – most participants shared the understanding that a nexus of activities that contributed to agency on their own behalf also contributed to agency on behalf of marginalized others. These participants expressed the belief, moreover, that advocacy efforts were properly exercised as part of their professional practice, and most treated professional advancement as a warrant for expanded advocacy on behalf of others.

Second, all of the participants recounted events in their personal histories that led them to treat advocacy on their own behalf and/or advocacy on behalf of others as a crucial part of their life's work and also to view the pursuit of higher education as a strategy for supporting their advocacy efforts. For these participants, all of whom worked in the education sector, schools, colleges, and other educational institutions were sites for advocacy; and educational processes such as teaching and mentoring were vehicles for promoting improvements in their own circumstances and the circumstances of marginalized students and clients.

Increased competence as a researcher accompanied by the attainment of an advanced degree, then, became a central force in moving forward most participants' advocacy: a mutually supportive agenda of continued advocacy on behalf of self and stronger advocacy on behalf of others, particularly within the workplace. In a sense, the enactment of advocacy as a two-pronged strategy of self-advocacy and other-advocacy represented what some writers have characterized as the "calling" that undergirds professional work (e.g., Burnett, 2003; Hall, 1969).

As noted above, both self-advocacy and other-advocacy represented responses to the participants' own life circumstances – in most cases as an enactment and extension of commitments that had been shaped in childhood by their families of origin. In two cases, by contrast, participants' advocacy for self and others represented an intentional rejection of the choices made by their families of origin.

Finally, we found that participants whose own backgrounds were sufficiently privileged to give them a sense of entitlement focused less attention than others on using their dissertations and related research efforts to achieve career advancement, acquire voice, gain entrée to positions that would continue to enable them to work as advocates, or sustain advocacy efforts beyond the workplace. In the discussion below, in which we elaborate findings from the two analytic categories, we explore these dynamics in greater detail.

## RESEARCH AS AN OPPORTUNITY FOR ADVANCEMENT (ADVOCACY ON BEHALF OF SELF)

All participants perceived their doctoral studies as stemming from dual motives, the commitment to social justice and the desire to gain greater authority. Attainment of an advanced degree became a means by which advocacy for others could be realized, but the personal benefits of advancing one's career and status also motivated participants, although to varying extents.

Although each participant's circumstance was unique, one similarity among them was the perceived importance of becoming a voice of authority. The following passage tells the story of one African American participant for whom the dissertation process was essential to her ability to advance her career as a professor. Despite her career advancement, however, she still experienced departmental inequities that she believed were related to her race:

> I'm a professor [now], and so I started off…as a part time instructor. I was working on my doctorate at the same time that I was teaching part time classes, and so once I finished up my coursework…I got a full-time, non-tenure track position . …When I was applying for that non-tenure track position, there [were] a lot of hurdles I had to jump…to even get the position. I interviewed three times for the position, and I was denied three times. Some of the people that had gotten the position before me weren't as qualified as I [was], in regards to education. People that had a bachelor's degree beat me out…. And by the third time, I was just fed up, and I decided to file a discrimination case against the school, and that's how I ended up getting my full time non-tenure track position, because I filed that discrimination case. I just became tenure-track. …And, I'll actually be the first African American tenure track in my department…When I applied for the position for tenure track, some of the faculty were saying they don't know if…I would be a good fit for the department. They were saying things like, "She's going to need a lot of mentoring in order for her to be able to get to her tenure, and I don't know if we have the capability to give her the mentoring that she needs." …my department director has tried to say to me…that race has nothing to with the situation. I feel like it does, because…out of the [department] faculty, there are only two individuals who have a Ph.D.: one colleague, and then myself. So, everyone else has a [master's], so they're still questioning me even after I've completed my Ph.D., saying, "we don't know if she's going to be qualified enough." (Wanda, Interview 1)

This participant had to seek additional education *outside of her professional field* (Interview 2, p. 5) in order to be accepted *by her professional field*, and she was willing to do so in order to obtain the authority associated with the status of a doctoral degree and a professorial position.

Furthermore, this participant was willing to make significant sacrifices in her life in order to reach this goal – sacrifices others may not have seen as tenable. She also suffered a range of frustrations associated with the membership and functioning of her dissertation committee. But she saw these sacrifices and frustrations as necessary to the cause of her advancement. In her case, the phrase, "the personal is political," seemed to apply. As an African American woman, this participant felt a responsibility to fight for authority, legitimacy, and equality for herself and for African American women in general, and everything about her story – from her choice of dissertation topic (which related to female African American high school students) to her focus on mentoring African American students – spoke to this mission.

For one White participant, doctoral study enhanced opportunities for advancement as a school administrator with increased influence in the district where she worked. Ironically, while completion of her degree enhanced her ability to serve the disadvantaged students and families about whom she was concerned, it also widened the distance between her and those children and families:

> It [the dissertation study] made me more aware that the students experience the school much differently than I perceived them to, as an administrator, and they feel somewhat disconnected, depending on their poverty, their race, their geographic location to the central school site. So, there [were] varying degrees of disconnectivity [sic]. And, a lot of that disconnectivity was blamed toward the "they." "They" did this to me; "they" did that. And, it made me…aware that I am perceived as the "they," because I'm a school official, and I'm a principal. And it wasn't specifically me that they were talking about, but that I'm in that group of people who have influence and power over schools, and they feel like that people do these things to them…That was disheartening—to feel lumped into that category. (Molly, Interview 3)

This participant welcomed the opportunity to develop authority through doctoral studies, particularly as a way to strengthen her influence in the region where she worked, but she also found it important to downplay the disconnects described above by identifying herself, not as a scholar, but as a "practitioner" (Molly, Interview 2).

For another White participant, becoming a voice of authority meant access to new networks and speaking opportunities, as well as to a new kind of respect she had not anticipated, but seemed to welcome. For this participant, being expert in a particular branch of African American women's history meant that she could fulfill an important academic function at the nearly all-White, rural college where she taught.

> I've met wonderful people, been networking, and folks just keep asking me to do things because of it, and just when I get to the point where I think I want to switch gears and do something else with my research interests, it pops back up, and I probably really should not put it away entirely…And certainly, when it [the dissertation process] was all over and they started inviting me to things …then you really feel, "I guess I'm the reigning expert on this." (Barbara, Interview 3)

For another participant, an African American male, self-advocacy, what he termed "self-sufficiency," was a central motive for educational advancement in general. For this participant, placing value on self-sufficiency had its genesis in his father's beliefs and manifested professionally as a commitment to serving in many different capacities in his career in academia.

> …my father talked about it in some of the other ways. Just from his upbringing…was the fact, in terms of dealing with—he dealt with race in another context, meaning that his family grew up in [a] rural [state], and so, as far as making the playing field equal, it was ownership—like property, and so forth. And, so, basically, instead of education being the value that we're talking [about], his focus was, "Well, you have to own property." And, property leveled the playing field, because if you owned property, you could dictate your future, either growing your own crops, build your own house, become self-sustaining…And, he became very, very sustaining. (Dwight, Interview 1)

For this participant more than others, attaining a Ph.D. helped him achieve a personal goal of being "self-sustaining." This motive, however, did not keep him from focusing his dissertation on the social justice issues to which he was deeply committed. Indeed, even though advocacy for self was the more salient motive for this participant, his dissertation concerned the marginalization of African Americans who were engaged in a graduate level program.

This participant's focus on having multiple means of self-sustenance translated into a drive for multiple sources of income, and he achieved this goal by working for not one but *three* different universities. Despite his extraordinary efforts, however, he acknowledged that he was often treated inequitably or with just a semblance of equity. Although he experienced the negative consequences of the White privilege and entitlement that pervades institutions of higher education as well as other social institutions, he nonetheless pushed forward so that he and his nuclear family would have more options and resources than were available to members of his extended family in the generation before.

## RESEARCH AS AN OPPORTUNITY FOR PROMOTING SOCIAL JUSTICE (ADVOCACY ON BEHALF OF OTHERS)

As was the case with their use of research for self-advocacy, participants' use of research for other-advocacy differed based on personal experience, temperament, and perspective. In this case, moreover, both race and social class seemed to be associated with evident differences in how participants viewed and enacted the connected work of research and advocacy.

Among the seven participants, six provided comments about how their ongoing professional practice would embed advocacy that had been informed by their dissertation research. For two participants, one White, one African American, continuing research was part of that advocacy. In particular, one anticipated that her role as a faculty member would entail research that expanded on her dissertation work:

> I'm still quite interested in why is it that some inner city kids make it, and why other don't. So many others don't. You know, very few make it out of the inner city, make it into successful jobs, you know, and you hear about those anomaly type stories every now and again, and then when you look at the overall inner city, a lot of those people are so stagnant, and just don't get that there's other things in this world besides what they see in their own neighborhoods. (Wanda, Interview 2)

And the other participant who spoke of continuing the research she had started with her dissertation study saw this effort as a way to discover more about African American educational leaders – a research agenda she pursued as the basis for helping mostly White colleagues and students increase their appreciation for the contributions of African Americans.

> This is, sort of, the dissertation that has never stopped. In fact, Friday, I'm presenting to the faculty forum … about this research, and I was quite surprised to be asked to do that so soon after just being hired. I got an email today asking me to be part of a grant … because they heard about my research through an email about my faculty forum presentation. (Barbara, Interview 3)

These two participants saw the role of researcher as deeply connected to their professional commitment to the role of advocate. For the other four participants who linked their dissertation research to their advocacy work, the linkage was less direct. Notably, these participants did not anticipate extensions of their dissertation research as a way to fuel continuing advocacy efforts but rather saw their dissertation research and subsequent degree completion as support for professional insights and expertise that enhanced their current advocacy efforts.

Although all four of the participants in this category made comments showing how dissertation work contributed to their credibility, the two from less privileged backgrounds were more vocal about the connection – a circumstance suggesting that the connection may have been more important to them than it was for the participants from more privileged backgrounds. Contrasting quotes from a school administrator (who came from a lower-SES background) and an elementary school teacher (who came from a higher-SES background) illustrate this difference:

> I think ever since I've done my dissertation, and I focused on minority groups, I'm more of an advocate, you know? I'm more informed. I realize that, that I come from a socioeconomic group that's very different, *as far as where I am as an adult—not as a child, but as an adult*—and so, my world views are so influenced by the people I'm around, and we have more assets and resources available to us, so it's, like, it helped me to be not so naive about what other people experience and what other people feel. (Molly, Interview 3, emphasis added)

> I think that that study and that experience really will change the way that I think about schools and how I share it with my students, you know, whether I'm in a K-12 school, whether I'm in a college setting, whether I'm an administrator. But, I really think that that experience will impact *others in my career*. (Robyn, Interview 2, emphasis added)

Note that, while both participants talked about how their dissertation studies would connect to their continuing advocacy, for the school administrator, personal social status (which had changed from lower class to middle class) was relevant to the conversation, but for the teacher it was not. This pattern was evident among other participants as well. As we discuss below, moreover, the school administrator alone among the White participants extended advocacy on behalf of others into her personal as well as her professional life.

Not only did participants' social class backgrounds influence how they connected research to advocacy, so too did race. For the African American participants, the connection was personal – and in two different ways.

First, their motives for studying particular groups came from their affinity with these groups. In particular, their own stories were integrally bound up with the stories of those whom they studied. One quote illustrates this perspective:

> I was a ... low-income and first-generation college student...and, I was actually in a Trio program.... But once I started to work in high ed., I noticed ... the program that I worked in, we tried to provide everything ... that was possible. And so I think ... my experience as an undergrad student at a predominantly White institution, and then, later on, working in the very same program ... I thought, well what, you know, what do these students think they need? And, especially, sometimes when they weren't using the services that we thought...were best. So, I was just curious to know, after working in the program for eight or nine years, you know, what do students think they need...just what could we do to offer what they need...? (Mary Lynne, Interview 2)

So too does a quote from another African American participant:

> That was a big thing for me because I just want to know more. I want to know more about myself, too. What was it that I had inside of me? And, that's the main reason why

> I did the dissertation topic that I did, is because I wanted to find out, you know, what
> was it about me [the drive to attend college]? (Wanda, Interview 2)

Second, for these participants, advocacy on behalf of others involved providing direct support to individual African American students – a stance that reflected the connections among their personal histories, the enhanced sense of personal agency resulting from their dissertation research, and their ongoing commitment to a social justice mission both in personal and professional life. One passage in particular characterizes this stance:

> If I had to think about a lot of the things that I've had to endure because of the fact that
> I am Black, I probably would favor my African American students a little bit
> more...than my other students. Because, you know, I feel like, you know, they've
> probably gotten so much unnecessary crap from other people, and need a little bit of a
> cushion. But because of the fact that I know that everybody needs to be treated equally
> and because of the fact that my moral standards just won't allow me, I wouldn't feel
> comfortable, even though I know they probably need a little bit of extra, you know,
> whatever they need...morally I just wouldn't feel comfortable doing that. I extend
> myself to them in other ways. (Wanda, Interview 1)

For the African American participants, direct support for students and clients involved mentoring and other forms of educational scaffolding. According to the same participant quoted above,

> I make myself available for mentoring kinds of things, like, if you want to go to lunch,
> let's go to lunch and talk, or, you know, if you need extra office hours, you know,
> assistance, you know, come to office hours. Come see me. So, I do extra things like that,
> and I make sure that they know that I'm present in the African American community on
> campus, so I make sure that I go to a lot of things where I might see my African
> American students. So they ... see that I'm ... on their side. (Wanda, interview 1)

In contrast to an intensely personal strategy for providing advocacy, White participants tended to favor a more diffuse, didactic approach. We use the word "didactic" here to refer to instructional events addressed to groups of people – most often people from dominant or mainstream groups. A small-group consciousness-raising session illustrates the didactic approach, as does a classroom lesson about the contributions of African Americans to educational leadership.

The White participants described their advocacy efforts as addressing two aims – broadening the perspectives of White people and enforcing equal opportunity. For one, work to broaden perspectives fit with a role he described as "being an ally:"

> A lot of it comes down to awareness raising, and there's always this question of, what's
> after awareness raising? [But] I'm not sure that we've been able to identify a whole lot

> past that. Specifically, what I'm talking about, though, in regards to the students and myself, is (1) self-awareness—increasing the (self) awareness of other peoples' experiences, and (2) your own role in privilege. Those are two of the big steps, I think, for allies of any sort. (Walt, interview 2)

According to this participant, not only did the ally role entail efforts to demonstrate solidarity with marginalized students, it also involved camaraderie with others who were taking on a similar role. Additionally, for this participant, broadening perspectives also involved expanding dialog beyond what was helpful in supporting the work of allies:

> [My dissertation] helped me identify that … probably the most important step that … I could take as a professional would be to support inter-racial dialogue on campuses, and so that's something that I'm working [on] now. (Walt, Interview 3)

Another's efforts to broaden perspectives functioned in somewhat different ways. Notably, this participant used her role as a school principal to expand the cultural sensitivity and reduce the racist behavior of White students. Note in the passage below that she talked about focusing her energy on combatting "race as a marker of difference," not on offering direct support to the African American student who was being bullied.

> I try to be very committed to making sure that race isn't a marker of difference that is used against them…. Like I had a parent this year come and report that their daughter was being made fun of on the bus because she does dreadlocks in her hair, and the daughter is Black. So, you know, I had to make sure that I really followed up on that and I monitored the situation, and not just say, "don't do that; don't call her that," explain why that's wrong and why that's not appropriate. (Molly, Interview 1)

One participant, who sometimes called herself an "advocate," also described her role as "being a mediator." She characterized this role in terms of speaking out *on behalf of* others – sharing with students and colleagues evidence of African Americans' significant contributions to the history of the United States. This role involved "mediation" in the sense of providing a bridge between the current perspectives of her White auditors and what she hoped would be a more enlightened future perspective.

Although this participant shared her research on African American leaders with various audiences, she seemed most passionate about using her research to augment class activities designed to expand the perspectives of undergraduates. She described the following activity as one she was going to use in the near future, and she also talked about her desire to find other ways that her research might inform what and how she taught.

> Then we're going to do a little study on the people [i.e., educational leaders mentioned in the course textbook] they picked, and we're going to say, "Who's missing from this?"

> Because, I know who's in that book. There aren't any ... Black women in there. (Barbara, Interview 3)

For some White participants, taking actions to ensure that all students had equal educational opportunities was as important as helping White people expand their perspectives. Quotes from two participants character-ized this perspective:

> ... I hope to be an administrator someday, and I think it really changed the way that I think about the responsibility of a school leader, to make sure that students are given equal opportunities—that it's a democratic educational environment where students are treated fairly, and that students are not discriminated against, and that students from privileged backgrounds, and students that are Caucasian are not given privileges and opportunities for education over students of color and students from ... economically disadvantaged backgrounds. (Robyn, Interview 3)

> I just think that, whether I were a teacher or whatever, I think it's my obligation morally to try to make the world a better place, and I think that the definition of a better place, for me, is a world where, you know, the playing field isn't based upon what color of skin you are. (Molly, Interview 1)

Contrasting with the direct ways that dissertation research supported the advocacy work of six participants was a less direct connection in the work of the seventh participant. For this individual, who worked as a faculty mem-ber and department chair, dissertation research gave him a strong basis for providing guidance to doctoral students with whom he had started to work:

> I've been able to apply, and actually guide, learners in the direction I've gone through. And, that's from opportunities from my original committee, and I still apply those rubrics, and so forth. And, I can understand their struggles, as well, when they have life issues and things that have come up. So, that's really been able to really assist me.

Note that for this participant, as for other African American participants, "advocacy" involved providing personal support to students. But in this case, advocacy had little connection to the race or social class of the people with whom he worked. Indeed, for this participant, there was value in "being invisible" (Dwight, Interview 1) – a circumstance that online teaching enabled both for him and for the students with whom he worked.

As the analysis showed, pursuit of a doctoral degree through the dissertation process was a simultaneous enactment of current commitments and a broadening of the toolkit for addressing those commitments. Curiously, despite the fact that all of the participants had recently come to embrace the role of researcher to some extent through completion of a doctoral dissertation, only two talked about the publication of their dissertation research as a way to enact their advocacy role, and these two saw the effort more as a way to advance their own careers than as a first step in engaging advocacy through ongoing dissemination of scholarship.

### *Potential Influence of Participants' Race*

In the context of the interview data, examination of scores on the WRIAS and BRIAS uncovered curious patterns related to the personal and professional advocacy of both groups of participants. These patterns suggested that White participants were more likely to confine advocacy to the professional realm, whereas African American participants were somewhat more likely to undertake advocacy that bridged personal and professional life. Nevertheless, for both groups, incomplete realization of the highest racial identity status appeared to make advocacy at work more comfortable and perhaps less threatening than advocacy in the personal domain of family and community.

These speculations were supported by evidence in the qualitative data suggesting that the RID of White participants may have been more consistent with the status of Pseudo-independence (a status supporting intellectualization) as opposed to Autonomy (a status supporting action).In fact, only one participant (Molly) provided concrete examples of continuing commitment to advocacy in her personal life. She described changes to her worldview, as a result of repeated interactions during her dissertation research with students and families from diverse racial, ethnic, and economic background. Viewing these interactions as eye-opening, she talked about applying what she learned not just to her work as a school administrator but also to her role as a parent.

For the African American participants, the qualitative data appeared to be consistent with a pattern of advocacy that aligned with their high scores on the Emersion subscale. In particular, these participants revealed a strong commitment to professional advocacy and a relatively weaker commitment to advocacy in their communities or in the wider political sphere. Notably, many of their efforts were confined to direct support to the African American students and clients to whom they provided service. Whereas this analysis certainly does not belittle their efforts, it does suggest that they may have felt some discomfort with direct confrontation of dynamics of oppression with co-workers in their places of employment and in their home communities.

Interpretations linking the participants' racial identity profiles with the interview data are, of course, tentative. Various limitations relating to instrument reliability, social desirability bias, and very small sample size suggest the need for caution in treating these findings as anything other than speculative.

# DISCUSSION

Findings from this study contributed to insights and conjectures about the ways RID and socioeconomic status intersected with the choice of dissertation topic, the challenges of dissertation research, and the outcomes of doctoral completion for a group of African American and White doctoral students in colleges of education. In particular, African American participants came to the study of a topic relating to dynamics of race and/or ethnicity from their own experiences of racism, and they decided to pursue doctoral work in response to their strong belief that the degree would provide them with both a measure of career security and a platform for continuing and expanding advocacy efforts – beneficial outcomes they saw as inter-dependent. In other words, for these participants the link between advocacy on behalf of self and advocacy on behalf of others tended to be close.

White participants, by contrast, were somewhat more varied both in the extent to which they linked the two forms of advocacy and in the strength of their ongoing advocacy efforts. Except for one of these participants, oppression was not an experience they understood emically, and therefore their advocacy was not constitutive of identity. This insight in no way minimizes the contributions of these professionals to social justice – either through their research or through their professional work. But it does suggest that deeper engagement with issues of oppression and ongoing relationships with people from other racial and ethnic backgrounds might be useful for encouraging them to pursue a more thorough-going approach to advocacy – an approach that might extend their commitments from what education researchers term "cultural competence" to something more radically transformative.

# IMPLICATIONS FOR EXPANDING AND MOVING BEYOND CULTURAL COMPETENCE

As our findings revealed, the seven participants used their dissertation studies to express and build on culture competence. Especially for the White dissertation researchers, investigations relating to the experiences of African American and multiracial individuals increased cultural sensitivity and knowledge. Molly, for example, came to understand the multiple disadvantages influencing the experiences of the low-income, multiracial families that she studied. Robyn's status as a White, middle-class teacher enabled her to learn about the debilitating racial prejudices and classism that prevailed in the school where she conducted her study; and Barbara's historical study exposed her to surprising information about how racial discrimination shaped the experiences of Black professionals even though these individuals were elite members of the African American community. Although their racial identity statuses, which tended to reflect Pseudo-independence and Autonomy, predisposed these dissertation researchers to understand and be sensitive to dynamics of racism and classism, their studies contributed to deeper and more systematic knowledge of the dynamics of racism and oppression. Nevertheless, given their prior commitments and the insights revealed by their studies, their plans to build on their dissertation work were, as we indicate above, somewhat modest and mostly confined to the professional domain.

For the African American participants, dissertation research confirmed but did not add to knowledge about such dynamics. This knowledge was already part of these participants' *own* experiences. Nevertheless, their dissertation research strengthened the resolve to use their professional roles to provide direct support to the students with whom they worked. Mary Lynn and Wanda, perhaps more than Dwight, saw immediate applicability of what they had learned both in their dissertation studies and in the complicated and often frustrating process of completing the doctoral degree. From their perspective, the experience added force to an existing commitment to provide mentoring to African American adolescents and young adults. Moreover, all three came away from the experience with insights about how educational attainment through conventional channels (e.g., completion of a doctoral degree in a mainstream institution) both contributed to and simultaneously undermined social transformation. Dwight and Wanda, in particular, had encountered significant impediments to the completion of their research, and both understood that their experiences and accomplishments had done little to change the structures and values of the institutions with which they had interacted.

This analysis leads to questions about whether or not curricular experiences to increase *cultural competence* among students in colleges of education – including support for their studies of racial and ethnic dynamics – are sufficiently powerful and far reaching. As we discovered, even intensive engagement with dissertation research focusing on racial and/or ethnic dynamics contributed primarily to strengthening already existing commitments. Notably, none of our participants came away from their dissertation work with an explicit plan for engaging advocacy in intensive ways, for example as grassroots organizers or public intellectuals. Whereas modest and somewhat circumscribed advocacy efforts, such as those undertaken by our participants, clearly contribute to social justice, they may not be sufficient to foster the sorts of social transformation that some colleges of education seek (see e.g., Cochran-Smith, 1995, 2004; Hayes & Juárez, 2012; Katsarou, Picower, & Stovall, 2010; Porfilio & Malott, 2011).

## ACKNOWLEDGMENT

The research team wishes to thank Longun Moses Lado for his help with data collection.

## REFERENCES

Abrams, L., & Trusty, J. (2004). African Americans' racial identity and socially desirable responding: An empirical model. *Journal of Counseling & Development, 82*, 365–374. doi: 10.1002/j.1556-6678.2004.tb00322.x

Adams, G. B., & White, J. D. (1994). Dissertation research in public administration and cognate fields: An assessment of methods and quality. *Public Administration Review, 54*, 565–576.

Andrews, R. (2007). Argumentation, critical thinking and the postgraduate dissertation. *Educational Review, 59*(1), 1–18.

Burnett, C. (2003). Passion through the profession: Being both activist and academic. *Social Justice, 30*(4), 135–150.

Canen, A. (2007). Multiculturalism and a research perspective in initial teacher education: Possible dialogues. *Policy Futures in Education, 5*(4), 519–534.

Carillo, T. A. (1990). Promoting multicultural dissertation research in a Eurocentric university. *American Behavioral Scientist, 2*(34), 181–187.

Carter, R. T. (1995). *The influence of race and racial identity in psychotherapy: Toward a racially inclusive model.* New York, NY: Wiley.

Carter, R. T., Helms, J. E., & Juby, H. L. (2004). The relationship between racism and racial identity for white Americans: A profile analysis. *Journal of Multicultural Counseling & Development, 32*, 2–17. doi: 10.1002/j.2161-1912.2004.tb00357.x

Chae, M. H., Foley, P. F., & Chae, S. Y. (2006). Multicultural competence and training: An ethical responsibility. *Counseling & Clinical Psychology Journal, 3*, 71–80.

Chao, R. C., Wei, M., Good, G. E., & Flores, L. Y. (2011). Race/ethnicity, color-blind racial attitudes, and multicultural counseling competence: The moderating effects of multicultural counseling training. *Journal of Counseling Psychology, 58,* 72–82.

Cochran-Smith, M. (1995). Color blindness and basket making are not the answers: Confronting the dilemmas of race, culture, and language diversity in teacher education. *American Educational Research Journal, 52*(3), 493–522.

Cochran-Smith, M. (2004). *Walking the road: Race, diversity, and social justice in teacher education.* New York, NY: Teachers College Press.

Creswell, J. W. (2009). *Research design: Qualitative, quantitative, and mixed methods approaches* (3rd ed.). Thousand Oaks, CA: Sage.

Cross, W. E., Jr. (1971). The Negro-to-Black conversion experience: Toward a psychology of Black liberation. *Black World, 20*(9), 13–27.

Davis, D. J., & Sutherland, J. (2008). Expanding access through doctoral education: Perspectives from two participants of the sisters of the academy research boot camp. *Journal of College Student Development, 49*(6), 606–608.

Dickson, G. L., Jepsen, D. A., & Barbee, P. W. (2008). Exploring the relationships among multicultural training experiences and attitudes toward diversity among counseling students. *Journal of Multicultural Counseling and Development, 36,* 113–126.

Festinger, L. (1957). *A theory of cognitive dissonance.* Stanford, CA: Stanford University Press.

Foldy, E. G., & Buckley, T. R. (2010). A pedagogical model for increasing race-related multicultural counseling competency. *The Counseling Psychologist, 38,* 691–713.

Gardner, S. (2008). "What's too much and what's too little?": The process of becoming an independent researcher in doctoral education. *Journal of Higher Education, 79*(3), 326–350.

Gonzales, J. C. (2007). Surviving the doctorate and thriving as faculty: Latina junior faculty reflecting on their doctoral studies experiences. *Equity & Excellence in Education, 40,* 291–300.

Hall, R. H. (1969). *Occupations and the social structure.* Englewood Cliffs, NJ: Prentice-Hall.

Hardiman, R. (1979). *White identity development theory.* Unpublished manuscript.

Hayes, C., & Juárez, B. (2012). There is no culturally responsive teaching spoken here: A critical race perspective. *Democracy & Education, 20*(1), 1–14.

Helms, J. E. (1984). Toward a theoretical explanation of the effects of race on counseling: A Black and White model. *The Counseling Psychologist, 12*(4), 153–165. doi: 10.1177/0011000084124013.

Helms, J. E. (1990). *Black and white racial identity: Theory, research, and practice.* Westport, CT: Praeger.

Helms, J. E. (1995). An update of Helms's white and people of color racial identity models. In J. G. Ponterotto, J. M. Casas, L. A. Suzuki & C. M. Alexander (Eds.), *Handbook of multicultural counseling* (pp. 181–198). Thousand Oaks, CA: Sage.

Helms, J. E., & Parham, T. A. (1996). The racial identity attitude scale. In R. L Jones (Ed.), *Handbook of tests and measures for black populations* (Vol. 2, pp. 167–174). Hampton, VA: Gobb & Henry.

Herman, C. (2009). Political transformation and research methodology in doctoral education. *Higher Education, 59*(4), 489–506. doi: 10.1007/s10734-009-9261-6

Horton, E., & Hawkins, M. (2010). A content analysis of intervention research in social work doctoral dissertations. *Journal of Evidence-Based Social Work, 7*(5), 377–386. doi: 10.1080/15433710903344066

Jackson, B. (1975). Black identity development. *Journal of Educational Diversity, 2*, 19–25.

Jackson, J. M. (2007). Reclaiming queerness: Self, identity, and the research process. *Journal of Research Practice, 3*(1)Retrieved from. http://jrp.icaap.org/index.php/jrp/article/view/66/87

Johnson-Bailey, J. (2001). The road less walked: A retrospective of race and ethnicity in adult education. *International Journal of Lifelong Education, 20*(1/2), 89–99.

Johnson-Leslie, N. A. (2009). Taming the 'beast': The dance of sustaining reflective practice of the dissertation process. *Reflective Practice, 10*(2), 245–258.

Jome, L. M. (2000). Construct validity of the White Racial Identity Attitude Scale. *Dissertation Abstracts International: Section B. Sciences and Engineering, 61*(2-B), 1133.

Kantawala, A., Hochtritt, L., Rolling, J. H., Jr., Serig, D., & Staikidis, K. (2009). Establishing collaborative dialogue: The mentor and the apprentice. *Visual Arts Research, 35*(2), 40–50.

Katsarou, E., Picower, B., & Stovall, D. (2010). Acts of solidarity: Developing urban social justice educators in the struggle for quality public education. *Teacher Education Quarterly, 37*(3), 137–153.

Katz, J. H. (2003). *White awareness: Handbook for anti-racism training* (2nd ed.). Norman, OK: University of Oklahoma Press.

Kirton, J., Straker, K., Brown, J., Jack, B., & Jinks, A. (2011). A marriage of convenience? A qualitative study of colleague supervision of master's level dissertations. *Nurse Education Today, 31*, 861–865.

Kurtzweil, P. L. (1996). The influence of life experience and social desirability on the development and measurement of the White racial identity attitudes. *Dissertation Abstracts International: Section B. Sciences and Engineering, 56*(10-B), 5836.

Lemon, R., & Waehler, C. (1996). A test of stability and construct validity of the Black Racial Identity Attitude Scale, Form B (RIAS-B) and the White Racial Identity Attitude Scale (WRIAS). *Measurement and Evaluation in Counseling and Development, 29*, 77–85.

Malott, K. M. (2010). Multicultural counselor training in a single course: Review of research. *Journal of Multicultural Counseling & Development, 38*, 51–63.

Martin, R. J. (2005). An American dilemma: Using action research to frame social class a an issue of social justice in teacher education courses. *Teacher Education Quarterly, 32*(2), 5–22.

McIntyre, A. (1997). *Making meaning of whiteness: Exploring racial identity with white teachers.* Albany, NY: State University of New York Press.

Nixon-Cobb, E. J. (2005). Humanizing the dissertation defense: One women of color's experience. *Feminist Teacher, 1*(16), 61–74.

Phinney, J. S., & Rotheram, M. J. (Eds.). (1987). *Children's ethnic socialization: Pluralism and development.* Newberry Park, CA: Sage.

Ponticell, J. A., & Olivarez, A. (1997). Dissertation quality and Kerlinger's methods myth. *Journal of Experimental Education, 65*, 113–122.

Porfilio, B. J., & Malott, C. S. (2011). Guiding white pre-service and in-service teachers toward critical pedagogy: Utilizing counter-cultures in teacher education. *Educational Foundations, 25*(1/2), 63–81.

Rosenthal, D. A. (1987). Ethnic identity development in adolescents. In J. S. Phinney & M. J. Rotheram (Eds.), *Children's ethnic socialization: Pluralism and development* (pp. 156–179). Newbury Park, CA: Sage.

Sugimoto, C. R. (2012). Are you my mentor? Identifying mentors and their roles in LIS doctoral education. *Journal of Education for Library and information Science, 53*(1), 2–19.
Watt, S. K., Robinson, T. L, & Lupton-Smith, H. (2002). Building ego and racial identity: Preliminary perspectives on counselors-in-training. *Journal of Counseling & Development, 80*(1), 94–100.

# CHAPTER 13

# PERSPECTIVE OF A MAJORITY STUDENT

Kathleen M. Kanz-White

## ABSTRACT

*This chapter examines the importance of social justice courses from a majority student's perspective and outlines some of the difficulties in offering these courses. It discusses the benefits of social justice courses for both minority and majority students and focuses on the challenges of understanding and acknowledging the impact of the types of privilege and power that majority individuals experience. The concept of intersectionality, the compounding of injustice for individuals who have multiple minority identities, is explored. Finally, a four-phase model is proposed that can be used to describe the journey that majority students experience as they begin to understand the impact of privilege both on a personal and societal level.*

## INTRODUCTION

In fairness to the reader, it is important for me to state that I write this chapter from a biased perspective. My perspective is that of a member of society's dominant and privileged groups. I am Caucasian, heterosexual, Christian and able-bodied, and educationally privileged. As a graduate

Social Justice Issues and Racism in the College Classroom: Perspectives from Different Voices
International Perspectives on Higher Education Research, Volume 8, 229–241

ISSN: 1479-3628/doi:10.1108/S1479-3628(2013)0000008015

student in education, I am an advocate for social justice themes and courses in the curriculum of wide-ranging academic disciplines. Courses focusing on social justice provide a forum for open dialogue and an opportunity to build allies and support systems to confront injustice.

## IMPORTANCE OF SOCIAL JUSTICE COURSES

Social justice is a topic that is becoming increasingly more popular in academia. While it is difficult to determine the exact number of colleges and universities that offer courses, a quick Internet search turns up an extremely large number of schools that offer classes or in some cases, a major or graduate program in social justice. As the demographics and dynamics of our society are changing, it is important to discuss the concept of social justice in a classroom setting. This allows for freer expression of ideas and debate and critiquing of ideas and experiences that society does not allow for. Within the larger society, most people have concrete entrenched ideas of race and equality and are not necessarily open to changing those ideas or even engaging in dialogue that would challenge them. Presumably, that is not the case in a college classroom, especially in a graduate program. Ideas can be contemplated, experiences reflected upon, and beliefs challenged. There is great power in the educational process that can lead to lasting change for some individuals.

Ideally, social justice issues should be woven through multiple courses leading up to a specific course in the curriculum that focuses on social justice applied to that discipline. It is important that social justice be addressed in multiple classes in multiple ways to help students see the breadth of issues where injustice is present. It is not enough to mention it off-handedly or as a tangent to the main point of discussion. Injustice, privilege and discrimination in all forms are so intertwined in the systems of our society that they must be addressed when teaching and learning about topics such as access to education, hiring practices, health care, legal issues, and poverty. These topics cut across so many academic disciplines especially in the social sciences and education. Graduate students have such varied backgrounds, cultural and geographical differences, professional experiences, age, and political interests and understanding. Students may need to have their thinking challenged, their world views questioned, and their experiences reframed in order for them to be prepared to assume their roles as socially and culturally competent professionals. Ideally, students would take it a step further to become advocates who are working to create a more just, equitable, and peaceful society.

## CHALLENGES IN OFFERING SOCIAL JUSTICE COURSES

There are a number of potential challenges when considering how a social justice course will fit into a graduate program. There may be trepidation on the part of some faculty and administrators to require a class on social justice; there can be great discomfort when addressing the principles of social justice. It may be difficult to find a faculty member brave enough to teach the course. If the course is part of the core curriculum and is valued and supported by the dean and department chair, it will likely be easier to find a faculty member willing to teach it. Moreover, if the course is taught by multiple faculty members or team taught, it may be perceived as being more valued than if it is taught by the one African American or Latino American professor in the department.

Another challenge is the degree to which the course will be accepted and embraced by students. Conservative students may be resistant to being required to take a course that they believe advances a liberal agenda. However, it is the responsibility of the graduate program to determine what experiences students need; we don't get to pick only the classes we want. If that were the case, there would be many fewer students taking research methodology and quantitative analysis classes. Additionally, it is always a challenge to fit another course into an established graduate program complete with core courses, prerequisites, and electives. From my perspective, while these challenges are legitimate, they are not insurmountable and all graduate programs in education, the social sciences, the law, and health care, should have a required course on social justice.

If social justice classes are not taught at the graduate level, students will be ill-prepared to assume professional positions upon graduation. Students will fail to recognize the larger context and societal systems that inherently oppress and separate those with privilege and those without. Institutional racism plays a major role in education, health care, housing, and the legal system (Wise, 2008). Students need to have that broader perspective in order to successfully navigate the systems and be effective in their professional positions, especially if they will be working with individuals from underserved populations.

# BENEFITS OF A SOCIAL JUSTICE COURSES

*For Students of Color*

Often students of color and other minorities may have a different experience in a social justice course than Caucasian and other majority students do. The perspective is different and the motivation for taking the course may even be different. Social justice courses can provide a validation of experiences, provide a safe space for dialogue, and allow students of color to connect to theories and research that can explain and validate their experiences for themselves as well as for others.

While participating in a graduate-level social justice course in education, I noticed a difference in the responses of the minority students and the majority students. It felt as if there was a sense of empowerment growing in the minority students in the class, like they were finally taking a course where their experiences and perspective mattered. One of the topics they seemed to connect with most strongly was the theories of racial identity development. I listened as they told of their childhood experiences, the hurts they experienced as teenagers, and their current professional and academic challenges. It seemed like they believed they had a sympathetic audience or at the very least, an audience who would listen to their perspectives. The students of color were eager to share their experiences to get support and help educate the Caucasian students. They wanted others to know and understand their experiences and challenges. A few students of color talked about the racism they experience daily in their jobs and on campus, and as they did so, other students shared similar experiences and support began to be generated for one another. As the course progressed over the semester, we looked at current events through a new perspective. As the Caucasian students began to see more and more instances of racism and discrimination happening in the news and in the world around us, the students of color seemed to express relief and excitement that others might be understanding a bit more about their lives and their daily experiences. The minority students expressed appreciation as majority students "got it" and communicated their support. Experiences were validated, allies were created, and support for individuals and the goal of social justice generated.

*For Majority Students*

One of the major accomplishments for majority students in a social justice course can be the identification of a racial identity. Most white students don't identify themselves as white, but as Irish, German or English or whatever nationality their ancestors were. Exposure to racial identity models can be an excellent step in connecting with their whiteness and recognizing the impact of it. For many majority students it is the first time they have had their whiteness pointed out to them. If they have never been placed in situations where they were different from others and became aware of that difference, their whiteness does not stand out as a defining characteristic. Once students begin to understand that their racial identity is part of their overall identity, they can become more aware of the implications of their whiteness and other majority statuses. Ideally, racial identity should be covered in an undergraduate psychology or sociology course to expose students to these concepts at an earlier stage in their development, but most often that is not the case and the first exposure comes in graduate school.

### Power and Privilege

Power and privilege are inextricably tied together. The more privilege one experiences, the more power one has. For many students of color this is a concept they are very familiar with; however, for many majority students, it is a concept that they have not even considered. Most majority students do not see themselves as privileged, and they are essentially unaware of the power that they possess. Most likely they would argue that as students they have no power to affect change, especially in a large bureaucracy like a university. The reality is that majority students do have the power to affect change both in the university and the broader society. It takes repeated, systematic exposure to these ideas of power and privilege for them to be recognized and acknowledged.

### Intersectionality

One of the experiences in the social justice course that generated the most amount of critical thinking and dialogue was based on Critical Race Theory (CRT). CRT states that one must look at the intersectionality of identity and categories and how those categories interact on simultaneous levels to determine inequality (Crenshaw, 1991). Essentially, injustice is compounded when individuals have multiple minority identity statuses and it is important to look at that intersection in order to get a full view of that individual's experience. This powerful concept was demonstrated through an activity in which students portrayed characters and were asked to line themselves upon a continuum of privilege. Initially students were only given one or two pieces of information such as name and gender. As more information about the character was revealed, such as age, education, sexual orientation, and income, students were asked to realign themselves on this continuum. This produced a great deal of discussion and examination about privilege and what types of privilege are most influential. Is race more powerful than gender? Is sexual orientation more powerful than education? What role does income play in privilege? It also strongly reinforced the point that privilege and minority statuses do not exist in a vacuum. As an example, we cannot just look at an individual's sexual orientation to determine privilege without also looking at race and education to determine how these identities interact. An individual who is gay and white and well educated may experience less injustice than an individual who is gay and African American and less educated. Identities intersect to determine privilege and injustice (Crenshaw, 1991). It is critical for majority students to be exposed to this concept. As difficult as it is for Caucasian students to grasp the concept of white privilege, it can be especially challenging to recognize how different identities combine to give more privilege or reduce privilege. If they don't see themselves as having white privilege, they will most likely also reject the idea of privilege based on heterosexuality and Christianity, as an example. The individuals with the privilege are also most likely to be in the position of being able to influence change, but the first step is to get them to recognize the privilege that they have and then recognize the injustice that exists in order to motivate them to want to make changes.

One other important point came out of this activity that is described by Chater (1994); privilege can be relative and can shift with changing societal perspectives and world events. There are numerous instances in US history where certain ethnic or religious groups have been treated unjustly because of the actions of a few terrorists who have unfairly represented those groups. An example of this is the manner in which many Muslim Americans were treated after the September 11, 2001 attacks. These individuals, who already experience less privilege than Christians in this country, lost privilege because of the actions of terrorists from another country who happen to share the same religion. Muslims in the United States were treated with contempt and suspicion, communities rallied to keep mosques from being built (Carty, 2011), and hate crimes were perpetrated against Muslims at an increase of 1,600% over rates in the year 2000 (United States Federal Bureau of Investigation, 2001). Another example of shifting societal perspectives is attitudes about gay rights and specifically gay marriage. This shift could result in a change in privilege for gays and lesbians. Newport's (2011) analysis of Gallup polling data showed that for the first time in history, the majority of Americans favored legal gay marriage. These examples illustrate that privilege can be gained and lost based on world events and shifting viewpoints in society.

As I contemplate what I gained from discussions of social justice in a classroom setting, I focus on my journey to understanding the impact of privilege both on a personal and societal level. The four phases in my journey were awareness, accountability, action, and advocacy. I am not suggesting that this is a universal model, merely a description of my personal experiences. It may well apply to other majority students, but I will leave that to their determination.


*Awareness*

The concept of privilege is a difficult one for many majority students to fully understand and embrace. Even the most socially aware individuals sometimes don't fully recognize the impact or extent of privileges that they experience. Circumstances and opportunities are taken for granted and expected. Chater (1994) made this statement about the nature of privilege:

> What is privilege? How is it defined or measured? Privilege can be a problematic term, it seems to me, because material conditions that all peoples inherently deserve, have a right to, when not available to all, become a privilege. Food, housing, health care, education, bodily autonomy, love, respect, and self-determination as peoples can be termed privileges because of their inequitable distribution. Having access to them, however, is not necessarily experienced as a privilege. (p. 102)

Majority students may not see basic things like a quality public school education, access to health care, or living in a neighborhood free of violence as privileges. They expected those things growing up, were given them, and most likely assumed that everyone else they came into contact with had the same experiences. Certainly this was true for me growing up in a small, middle class, homogeneous, rural community. All the children in the community attended the same public school, we did not see great variations in education levels or income, there was no racial or ethnic diversity in our community, and the only places of worship in the community were Christian. I did not have to come face to face with anyone who made me aware of all the advantages I had that came without effort.

Privilege allows the advantage of never having to confront issues and feelings that others have. Confronting instances where someone lacks privilege or is being oppressed can make those of us with privilege so uncomfortable that we need to reinterpret it, minimize it, or describe it in ways that do not threaten our privileged status. I had never really considered how frequently and how dramatically this happens until an interaction took place during a class discussion. We were talking about the concept of in-group prejudice and discrimination and that even within a racial group there can be discrimination based on a physical characteristic. A young African American student was describing how her extended family treats her very differently than her sisters. The family members know her name and ask about what she is doing with her life, but don't know her sisters' names or care about their life activities. The student was describing that this difference was based on skin color; she was much lighter skinned and considered much more attractive and successful than her equally successful and attractive sisters. A white student in the class began to challenge her experience and tell her that there must be some other reason, personality characteristics, levels of success, etc., that could account for the differences in treatment. When the African American student attempted to assure her that the only reason was based on skin color, the white student began to argue with her. She just could not accept that experience which was so different than her privileged experience. This white student could not even begin to acknowledge that people may be treated differently because of skin color within a race different from her own. She was not mean-spirited, she was just so oblivious that she could not even acknowledge or validate another's experiences. She could not see beyond her own privileged existence to view someone else's experience from their perspective.

These types of situations happen all the time, albeit in more subtle ways. It happens when white people tell tribal community members not to make such a big deal about college mascots they find offensive. It happens when we tell people not to be "so sensitive" about Halloween costumes that reinforce stereotypes. It happens when we say "words don't really have meaning, and he didn't really mean anything by what he said." We attempt to reinterpret meaning from our all-knowing, privileged perspective, and completely invalidate the experiences and feelings of people of color.

A graduate student who is a member of the majority could never encounter the concept of privilege, living in a bubble isolated from the experiences of those in the minority. We can tell ourselves that all is right with the world; racism, ableism, homophobia, and the like aren't really a problem in our society. We can isolate ourselves from those things that make us uncomfortable. However, when challenged with these concepts in an academic setting, we are forced to confront them. It may not cause an immediate change in behavior, it may not be acknowledged or accepted as a reality at the first exposure, but with repeated exposure, hopefully the concept can slowly become recognized and acknowledged.

Self-reflection can be a significant tool in this awareness phase, and it was utilized successfully by the professor teaching my social justice class. It was important to reflect upon the messages I had heard and internalized in childhood that were racist or discriminatory in some way. Understanding the impact of those early messages was a significant component in developing a sense of awareness of my own white, heterosexual, Christian privilege. It also is important to reflect upon the first instances of being aware of the privilege we individually possess. For me, the first time I really came face to face with my privilege was when I had heard that an African American coworker of mine was absent from work because she had a cross burned on her front yard the previous night. I knew that experience was something that was never going to happen to me and it was never something that I even considered could happen nor is it something that I worried about. That is privilege. Reflecting back on that event and the feelings associated with it have allowed me to become more aware of many other instances of privilege in my life. It is unlikely that most of us will live our life being cognizant of the all privilege we experience every day, but without a general awareness of privilege in our lives, we never even know to look for the myriad of ways in which we are privileged.

*Accountability*

Once we have an awareness of our privilege we need to be accountable for it. McIntosh (2003) describes the difficulty in recognizing oneself as an oppressor because of privilege; she describes viewing herself as a moral person based on her own individual moral behavior. This is a definite challenge for those with privilege. Even individuals who are sympathetic to equality and justice may view themselves in terms of their own behavior and judge themselves accordingly. It is common to hear someone say "I am not prejudiced or racist, I have friends that are…." or "I didn't own slaves, I am not responsible for the oppression of others." We have been taught that our personal accountability and action are important, and rightfully so. We are responsible for our own actions and our own moral or immoral choices and the consequences of those choices. That is a powerful principle. However, the problem is that when addressing social justice issues, we cannot stop with our own behavior. We need to move beyond this individual perspective. We must move toward looking at our role and place in the larger society (McIntosh, 2003) and be accountable for the privilege that comes with our identities. The challenge becomes helping people realize that while they personally may not have made decisions to support slavery during the civil war or oppose human rights in the 1960s, they have responsibility now to improve conditions for those who were oppressed as a result of those decisions.

Wise (2008), an antiracist author and educator emphasizes that the focus should not be on creating guilt among the privileged, but on creating a sense of responsibility. He uses a powerful analogy to demonstrate this point. A new chief executive officer (CEO) takes over a company and asks for a presentation from the chief financial officer who brings detailed information about the company's assets, revenue, debts, and general financial strength; all of which were accumulated before the new CEO took over. The new CEO then says, "that was great, but from here on out, I don't want to hear about those debts, I had nothing to do with accumulating them, those that have gone before did that, it wasn't me. I am going to use the assets to take us to achieve great things and make this company even more successful than it has been, but I am not planning to pay the debts and I don't want to talk about them anymore" (Wise, 2008, p. 13).

We would question the sanity of that CEO, but in many ways we are doing the very same thing with social justice in our country (Wise, 2008). Those of us with privilege have benefited in countless ways in our life time, often because of the oppression of others. To ignore the inherent flaws in the systems of society perpetuates unjust treatment, and ignoring the debts owed only creates more injustice and inequality. For me, accountability comes down to recognizing that if I want my campus, my community and my world to be more socially just, I play an integral role in creating change. I am accountable not just as an individual but as a representative of privileged groups to which I belong: white, heterosexual, Christian, able-bodied, etc. It is extremely difficult for those who do not hold the power and privilege in society to make changes. It is infinitely easier for those in privileged positions to make changes. Accountability carries with it responsibility not just on a personal level but also on a societal level. Once we embrace a sense of accountability, the next phase is action.

*Action*

Action requires an individual to do something about the injustices and inequalities in society. Action at this phase is usually reactive rather than proactive, but actions, even simple ones can be powerful and dramatic. It usually starts with small but significant events such as not laughing at a racist or sexist joke. It may then advance to telling the person making the joke that it is offensive. The actions may become bolder such as confronting coworkers, friends, and family about the language they use, or engaging them in discussions that challenge their viewpoints and perspectives. Actions may progress to defending the rights of others in one's workplace or community as circumstances arise where individuals or groups are being treated unjustly.

It is a challenge to speak up when we hear words that are derogatory, racist or sexist, especially when it comes from those whom we have been taught to respect based on their position; parents, bosses, teachers, etc. However, if we fail to speak up, we are communicating agreement or at least passive acceptance of language and ideas that are designed to oppress and marginalize groups and individuals. In addition, it is common for individuals to feel guilt and remorse due to their lack of assertiveness in these situations. Social justice courses can provide great support and encouragement for students as they take initial actions in confronting oppression and inequalities. Typically, confidence begins to grow as we speak up in defending others. As that confidence grows, it becomes easier and we become more willing to speak up and speak out. Once we begin speaking out, we enter the last phase, advocacy.

### Advocacy

Advocacy moves beyond action. It is proactive; it involves not just defending the rights of marginalized groups, but seeking to gain more rights and privileges for them. It includes activities such as: signing petitions, participating in protests, lobbying legislators, attending rallies, joining advocacy organizations, creating blogs, etc. Students can become most effective as they join forces to unify their voices and develop a commitment to advocacy. Bettez (2011) describes the important task of building critical communities to support graduate students in the work of social justice, especially given the "socially isolating, intellectually challenging, and emotionally taxing nature" of the work (p. 102).

One of the main components of advocacy is giving up privilege in order to create a more just society. Not only is it difficult to be aware of all the ways in which privilege affects one, it is difficult to know how to give up privilege, and to predict what impact less privilege will have on one's life. As one reaches this phase, there may be a genuine desire to give up privilege, but how to do that and at what cost are still difficult questions. It may be easier to give up privilege that is more symbolic in nature rather than tangible. If giving up privilege means it will impact one financially, for example, a majority student receiving less financial aid to create more assistance for minority students, will that student still be willing to give up privilege? What if giving up privilege means that a highly desirable career opportunity goes to a minority candidate instead of the majority candidate? Will that individual still embrace the idea of reducing her privilege? These are questions that need to be examined and discussed. Many individuals need support in determining ways in which to give up privilege and encouragement to do so in the face of real tangible losses for themselves. Advocacy requires ongoing effort and continual self-monitoring to bring about real sustainable change in society. Critical communities fostered through social justice courses can enhance an individual student's commitment to advocacy.

## CONCLUSION

The study of social justice is extremely beneficial for graduate students. In order for students to become socially and culturally competent professionals, they need to have exposure to the ideas of social justice and privilege and have a safe space for open dialogue and self-reflection about their beliefs and biases. It is through the processes of reading, writing, and dialogue that students can begin to develop the awareness and accountability for social justice and be willing to take action to become advocates for a more harmonious, just, and equitable society.

I have seen social justice discussions and activities make a difference in the lives of a number of students. On a personal level, I have had experiences as a result of classroom discussions and assignments in social justice courses that will stay with me the rest of my life. I also recognize that change happens for different individuals in different ways and at different times, but discussions of social justice principles and themes plant seeds and challenge viewpoints and that is how lasting change begins.

## REFERENCES

Bettez, S. C. (2011). Building critical communities amid the uncertainty of social justice pedagogy in the graduate classroom. *The Review of Education, Pedagogy, and Cultural Studies, 32*, 76–106. doi: 10.1080/10714413.2011.550191

Carty, D. (2011). "Mixed bag" for U.S. Muslims since 9/11. Retrieved from http://www.cbsnews.com/8301-201_162-20104307.html

Chater, N. (1994). Biting the hand that feeds me: Notes on privilege from a white antiracist feminist. *Canadian Woman Studies, 14*(2), 100–104.

Crenshaw, K. (1991). Mapping the margins: Intersectionality, identity politics, and violence against women of color. *Stanford Law Review, 43*(6), 1241–1299.

McIntosh, P. (2003). White privilege and male privilege: A personal account of coming to see correspondences through work in women's studies. In M. S. Kimmel & A. L. Ferber (Eds.), *Privilege areader* (pp. 147–160). Boulder, CO: Westview Press.

Newport, F. (2011, May 20). For first time, majority of Americans favor legal gay marriage. Retrieved from http://www.gallup.com/poll/147662/first-time-majority-americans-favor-legal-gay-marriage.aspx

United States Federal Bureau of Investigation. (2001). *Unified crime reports 2001.* Retrieved from http://www.fbi.gov/about-us/cjis/ucr/hate-crime/2001

Wise, T. (2008). The pathology of privilege: Racism, white denial & the costs of inequality. Retrieved from http://www.mediaed.org/assets/products/137/transcript_137.pdf

# CHAPTER 14

# REFLECTIONS ON A CRITICAL RACE THEORY PROJECT WITH EDUCATIONAL LEADERS

Abul Pitre

## ABSTRACT

*This chapter highlights the experiences of a professor who taught a cultural diversity class to doctoral students in an educational leadership program. During the course students were engaged in the study of critical educational theory with a component of the course focusing on critical race theory. Some of the examples in this chapter illustrate how educational leaders despite initial difficulty with confronting issues of racism were able to overcome years of mis-education to become educational leaders for social justice. Moreover, the chapter highlights the difficulties and challenges that professors who engage in critical race theory encounter. The chapter pointedly discloses why there is a need for professors to engage students in conversations around racism and social justice.*

Social Justice Issues and Racism in the College Classroom: Perspectives from Different Voices
International Perspectives on Higher Education Research, Volume 8, 243–254
Copyright © 2013 by Emerald Group Publishing Limited
All rights of reproduction in any form reserved
ISSN: 1479-3628/doi:10.1108/S1479-3628(2013)0000008016

# INTRODUCTION

In this chapter, I reflect on experiences with doctoral students in a cultural diversity. As a major part of the course, students were required to write a paper that would later be used as a contribution for a book addressing multicultural education for educational leaders. During the course, several of the conversations presented a type of shock and awe for these educational leaders. Shields (2011) captures from her experiences in part some of my own experiences when she says she was dumbfounded that her students had not had conversations about racism, social class, and deficit thinking: "You mean, you did not have discussions like this at the beginning of the year at your opening faculty meeting? You never had conversations about privilege, racism, sexism and so forth, and how different practices and beliefs affect the ability of your students to achieve" (p. 7). For the most part, the students in my class replied as Shields did, "We have never discussed these topics-not at our schools, nor in out teacher training programs- so how are we supposed to know how to address them when we become principals and leaders" (p. 7).

In part, much of the dilemma lies in the fact that professors in educational leadership programs may have limited knowledge in multicultural education and critical theory. What I have come to find from my colleagues at some universities is that the body of knowledge used to teach leadership courses is based primarily on technical knowledge that is not linked to critical discourse that would disrupt the status quo. Thus, not only is there the challenge of working with students in courses that deal with issues of equity, diversity, racism, and social injustice, but there is also the challenge of working with faculty as eloquently noted by one of my colleagues who confronted a student about the critical race theory (CRT) discourse in my class chiming "all you all are doing is having black talk."

Introducing students to concepts about racism, white privilege, and social injustice can be very draining to say the least but it can also be very rewarding. What you will read in this chapter is a brief description of the evolution of a book that would later be titled: *Educational Leaders and Multicultural Education: Critical Race Theory and Anti-Racist Perspectives in Multicultural Education*. The comments by students in the course highlight the need to have these critical conversations that offer an opportunity to produce transformative educational leaders. If professors are afraid to have these conversations then chances are we have not come to truly understand the tenets of transformative leadership. In summary, what you will find in this chapter is a reflective writing where I provide an understanding of CRT, the historical origins of CRT combined with reflections from students, and elements of a case study to illuminate the dynamics of racial discourse in the classroom.

# REFLECTIONS

In the summer of 2009 a group of educational leaders took a course titled "Cultural Diversity in American Education" and as part of the culminating class project, students were required to write a publishable paper that could later be turned into a book. However, because the course lasted only four weeks, the students were unable to complete their final papers. Despite its short length, the course covered several major topics, including race, racism, social class, special needs, religion, and gender issues. Several class sessions seemed to alarm some students, creating what might be termed a crisis and exacerbated when the topic of racism and critical pedagogy were the center of discussion. Students were troubled by the ways racism and social class inequities were perpetuated in schools, and through deeper reading and reflecting on their work as school leaders, they began to see the depth of the systemic inequities permeating educational institutions.

The following semester, the same educational leaders were engaged in a course titled "Legal and Ethical Issues." During the course of the class, an epiphany occurred through the text, *Foundations of Critical Race Theory in Education*, which seemed to summarize the conversations from previous semester's diversity course. I was amazed that the students had come to realize that race does matter in schools. As a follow through on the agreement to write a book on educational leaders and multicultural education, they soon completed preliminary drafts. Initially the book was titled *Educational Leaders and Multicultural Education*; however, as the articles were edited, it became apparent that the students had produced something extraordinary during their research on multicultural education, adding a rare but much-needed perspective for school leaders. The book's title became *Educational Leaders and Multicultural Education: Critical Race Theory and Anti-Racist Perspectives in Multicultural Education*.

In his book *Race Matters*, Cornell West (2003) highlights the significance of race in the American society. He argues, "To engage in a serious discussion of race in America, we must begin not with the problems of [B]lack people but with the flaws of American society flaws rooted in historic inequalities and longstanding cultural stereotypes" (p. 53). A major flaw in the American society can be traced back to its educational process, which has had a "double consciousness." In his book, *Mis-Education of the Negro*,

Carter G. Woodson (1933/2008) wrote on double consciousness: "The same educational process which inspires and stimulates the oppressor with the thought that he is everything and has accomplished everything worthwhile, depresses and crushes at the same time the spark of genius in the Negro making him feel that his race does not amount to much and never will measure up to the standards of other people" (p. xiii).

With all of the current educational debate focusing on the inequitable schooling experience of non-White children and the existence of the so-called achievement gap, there remains a great deal of misunderstanding, and perhaps even denial. History has shown that "the conditions of today have been determined by what has happened in the past" (Woodson, 1933/2008, p. 9). Thus, if we are to move forward in the creation of a balanced education system, we must accept that at the center of American life are the issues of race and racism; racism is as American as apple pie.

It could be argued that one of the primary reasons race has continued to play a major part in the American landscape is because the overarching educational system reinforces White supremacy. This ideology has shaped curricula, student–teacher interaction, school policies, and community relations, to mention a few. To effectively dismantle racism in the American educational system, a complete overhaul of the current system is a must. Colleges of education would have to be at the forefront of this paradigm shift because the death of racism would require teacher educators and educational leaders to be prepared to undertake a critical study of the social order and the schools' role in shaping that order. Educational leaders should serve as visionaries, but what happens when those would-be leaders enter graduate programs that are primarily focused on teaching skill sets? In describing the educational leadership dilemma, Lopez (2003) writes, "… and the important stuff in educational leadership is not about creating schools that work for all children but rest in the more technical matters of school finance, organizational theory, leadership theory, and other staple topics" (p. 70). This type of vocational training produces commissar administrators who seek to maintain the existing order as opposed to producing school leaders who transform schools into just, equitable, and powerful catalysts for social change.

While most colleges of education are accustomed to facing accreditation issues related to diversity, educational leadership programs have been able to skirt specific diversity issues regarding race and racism. Though progress in addressing diversity remains stagnant at an additive approach, some colleges of education have been compelled to offer courses that address multicultural education. Moreover, some teacher education programs offer courses solely focused on the topic of racism; for example, a major

Midwestern university offers a course titled "Race and Inequality in American Education," and another major West coast university at one time offered a course titled "Pedagogy of Malcolm X." Additionally, some urban education programs also address issues related to race and racism. However, for the vast majority of students in educational leadership programs, there seems to be minimal discussion about racism. If in a room of educators and a discussion about eliminating racism ensued, most educational leaders would be disturbed by the discourse, as evidenced by a recent meeting of educational administrators where a participant suggested changing the admission requirements for an educational leadership program. The proposed change would eliminate the program's process of self-nomination and require an administrator to nominate potential candidates into the master of school administration program. When questioned about available mechanisms to ensure diversity in the applicant pool, one Black superintendent responded, "I don't look for diversity; I look for people who can do the job." This comment and others made it apparent that administrators across the country may share this Eurocentric thinking, which contributes to the structure of White supremacist schools.

The few non-Whites who do enter into administrative positions may have fulfilled Woodson's (1933/2008) prophetic utterance regarding the education of African Americans.

> With mis-educated Negroes in control themselves, however, it is doubtful that the system would be very much different from what it is or that it would rapidly undergo change. The Negroes thus placed in charge would be the products of the same system and would show no more conception of the task at hand than do the Whites who have educated them and shaped their minds as they would have them function. (p. 23)

Educational leaders and the programs that have shaped their thinking do not allow for critical dialogue that could be transformative. In this chapter, you will find compelling reasons for why educational leaders need to engage in CRT and antiracist conversations in their graduate programs. If the vast majority of educational leaders are trained in postsecondary programs that do not address racism, it is highly likely that racism will continue to be perpetuated in America's schools.

## UNDERSTANDING CRITICAL RACE THEORY

In 1995, Ladson-Billings and Tate wrote one of the first major papers on the idea of CRT in education. In a subsequent book titled *Critical Race Theory*

*Perspectives on Social Studies* (2003), Ladson-Billings, along with other teacher educators, specifically discusses the pervasiveness of race in the teaching of social studies. The author writes, "And for the purpose of this discussion I want to suggest that race is an ever present concept in the social studies in the curriculum, the profession, and its policies, and practices" (p. 2). Similarly, the issue of race and racism should be an important topic of study in the area of educational leadership.

Educational leaders and leadership programs should form the bedrock for issues related to race and racism in schools. Historically, educational leaders are shaped or birthed into a profession that is dominated by Whiteness. The vast majority of school leaders in this country are White. In addition, an examination of the racial dynamics of school boards might result in the surprising find that in some cases the school board is majority White even though the student population is majority non-White, leaving the educational decisions of Black and minority students in the hands of people outside their race. Another factor worth exploring is the race of leaders in state departments of education. The selection of these leaders reveals that beyond the local school and school board is the state legislature, which is a major player in determining how schools will operate in a particular state. Examining state legislatures will result in the finding that the majority of state legislatures are again White. The problem is not skin color as such but the ideology that has historically embodied these lawmaking sanctuaries and the people who work in them. All of these factors play a significant role in revealing the need for CRT in educational leadership. Lopez (2003) argues, "quite simply, preparation programs across the nation do very little to equip students with a cogent understanding of racism and race relations. Moreover, when these topics are introduced, they are often relegated to special topics courses or seminars that are not a part of the core curriculum of leadership preparation" (p. 70).

## HISTORY OF CRITICAL RACE THEORY IN EDUCATION

Understanding the origin of critical race theory is significant so let us briefly consider it and its application for educational leaders. CRT has emerged to inform our understanding of race and education. CRT is primarily concerned with the race and its impact on American life. Ladson-Billings (2003) notes the origin of CRT: "Critical race theory sprang up in the mid-1970s with the early work of legal scholar Derrick Bell and Alan Freeman, both whom were distressed over the slow pace of racial reform in the United States" (p. 8). CRT considers racism to be a normal part of American life. More importantly, critical race theorists seek to expose racism and its impact on American life. Gollnick and Chinn (2009) point out that CRT "focuses on racism in challenging racial oppression, racial inequities, and White privilege" (p. 11). Stovall (2005) identifies two major aspects of CRT as educational protest and scholarship. More importantly, Stovall links CRT to identification of White supremacy in education and methods used to eradicate its dominance in education. For the most part, racism is everywhere in the education world and educational leaders, the people who could play a major role in dismantling it are not cognizant of its existence.

In the courses I taught that became the basis for a book I wanted to test the understanding of educational leaders relating to racism. We started our conversation in an organizational theory and cultural diversity course that lent itself to the discussion of racism. Using Nieto and Bode's (2012) framework in *Affirming Diversity*, I was amazed that these educational leaders had never thought about racism to this degree. Nieto and Bode (2012) define racism as prejudice plus power and they point out two forms of racism: individual racism and institutional racism. They contend, "Although the beliefs and behaviors of individuals may be very hurtful and psychologically damaging, institutional discrimination- that is, the systematic use of economic and political power in institutions(such as schools) that leads to detrimental policies and practices—does far greater damage" (p. 64). This argument suggests that it is necessary for educational leaders to understand racial inequality and its systematic inherency in school policy and practice.

While having these conversations about race and racism, some of the educational leaders had difficulty comprehending how schools produce race and social class inequalities. One leader (a White female) had grown up in the Midwest region of the United States and could not understand Nieto's argument to dismantle tracking. She argued that tracking was necessary, but as she begins to speak more about her experiences it became clear that she could not grasp the concept of tracking and racism because she had never been around people outside of her race in a meaningful way. Her first real encounter with Black people came as result of being placed in a majority Black school as a teacher, an experience of which she expressed, "I was terrified." At the end of the course she made the following comments:

> My doctoral coursework introduced to me to institutionalized racism in the educational
> system and the idea that although I genuinely had no idea what I was doing was racist,
> I had contributed to racism against children for many years as a teacher and
> administrator. My immersion in critical educational theory and multicultural education

has led me to read books and articles by scholars in critical multicultural education 1933/2008, which has really resulted in personal epiphanies and growth. I do not for a second think my journey is complete; rather, it has only just begun.

One of the scariest thoughts about this whole process has been the "what if?" What if I had stayed in the Midwest town in which I grew up? Would I have ever learned these things or would this process have just occurred much later in life? Even scarier is the fact that I made it through almost 12 years in a very diverse environment surrounded by a multitude of races and yet I still managed to be oblivious to much of what really happens and why it happens. I never gave thought to the fact that the first people educated were rich, White male property owners. We are still using a lot of their ideas to teach non-White students, which is problematic because it means that we are trying to educate everyone according to a Euro-centered perspective. If school leaders are really going to transform schools so that they are just and equitable, they will need to reexamine the history of the United States. It is in critiquing the lies we have been told that White school leaders can develop an understanding of the diverse student groups who have historically been disempowered through what has been called education. Our job as educators in the new century will be to learn more about the experiences of marginalized students that enter our schools. It is the only way that we can truly lead students, besides We Can't Lead Students We Don't Know!

In addition to using Nieto and Bode's framework of the sociopolitical nature of multicultural education I wanted to use elements of Asante's *Afrocentric Idea.* Prior to assigning Asante's reading, I needed the students to develop some understanding of the historical issues that gave birth to multicultural education. Even more importantly, I wanted the students to take a historical journey to the period when the first Blacks arrived in America to be made slaves. I asked them to read the *Willie Lynch Letter and The Making of Slaves* (Hassan-EL, 2007), a work that has been argued is a fabrication but nonetheless created shock for the educational leaders. They began to see elements of Lynch's ideas being played out in the educational arena. At this point they began to ask questions and make comments like,

If Lynch was right about the sustainability of his conditioning process, then educators of today must realize their responsibility to make changes and end the process. Lynch makes it clear that "values are created and transported by communication through the body of the language. A total society has many interconnected value system." Educational leaders should heed his message, and begin to use his method for positive efforts towards racial unity and acceptance. This concept validates the importance of spreading multicultural education across the curriculum so that the underlying values can be instilled in more deep and meaningful ways.

Regarding its application for educational leader's one student wrote:

It is important for this letter to be read and taught to school-aged children so they can begin to understand the construct of the Black individual, family, and community.

> I believe it is particularly important for Black children to understand this letter. Educational leaders are in some ways being controlled by not having the flexibility to teach certain material and content. It is highly unlikely that this material will be taught in detail to K-12 or even to college-level students, but it should be taught in the home and in the community. As an educational leader, this letter has allowed me to look through a different lens within my own educational system. I began to count the number of Black upper-level managers within my Institution. There are three Black directors (to include myself), one assistant VP, and one VP in a total of 200 full-time employees. How does this happen? I have noticed this issue in the past, but this letter has made me more aware of the fact. It's quite unsettling yet motivating at the same time. This is a paradox that will force me to continue moving in a direction of empowerment by educating myself to help others.

It could be argued that what is needed in conjunction with CRT is a component that could be called Black studies for educational leaders. Asante (1991) argues, "... multicultural education is thus a fundamental necessity for anyone who wishes to achieve competency in almost any subject...The Afrocentric idea must be the stepping stone from which the multicultural idea is launched" (p. 172). Asante's ideas for Afrocentricity as the launching for multicultural education would be especially important for educational leaders who may have historical amnesia. Because the overwhelming number of schools that are considered failing are predominately Black and Hispanic, this requires educational leaders to have some understanding of the historical plight of these groups. Black studies could provide a stimulus for ameliorating the problem addressed by Butterfield: "Knowledge of the sins of the fathers is a terrible burden for the children of pirates, murderers, kidnappers, rapists, for the children of those who received the benefits of stolen labor and genocide and closed their eyes, perhaps with humanitarian shudder, to its effects" (cited in Pinar, 2004, p. 41). This is a point where educational leaders would have to face the demons that have haunted the sociopolitical nature of education.

Historically, confronting this truth has been very difficult for educators and I suppose it is even more daunting for those leaders who have played a role in the deep forgetting described by Pinar (2004) in what he calls an official story:

> The official story a nation or culture tells itself-often evident in school curriculum-hides other truths. The national story also creates the illusion of truth being on the social surface, when it is nearly axiomatic that the stories we tell ourselves mask the unacceptable truths. What we as a nation try not to remember—genocide, slavery, lynching, prison rape—structures the politics of our collective identification and imagined affiliation. (p. 38)

Pinar's exegete of the official story can clearly be seen in events described in *Freedom Fighters: Struggles Instituting the Study of Black History in K-12*

*Education* (Pitre, 2011). In this book, Pitre discloses how CRT was played out in the context of a school's Black History program that became controversial when a few White teachers walked out. One of the White teachers who disagreed with the contents of the guest speaker's address is believed to have phoned the school board to intercede on behalf of the student unrest that he perceived would take place as a result of the Black History program. The next day the majority White school leadership of the central office, along with sheriff's deputies, descended on the majority Black school. One of the major underpinnings of Pitre's work was that it used a case study and student interviews illuminating the role of racism, privilege, and White supremacy in school. In the case study, concerned parents pointed out that "racism was and is the basis used in past historical events that caused races to be intimidated and deprived of human dignity" (Pitre, 2011, p. 74). The head of the NAACP also discussed the institutional role of racism in this particular school district noting the role of the educational leaders:

> The system is racist for allowing those types of things to happen. …We met with the superintendent last year about White teachers leading White students out of those programs. We approached the superintendent a week prior to the assembly and asked that a policy be established. (p. 22–23)

The study also made connection between CRT and White privilege, which was clearly observed in the case study and student narratives. This privilege was manifested as some teachers who walked out of the program did so knowing they would not be reprimanded; indeed, walking out of Black History programs had been an ongoing phenomenon prior to this particular incident. White privilege was illuminated when White school administrators showed up the day after the program with sheriff's deputies – a show of force that has been attributed to one teacher who phoned the school board indicating there would be violence at the school. The privilege of having White skin afforded these teachers with a level of comfort that paved the way for them to openly display racist attitudes. In fact, one teacher had the audacity to tell the Black students he felt bad for them because they had to hear another Black person talk like that. Perhaps more insulting and illuminating was the ensuing apology by the school principal, who was forced by the Whites in power to hold an assembly apologizing for the Black History program. This apology crystallized the racism, power, and privilege afforded to those in the dominant group. The Black History program, despite being a powerful tool for constructive change among the students, was seen as threatening to the majority White school leaders and prompted parents to form a group called the Concerned Parents Organization that challenged the practice of racism at the school. In a letter to the local newspaper, the parents pointed out, "We have some racist teachers in our public schools, those who send their children to private schools because a Black teacher isn't good enough to teach their children but they teach ours" (Pitre, 2011, p. 76). The parents in this study were in the forefront of identifying and challenging the unjust and inequitable school policies in this school district.

The students were also very active in this challenge, displaying their anger by walking out of school for several days and attending school board meetings to protest the board's decisions. The students' protest demonstrated a newfound consciousness of the individual and institutional racism. What seemed to emerge was that the students were protesting against a system that had sought to reduce them to beings for others. They realized that they had been made victims of what Freire (2000) called "domestication" and Woodson (1933/2008) called "mis-education."

Educational leaders who are exposed to CRT as a component of Black studies could have a powerful impact on transforming schools. In the aforementioned study, leaders could have used the situation at this particular school to create a very powerful opportunity to eradicate racism and inequality in schools. However, blinded by what Howard (2006) describes as the luxury of ignorance and the White is right assumption, these school leaders instead revealed the racist ideologies that have historically impeded non-White students' quests for equality of education. Howard writes,

> This was real colorblindness: Whites seeing only in White...The luxury of selective forgetting is not afforded to those who have suffered the consequences of White dominance. For them, the American Dream has often become an unbearable nightmare... Through the luxury of ignorance, Whites for centuries maintained a view of reality that "makes sense" to us {Whites}. (p. 63)

Peter McLaren (2007) cogently asserts, "The specific struggle that I wish to address is that of choosing against Whiteness...My message is that we must create a new public sphere where the practice of Whiteness is not only identified but also contested and destroyed" (p. 261). What better place to start contesting racism than with the educational leaders who, like bus drivers, have the power to steer us onto new roads that bring us beyond the rhetoric of equality into the confines of the school where justice and equality could reign supreme.

# REFERENCES

Asante, M. (1991). The Afrocentric idea in education. *The Journal of Negro Education, 60,* 170–180.

Freire, P. (2000). *Pedagogy of the oppressed.* New York, NY: Continuum.

Gollnick, D., & Chinn, P. (2009). *Multicultural education in a pluralistic society* (8th ed.). Upper Saddle River, NJ: Pearson Education, Inc.

Hassan-EL, K. (2007). *The Willie Lynch letter and the making of slaves.* Besenville, IL: Lushena Books.

Howard, G. (2006). *We can't teach what we don't know: White teachers in multiracial schools* (2nd ed.). New York, NY: Teachers College Press.

Ladson-Billings, G. (2003). Lies my teacher still tells: Developing a critical race theory perspective toward the social studies. In G. Ladson-Billings (Ed.), *Critical race theory perspectives on social studies: The profession, policies, and curriculum* (pp. 1–14). Greenwich, CT: Information Age Publishers.

Ladson-Billings, G., & Tate, W. (1995). Toward a critical race theory of education. *Teachers College Record, 97,* 47–68.

Lopez, G. (2003). The racially neutral politics of education: A critical race theory perspective. *Educational Administration Quarterly, 39,* 68–94.

McLaren, P. (2007). *Life in schools. An introduction to critical pedagogy in the foundations of education* (5th ed.). Boston, MA: Allyn and Bacon.

Nieto, S., & Bode, P. (2012). *Affirming diversity: The sociopolitical context of multicultural education* (6th ed.). Boston, MA: Allyn and Bacon.

Pinar, W. (2004). *What is curriculum theory.* Mahwah, NJ: Lawrence Erlbaum Associates.

Pitre, A. (2011). *Freedom fighters: Struggles instituting the study of Black history in K-12 education.* San Francisco, CA: Cognella Academic Publishers.

Shields, C. (Ed.). (2011). *Transformative leadership. A reader.* NY: Peter Lang.

Stovall, D. (2005). Critical race theory as educational protest: Power and praxis. In W. Watkins (Ed.), *Black protest thought and education* (pp. 197–211). Oxford: Peter Lang.

Taylor, E., Gillborn, D., & Ladson-Billings, G. (Eds.). (2009). *Foundation of critical race theory in education.* New York, NY: Routledge.

West, C. (1993). *Race matters.* New York, NY: Beacon Press.

Woodson, C. G. (2008). *The mis-education of the Negro.* Drewryville, VA: Kha.

# INDEX